135.

THE WORLD'S FINEST HORSES AND PONIES

Principal Contributors

YURI BARMINTSEV	*(U.S.S.R.)*
RICHARD GLYN	*(Great Britain)*
HANS LÖWE	*(Germany)*
PAMELA MACGREGOR-MORRIS	*(Great Britain)*
DAPHNE MACHIN GOODALL	*(Great Britain)*
ALEXANDER MACKAY-SMITH	*(U.S.A.)*
HEINO H. MESSERSCHMIDT	*(Germany)*
MAURICE O'NEILL	*(France)*
BARBARA VAN TUYL	*(U.S.A.)*
DORIAN WILLIAMS	*(Great Britain)*

THE WORLD'S FINEST
HORSES AND PONIES

Edited by

COLONEL SIR RICHARD GLYN Bart
O.B.E. T.D. D.L.

Photographs by

SALLY ANNE THOMPSON

GEORGE G. HARRAP & CO. LTD
LONDON   TORONTO   WELLINGTON   SYDNEY

To Barbara, my wife — with love

First published in Great Britain 1971
by GEORGE G. HARRAP & CO. LTD
182–184 High Holborn, London, W.C.1

Text © *George G. Harrap & Co. Ltd* 1971
Photographs © *Sally Anne Thompson* 1971

ISBN 0 245 59267 9

Composed in Baskerville type and printed by Morrison & Gibb Ltd, London and Edinburgh

Made in Great Britain

PREFACE

This book provides a world-wide survey of the breeds and types of horses and ponies which are significant today, and it is designed for readers in every continent. Special editions are being prepared in six different languages. It does not provide details of breeds which are no longer viable, unless they are of particular historical importance, nor is it a catalogue of varieties which are of purely local interest.

I am enormously indebted to my principal collaborators, Professor Yuri Barmintsev, Dr Professor Hans Löwe, Miss Pamela MacGregor-Morris, Miss Daphne Machin Goodall, Mr Alexander Mackay-Smith, Professor Heino Messerschmidt, Monsieur Maurice O'Neill, Miss Barbara Van Tuyl, and Mr Dorian Williams, surely the strongest international team ever to co-operate in the production of a book on horses and ponies. I am particularly grateful to Miss MacGregor-Morris who, in addition to contributing valuable articles on breeds and aspects of horsemanship of which she has special knowledge, also gave invaluable assistance in sub-editing sections of the book which had suffered in translation. I would also record my appreciation of the outstanding photographs by Miss Sally Anne Thompson.

I gladly pay tribute to the generous help given by my friend and neighbour Major Kenneth Wallis, one of the best-known and best-respected judges of hunters and ponies in Britain. But for his aid the British Isles section of this book could not have been so authoritative, and I gratefully acknowledge help and advice from my friends the Editor of *The Field* and Major Eric Rickman, for twenty years the senior Racing Correspondent of the London *Daily Mail*.

Important articles and valuable information were kindly provided by Mr Peter Burrell, Director of the British National Stud; Miss Judith Campbell, the well-known expert on horses in the Middle East, who was given special permission to ride and describe the horses at the Imperial Stud; Mr Anthony Dent, author of innumerable articles on Arabians and on the history of horses in general; Sir Andrew Horsbrugh-Porter, Hunting Correspondent of *The Field* and Polo Correspondent to the London *Times*; Mrs Virginia James, who fought many times on horseback in the bullrings of Portugal as Virginia Montesol (see Appendix III); Señor Leather de Macedo, who provided invaluable information about horses in the Iberian Peninsula; Dr Vladimir Matoušek of the famous Czechoslovakian Kladruby Stud; Mr W. J. B. Murphy of the Department of Agriculture of Australia; Major D. Satow, Public Relations Officer of the British Horse Society, and the veteran expert, Mr R. S. Summerhays, Past President of the Arab Horse and National Pony Societies, who edited *Riding* for thirteen years.[1]

The following have kindly contributed articles on breeds of which they have special knowledge: Colonel A. Stuart Bellingham, Mr Roy Charlton, Major Maurice Cox, Mr A. G. Holland, Mr Robert Jarvis, Mr M. R. J. McGregor, Miss M. H. Mole, Mr G. J. Mountain, Mrs Parsons, Mrs N. Pennell, Colonel F. H. Reekes, Dr Roberts, Mr Tom Ryder, Mrs Mary Sellar, Mr Warren, and Captain The Lord Westbury, M.F.H.

I am particularly grateful to my friend Sir Jocelyn Lucas, Bart, who made available rare books from his private library; to Mr H. Russell Robinson, Assistant to the Master of the Armouries in Her Majesty's Tower of London, whose contributoin is acknowledged in the text; and to Lt-Colonel John Miller, C.V.O., and Mr Anthony

---

[1] Author of *Summerhays' Encyclopaedia for Horsemen*, *The Observer's Book of Horses and Ponies*, etc.

Crossman for the trouble they took in making arrangements for the photographing of horses of special interest.

I also thank the staffs of the British Museum and of the Library of the House of Commons, who spared no effort to procure old books and documents not otherwise available. I am indebted to Messrs Weatherbys, Publishers of the Stud Book, and to the Research Department of Olympia Limited, both of whom went to trouble to provide information unobtainable from any other source.

I received invaluable information as to Stud Books, methods of registration, horse populations, and the degree of Government support for horse breeding in the countries concerned from Their Excellencies the Ambassadors, and members of the staff of the American Embassy, the Argentine Embassy, the Austrian Embassy, the Royal Belgian Embassy, the Brazilian Embassy, the Royal Danish Embassy, the Finnish Embassy, the French Embassy, the Imperial Iranian Embassy, the Italian Embassy, the Royal Netherlands Embassy, the Royal Norwegian Embassy, the Peruvian Embassy, the Embassy of the Polish People's Republic, the Embassy of the Republic of Indonesia, the Soviet Embassy, the Spanish Embassy, the Swiss Embassy, the Venezuelan Embassy, and the staff of the Legation of the People's Republic of China.

I am grateful also to the High Commissioners of Australia, Canada, India, and Pakistan for the information they and their staffs provided. I am greatly indebted to the Ministries of Agriculture of Britain, Eire, and Morocco, and in particular to that of the U.S.S.R. who, for the first time, provided a Western editor with official information concerning Russian breeds and breeding methods, and also assisted Miss Sally Anne Thompson to obtain her unique photographs of Russian horses.

The photographer and I would also like to thank all those who showed her such kind hospitality and who helped her in every possible way.

No international book of this compass could ever have been completed without the assistance of a host of translators among whom I am particularly indebted to Señora Manuella Leather de Macedo, Mrs Fiddick, Mr Tavakkoli, and Miss Norma Stark of the Peruvian Embassy. Finally, like all authors who attempt to portray events of long ago, I must express my gratitude to earlier writers, and to the scientists whose discoveries have indicated what was happening long before writing was invented.

RICHARD H. GLYN

THE FARMERS' CLUB,
3 WHITEHALL COURT,
LONDON, S.W.1

CONTENTS

Breeds and Types Described or Mentioned   8

List of Monochrome Plates   10

Introduction   11

The British Isles   37

Central Europe   52

The Federal Republic of Germany   63

The French Republic   70

Northern Europe   77

Southern Europe   85

North America   90

South America   101

U.S.S.R.   105

Other Nations with Breeds of Importance   115

Appendices   121

Horses and Ponies Illustrated and their Owners   127

Acknowledgments   128

BREEDS AND TYPES DESCRIBED
OR MENTIONED

References to pages in the text are given in roman type
Numbers of illustrations are given in italics

Adaev — 107
Akhal-Teké — 107, *121*
Albino — 92
Alter-Real — 87, *94*
American Quarter Horse — 93, *102*
American Saddle Horse — 93, *106*
American Shetland Pony — 94, *97*
American Standardbred (*see* Standardbred)
American Thoroughbred — 95, *104*
American Trotter (*see* Standardbred)
American Welsh Pony — 95
Andadore (*see* Llanero)
Andalusian — 89, *95*
Andalusian-Carthusian — 88
Anglo-Arab — 73
Anglo-Kabardin — 106
Anglo-Norman — 71, *73*
Anglo-Persian — 119
Appaloosa — 96, *99*
Arabian — 39, *1*
Aragon — 88
Ardennais — 72, *74*
Ardennes — 77
Avelignese Horse — 86
Azerbaijanian — 107

Barb — 117, *127*
Bashkir — 106
Bavarian Warm Blood — 64
Belgian Heavy Draught Horse — 77
Bigourdane (*see* French Anglo-Arab)
Bosnian Pony — 57
Boulonnais — 72, *76*
Brabant — 77, *77*
Breton — 73, *68*
Budenny — 108, *122*
Buriat — 107

Calabrese — 85
Campolino (*see* Mangalarga)
Canadian — 96
Canadian Cutting Horse — 92, *108*
Canadian Hunter — 92
Chickasaw Horse (*see* American
  Quarter Horse)
Children's Riding Pony — 40, *10*
Cleveland Bay — 40, *8*
Clydesdale — 41, *36*
Cob — 42, *4*
Connemara Pony — 42, *15*
Costeño — 103
Courraleiro (*see* Crioulo)

Covert Hack (*see* Hack)
Criollo — 101, *113*
Crioulo — 103

Dabrowsko-Tarnowski — 59
Dales Pony — 43, *12*
Dartmoor Pony — 43, *34*
Desert-bred Arab (*see* Jordanian Arab)
Døle — 82, *81*
Don Horse — 108, *123*
Dulmen Pony — 64
Dutch Draught Horse — 80, *78*

East Friesian — 65, *59*
East Prussian — 65, *61*
Einsiedler — 62, *56*
English Trotting Horse (*see* Hack)
Estonian Klepper — 107
Exmoor Pony — 44, *35*

Fell Pony — 44, *13*
Finnish Horse — 79, *86*
Five-gaited Saddler (*see* American
  Saddle Horse)
Fjord Pony — 83, *80*
Flanders Horse (*see* Brabant)
Franches-Montagnes — 62, *57*
Fredericksborg — 78, *83*
Freiberger (*see* Franches-Montagnes)
French Anglo-Arab — 73, *67*
Frencher (*see* Canadian)
French Thoroughbred — 74, *66*
French Trotter — 75, *65*
Friesian Horse — 80, *79*
Furioso — 56, *42*

Garrano Pony — 88
Gelderland — 81
German Thoroughbred — 66
German Trotter — 66, *64*
Gidran Arabian — 56
Great Horse (*see* Shire; *see also* p. 28)
Gronigen — 80
Gudbrandsdal — 82

Hack — 45, *3*
Hackney — 45, *6*
Haflinger Pony — 52, *55*
Hanoverian — 67, *63*

Harness Horse (*see* American Saddle Horse)
Highland Pony 46, *16*
Hispano AngloArab 89, *96*
Hispano-Breton 88
Holstein 67, *62*
Hucul 59, *46*
Hungarian Trotter 56
Hunter 46, *5*

Iberian (*see* French Anglo-Arab)
Icelandic Pony 82
Irish Draught Horse 47, *9*
Italian Heavy Draught Horse 86, *87*
Italian Trotter 85

Jaf 120
Jomud Horse 106
Jordanian Arab 116
Junqueira (*see* Mangalarga)
Jura (*see* Franches-Montagnes)
Jutland Horse 79

Kabardin 109, *117*
Karabair 109, *120*
Karabakh 109, *118*
Karaçabey 120
Kazakh 110
Kentucky Saddle Horse (*see* American Saddle Horse)
Kisbér 56
Kladruber 54, *39*
Klepper (*see* Estonian Klepper)
Knabstrup 78, *82*
Konik 59, *47*
Kopczyk 58
Kushum 107
Kustanair 106

Latvian Harness Horse 106
Lipizzaner 54, *40*
Lipizzan (*see* Lipizzaner)
Lithuanian Heavy Draught Horse 110, *115*
Llanero 104
Lokai 111, *119*
Lusitano 86, *93*
Lyngen 82

Malopolski 59
Mangalarga 103
Masuren 58
  (*and see* Wielkopolski)
Mezien 107
Minusin 107
Morgan 97, *103*
Morochuquo 104
Murakosi 56, *41*
Murgese Horse 86
Mur Insular 58

Narragansett Pacer 99

Navarrese (*see* French Anglo-Arab)
Neapolitan 85
New Forest Pony 48, *14*
Nonius 57, *43*
Nordestino (*see* Crioulo)
Norfolk Cob (*see* Hackney)
Noric 53, *54*
Northland 83
North Star (*see* Furioso) 56
North Swedish Horse 84, *84*
Novokirghiz 111

O'Bajan Arabian 55
Oberlander 52
Obvin 107
Oldenburg 68, *60*
Orlov Trotter 111, *124*

Paint Pony (*see* Pinto)
Palomino 98, *100*
Park Hack (*see* Hack)
Pechora 106
Pembrokeshire Packhorse (*see* Welsh Cob)
Percheron 76, *75*
Persian Arab 119, *128*
Peruvian Stepping Horse 104
Pinto 98, *101*
Pinzgauer 52
Polish Anglo-Arab 59, *48*
Polish Arab 60, *45*
Polo Pony 102
Pony of the Americas 99, *98*
Posavac 57
Poznan 58
  (*and see* Wielkopolski)
Prejvalski's Horse 14

Quarter Horse (*see* American Quarter Horse)

Rhenish-German Cold Blood 68
Rio Grande do Sul (*see* Crioulo)
Roadster (*see* Hackney)
Rottaler (*see* Bavarian Warm Blood)
Russian Arab 105
Russian Heavy Draught Horse 112
Russian Trotter 112

Sadecki 58
Salerno 85, *88*
Salteno 103
Schleswiger 68, *58*
Senner (*see* East Friesian)
Serrano 103
Shagya Arab 55, *44*
Shetland Pony 48, *33*
Shire 49, *38*
Siebenburger (*see* East Friesian)
Siglavi-Gidran 56
Slaski 60
Sokolski Horse 59

Sorraia 87
South German Cold Blood (*see* Noric)
Soviet Heavy Draught Horse 113, *116*
Spanish Arab 88
Standardbred 99, *105*
Strelets 106
Suffolk Punch 49, *37*
Swedish Ardennes 84
Swedish Warm Blood Horse 84, *85*
Swedish Trotter 83
Swiss Anglo-Norman (*see* Einsiedler)
Swiss Holstein 61
Sztumski 59

Tarbaise (*see* French Anglo-Arab)
Tarpan 14
Tawda 107
Tennessee Walking Horse 100, *107*
Tersk 113, *125*
Three-gaited Saddler (*see* American Saddle Horse)
Thoroughbred Horse 50, *2*
Toric 114
Trakehner (*see* East Prussian)
Transbaikal 107
Turkmene (*see* Turkoman)
Turkoman 119
Turn-Row Horse (*see* Tennessee Walking Horse)

Tushin 107

Ukranian 107

Viatka Horse 106
Vladimir Heavy Draught Horse 114, *114*

Waler 115, *126*
Welsh Cob 50, *7*
Welsh Mountain Pony 51, *11*
Welsh Pony 51, *11*
Welsh Pony of Cob Type 50, *7*
Westland (*see* Fjord Pony)
Westphalian (*see* Hanoverian)
Wielkopolski 61, *53*
Württemberg 69

Yakut 114
Yorkshire Coach Horse (*see* Hunter)

Zapateros 88
Zhmud 106
Zweibrücker 69

LIST OF MONOCHROME PLATES

PLATE

17 The Great Italian War-horse
18 The German War-horse
19 Flanders and Spanish stallions
20 The Capriole
21 Ménage by the Duke of Newcastle
22 A Friesian horse
23 The Byerley Turk
24 The Darley Arabian
25 The Godolphin Arab
26 Flying Childers
27 Eclipse
28 Unknown grey
29 Grey Diomed
30 The original steeplechase
31 Merry Tom
32 American Trotter and Orlov Trotter

PLATE

49 Ottawa Valley Hunt
50 Shires harrowing
51 A Tachanka team of Don horses
52 Circus horses
69 Point-to-pointing
70 The Spanish Riding School, Vienna
71 Bulldogging at Calgary
72 The Cadre Noir, Saumur
89 A Hackney at Windsor
90 Sun and wind in Southern France
91 Orlov Trotters at the Moscow Stud Farm
92 A four-horse team
109 Polo at Windsor
110 Jumping
111 Eventing at Badminton
112 The 1970 Epsom Derby

INTRODUCTION

The Little 'Dawn Horse'

THE HORSE has served man for over four thousand years. For centuries he carried kings, conquerors, and all the great captains of war. Thundering into battle, he helped to decide the destinies of Empires. The "Age of Chivalry" was named after him (from the French *cheval*) and, before being made a knight, every aspirant had to 'win his spurs' by some feat of arms.

The horse was man's first source of power combined with speed. Until a mere 130 years ago he provided the most efficient method of travelling on land. Now, in this age of mechanization, he is used more for pleasure and sport, but he remains man's loyal servant and friend—asking so little and giving so much.

The four thousand-odd years during which the horse has been associated with man cover only a tiny fraction of his history, which has been traced back for seventy-five million years to the condylarth family, a prehistoric group which varied in size from a cat to a collie dog and had five toes on each foot. At the end of each toe was a thickened nail. These condylartha were not horses, but they were the ancestors of our horses and of all hooved animals.

Our modern horse, *Equus caballus*, is the direct descendant of *Eohippus*, the 'Dawn Horse' (see Fig. 1), which flourished about sixty million years ago. In those days, man had not yet descended from the trees, where he was merely "an unidentified lemuroid".[1] Few other species of that far distant time survive today.

The differences between *Eohippus* and our modern *Equus caballus* are so great that when fossil remains of the former were first discovered in 1839 at Studd Hill in Kent, England, archaeologists did not recognize them as belonging to an ancestor of the horse family, and named them after an entirely different species. In 1876, when a more complete skeleton was unearthed in the United States, American scientists identified this as an ancestor of our modern horse and named it *Eohippus*. They proved by a series of intermediate forms that *Eohippus* had developed into *Equus caballus* in North America, and had travelled thence into other continents.

No-one could blame scientists for failing to connect the Studd Hill fossils with our modern horse because the animals were so very different. For example, *Eohippus* varied between the height of a fox terrier and that of a foxhound. It had four toes on each fore foot and three on each hind. These toes ended in a miniature hoof rather larger than a dog's claw, and each foot had a pad—again like a dog—which carried most of the weight. Moreover, the teeth of the *Eohippus* could never have grazed grass and were only suitable for browsing shrubs.

Not until 1932 was it pointed out by the late Sir Clive Forster-Cooper that the Studd Hill fossils and the *Eohippus* "were so extremely similar" that they could not "reasonably be separated genetically".[2] In other words, the Studd Hill bones represented the European variety of the *Eohippus* species.

[1] George Gaylord Simpson: *The Story of the Horse Family* (Oxford University Press, New York, 1951) pp. 76 *et seq.*
[2] *Ibid.*, p. 115.

Sixty million years ago the sea-level was lower than at present and there were land bridges across what is now the Bering Strait between Asia and North America, across the Mediterranean in the neighbourhood of Italy, and across the English Channel. So *Eohippus* and its descendants could travel freely throughout Asia, Europe, and the Americas. Only Australasia and other islands were barred to them.

Fig. 1 Eohippus, *c*. 60 million years ago

As thousands of centuries passed, the descendants of *Eohippus* gradually became more like our modern horses. They acquired an equal number of toes—three on each foot. Then, perhaps about twenty-five million years ago, grass appeared. Few horses of that time could chew tough herbage like grass because their teeth were not suitable. Gradually, however, some horses developed stronger and better teeth, protected by cement, enabling them to eat grass, which grew on open spaces where enemies could be seen some distance away, and gave less cover to predators than the undergrowth browsed by older types of horses. The horses able to graze and digest grass grew stronger and more efficient than the other horses, which eventually died out.

An important three-toed grass-eating ancestor of our modern horses and ponies was *Hipparion* (see Fig. 2) which appeared about ten million years ago. It was larger than *Eohippus* and built more like a modern horse. It was a great traveller and its remains have been found throughout Asia and Europe, as well as in Africa. It seems to have founded dynasties wherever it went, but its descendants died out eventually, except in North America.

Some six million years ago, a horse called *Pliohippus* appeared in what is now the United States. It was the first horse to have only one toe on each foot—that is to say, a hoof like our modern horses. *Pliohippus* was a recognizable, but smaller, edition of its direct descendant, our *Equus caballus*.

Equus Caballus

Genetically, *Equus caballus* is the horse we ride and drive today, but when it first appeared about a million years ago its make and shape were very different from those of modern horses and ponies. It varied in size, but in general was about the height of the small Island-bred Shetland Pony, and probably equally as shaggy, but it had not yet acquired the turn of speed achieved by the modern Shetland.

Being without any effective means of defence against the carnivores which preyed on all grazing animals, it depended for survival on constant vigilance and the ability to out-wit pursuers. Its eyes were set so that it could see an enemy approaching from either side, and it bolted immediately at any suspicious sound or sudden movement.

For the first quarter of a million years of its existence, *Equus caballus* was able to travel freely from its birthplace in North America through Asia to Europe and Africa as its ancestors had done, but, gradually, horses and all grazing animals were driven many hundreds of miles southwards by sheets of ice which slowly, over the course of many centuries, advanced from the North Pole and, much later, receded to approximately their former positions. Over a period of about six hundred thousand years, the seas of ice advanced and retreated at least four times; at their farthest point south they reached the present-day sites of London and New York. The grass on which horses and their relatives depended was driven hundreds of miles still farther south. During the Ice Ages many varieties of horses and other species of animals became extinct.

Fig. 2 Hipparion, *c.* 10 million
years ago

At some stage during the Ice Ages, *Equus caballus* became aware of a new enemy—man. Cave-men left many drawings of horses being attacked by spears and arrows, and Professor Ridgeway states that "horses provided an important part of the food supply" of stone-age man.[1] Great piles of horse skeletons have been found near some cave dwellings. By measuring these, we find that the biggest horses of that period were still under 13·3 hands high.

Eventually the earth seems to have become warmer. The ice crept back for the last time and much of it melted, raising the sea-level so that, perhaps about ten thousand years ago, the land bridges between Asia and America and across the Mediterranean Sea and the English Channel were submerged for ever. Since then, no horse has crossed from Europe into the British Isles, or vice versa, except by the intervention of man.

The Horses which Survived

When the lethal ice sheets had finally retreated to their present positions, just over ten thousand years ago, only four groups of the descendants of *Eohippus* remained alive: the horse, the ass, the zebra, and the onager, the latter being a species between the horse and the ass and sometimes known as the hemione. Its fossil remains have occasionally been mistaken for those of horses. Professor Zeuner[2] suggests that these groups may have been distributed as shown on the map, Fig. 3, which does not show the equines who survived on the other side of the Atlantic as these were destined soon to become extinct (see p. 90).

Fig. 3 Locations of Equines, *c.* 10,000 years ago

This map shows the surviving horses in the Old World as being distributed throughout a wide belt north of the great mountain chains which run roughly from east to west across Europe and Asia. Possible exceptions to this general rule are discussed below. The territory shown as containing horses comprises various regions which differ in altitude and in climate, both of which factors would have affected the horses or ponies which developed in them. For example, temperate climates and moderate altitudes tend to promote size in horses, while very high altitudes and extremes of climate tend to produce ponies rather than horses. In some cases, the various regions had different types of soil and so would have produced grasses which differed in quality —that is to say, in mineral and vitamin content. Again, heavy rainfall, resulting in moist, succulent pastures, would have tended to produce heavy horses while drier areas, with sparser grazing, would have tended to produce lighter, faster-moving animals.

Gradually, different types of horses and ponies developed and became established in these various regions, which were generally separated by some geographical barrier. All horses will interbreed and produce fertile offspring, which makes it impossible for

[1] W. Ridgeway: *The Origin and Influence of the Thoroughbred Horse* (Cambridge University Press, 1905), pp. 483 and 484.

[2] F. E. Zeuner: *A History of Domesticated Animals* (Hutchinson, London, 1963), p. 300.

different varieties of wild horse to occupy an area at the same time "without inter-breeding and thus mixing their racial characteristics"[1] —in other words, without merging into a single breed. When the remains of several species of horses or ponies are found in an archaeological deposit covering a relatively short period of time, scientists presume that all except one of the species had been brought there by man.

Of the four or more varieties of horses which survived the Ice Ages, only one still exists untamed. About ninety years ago Colonel N. Prjevalski discovered a herd of wild ponies in the depths of Mongolia which differed from domesticated horses in various ways—to give one example, they had erect manes. They were compact, generally dun in colour, with a narrow, dark dorsal stripe and occasional faint leg stripes. The adults varied between 12 and 14 hands high. This variety still exists in a wild state for, quite recently, Russian naturalists have reported sighting a small herd near the Yellow Wild Horse Mountains which lie between China and Mongolia. These are believed to be the only horses existing today whose ancestors have never been domesticated. The breed appears to have originated in the Asiatic Steppes where climate, altitude, and sparseness of grazing combined to favour the evolution of a superior type of pony, and where the flat steppe favoured the survival of the fastest as well as of the fittest.

This breed has been hunted by man ever since he learned to hunt, and innumerable specimens had been caught and tamed before written records were being made anywhere on earth. These ponies form part of the foundation stock from which sprang the ancestors of the Arabian and other Eastern horses, and are therefore, although far removed, ancestors of our modern Thoroughbreds. Many of them survive in zoos throughout the world; the *International Zoo Year Book* reported over 140 in 1967. This figure did not include the herd known to exist at Askaniya-Nova, in the Russian Ukraine, which did not then publish statistics.

Another Ice Age breed which survived in a wild state until modern times is the Tarpan, whose original home was farther west than Prjevalski's Horse. There seem to have been two branches of the Tarpan family, one grazing the steppes of the Ukraine and the other in Eastern Europe. Both groups were hunted long before history began, just as deer and wild oxen were hunted, but with more venom, because the wild stallions attacked and sometimes killed their domesticated rivals. Both branches of the Tarpan family were almost (some experts say entirely) exterminated by the end of the last century, when steps were taken to preserve (some experts say to restore) the breed. The most typical specimens which could be found were collected into reserves, where a substantial number still survive in a semi-wild state. At Popielno, in Poland, there is a famous domesticated herd of Tarpan used for experimental breeding.

Whether or not the present-day animals are of pure Tarpan descent is a vexed question, but they certainly bear a marked resemblance to their Stone Age ancestors. They are about the same size as Prjevalski's Horse and are generally brown in colour, with a dorsal stripe and black mane and tail.

It is generally agreed that Prjevalski's Horse and the Tarpan are joint ancestors of our present-day 'warm-blood' breeds—an expression which refers not to the body temperature but to the presence of Thoroughbred or Eastern blood. For example, Thoroughbreds, Arabians, and their near descendants are described as 'warm-blood' breeds, while heavy draught horses are generally supposed to be descended from 'cold-blood' stock. There are many intermediate breeds whose different ancestors contributed warm blood and cold blood in different proportions.

Another breed of horse which survived the Ice Ages and contributed to the ancestry of many of our modern breeds was the Forest or Diluvial Horse, which seems to have acquired a massive body and a passive temperament while grazing lush European pastures. Archaeologists have found traces of a heavy breed of wild horse which existed in Scandinavia nearly ten thousand years ago and seems to have been domesticated

[1] *Ibid.*, p. 308.

[14]

Fig. 4   Heavy Horse, c. 9000 years ago

about three thousand years ago. Excavations at Dümmer Lake in north-west Germany disclosed remains of three types of horses; the most common, only pony-sized, is thought to have been a native wild horse hunted for food. The other two were probably domesticated Forest horses. One was of intermediate size, while the other, a large, heavy horse, may have been related to the Swedish Heavy Horse mentioned above.[1]

Realistic cave drawings of numerous types of horses have been found. Some of these may have been of varieties which became extinct during the Ice Ages and could not have played any part in the development of our existing breeds, but an interesting drawing of a heavy horse (see Fig. 4) from the cave of Cambrelles, Dordogne, France, is considered to be dated from after the glacial period, and might well portray a relative of the Swedish Heavy Horse and of the Forest Horse whose remains were excavated at Dümmer Lake, in which case the drawing illustrates an ancestor of the heavy 'cold-blood' horses of today.

Professor Zeuner considers evidence of the survival of a fourth wild horse in eastern Siberia, but is of the opinion that it "has almost certainly not contributed to the domestic stock of horses".[1] This view conflicts with that of Russian horse-breeding specialists who believe that one of their modern breeds may be descended from it (see p. 114). Zeuner also considered the possibility of the survival of wild horses in south-western Europe and/or north-western Africa, at one time linked by a land bridge. He did not discard this possibility, but felt that more research in the area was needed before a definite opinion could be given. Since he wrote, the discovery of post-glacial reproductions of horses in cave-dwellings in the Sahara area and in Spain has given support to the belief that wild horses did survive in these parts of the world.

Horses become Domesticated

No clue so far discovered gives any clear indication of when and where the horse was first tamed, and it seems probable that the tribes or nations who first learned to catch young foals and rear them, and who gradually realized the horse's potential, were nomads—ideological ancestors of our modern gypsies—who lacked the wish (and perhaps also the ability) to leave records of their achievements in the field of horse management. It seems probable that these wanderers had no fixed habitation of any kind and that their horses, no more than ponies by modern standards, were at first herded like cattle. These small horses were not capable of carrying heavy burdens, but would have provided meat and milk, and perhaps also butter and cheese, just as Russian horses like the Bashkir do today (see p. 106).

It is certain that when horses first came to the knowledge of nations who kept records they had already been domesticated for generations, perhaps for centuries. The earliest written reference so far deciphered comes from China, where approximately 4250 years ago a scribe reported raids by nomad horsemen, said by subsequent writers to have had "the same customs as the latter-day Huns".[2] The original writer did not specifically state that the nomads rode their horses, but the later comparison with Huns (who never fought or even travelled except on horseback) makes it almost certain

[1] *Ibid.*, pp. 303 *et seq.*
[2] *Cambridge Ancient History* (Cambridge University Press, 1939), vol. iii, pp. 187 *et seq.*

that they were mounted. If so, this is not only the earliest reference to domesticated horses, but by far the earliest reference to horses being ridden.

Because the earliest mentions of domesticated horses come from the Old World, it is usually assumed that the horse was first tamed on this side of the Atlantic. This assumption overlooks the fact that man co-existed with horses in North America for centuries before the latter died out, which took place before horses were tamed in Asia.

The American bison (often wrongly called the buffalo) was never domesticated by the American aborigines, and if they had any draught animal larger than the dog (still used to pull sledges over the snow) it can only have been the horse. From the horse-mastership of their remote descendants, the Plains Indians, it is at least possible that these first Americans tamed horses; if so, they must have been the first men to do so.

Although the earliest Asiatic horse-masters left no tangible records, philologists (students of language) have pointed out that in parts of northern Europe, northern India, and Iran (formerly known as Persia) certain words are very similar. These include many words concerning domesticated horses as, for example, the words for "mare" and for "mare's milk".[1] Each of these regions is occupied by descendants of one or other branch of the great Indo-European nation called "Aryan" which, over four thousand years ago, was situated in what is now Asiatic Russia, and which later divided to conquer and occupy the regions concerned. This suggests that the Aryans must have had domesticated horses before they split up and began their career of conquest, a theory which chimes in with other faint indications that Aryans were among the first horse-masters on this side of the Atlantic.

Although it appears that these first owners of horses may have lacked the art of writing, in other respects they were more advanced than their contemporaries because, at some time during their wanderings on the Asiatic Steppes, they discovered how to make spoked wheels with hubs that turned freely on their axles—an art not then understood anywhere else in the world. This represented not only a great technical advance requiring skills and tools previously undreamed of, but also (in conjunction with the possession of horses or oxen) the ability to move loads at a relatively fast rate across the great plains of western Asia. This combination of horses and spoked wheels was destined to change the course of history and to disrupt the civilized world.

The "Ass from the Mountains"

Forty centuries ago there were three great civilizations whose remains have been excavated and whose customs are known, at least in part. The oldest, in Mesopotamia, was founded on Ur of the Chaldees (described in the Old Testament as the birthplace of Abraham) and on the fabulous Babylon. This group of City States traded over a wide area and did business with the second civilization, another group of City States in the Indus valley in what is now western Pakistan. The third, Egypt, was isolated behind the natural barriers of the sea and the great deserts. From their records and from the carvings and illustrations which have been discovered, we know that all these civilizations used oxen to draw ploughs and sledges. In Egypt and in the Indus valley wheels had not yet been invented; asses were used for pack purposes and also for riding. In the Mesopotamian civilization rudimentary wheels were known, and the onager, a species between the horse and the ass, was used as described below.

None of these civilizations had any knowledge of the existence of horses until about four thousand years ago when a scribe in Ur of the Chaldees reported what was to him a new kind of animal which he called the "Ass from the Mountains". This is the first known written reference to the horse outside China (see p. 15). Later, we have Babylonian references to the "fast horse with a wavy tail".

[1] *Encyclopaedia Britannica*, 1968 edition, vol. xiii, p. 717, Note I.

[16]

1 *ARABIAN*

2 *THOROUGHBRED*

3 *HACK*

4 *COB*

5 *HUNTER*

6 *HACKNEY*

7 *WELSH PONY OF COB TYPE*

8 *CLEVELAND BAY*

9 *IRISH DRAUGHT HORSE*

10 *CHILDREN'S RIDING PONY*

11 *WELSH MOUNTAIN PONY*

12 *DALES PONY*

13 *FELL PONY*

14 *NEW FOREST PONY*

15 *CONNEMARA PONY*

16 *HIGHLAND PONY*

The Mesopotamian army of those days was highly organized. The pick of the infantry, equivalent to present-day Commandos, were carried into battle in special carts which creaked into action on solid wheels fixed to revolving axles (see Fig. 5).

Fig. 5 Mesopotamian Chariot drawn by Onagers, *c*. 4000 years ago

Each of these carts was drawn by four onagers, harnessed by a type of ox yoke, with a throat strap. This was quite unsuitable for animals of the equine type as it pressed on their windpipes, making it impossible for them to throw their full weight into the traces for more than a few moments at a time. Recent experiments have shown that horses so restricted could pull less than one quarter of the load which they could move easily with a more suitable harness. Moreover, the solid wheels with revolving axles made the vehicles so uncomfortable that when a Mesopotamian monarch of this period offered his glamorous consort, Queen Shub-ad, a new pleasure car, she asked that this should be mounted on sleigh runners rather than on the uncomfortable solid wheels.

A hundred years after this first record of horses in Mesopotamia the first horse was imported into Egypt, where it was such a novelty that it was eventually given an honoured burial.[1] At about the same time a nation called the Mittani were introducing horses into eastern Turkey, which was then inhabited by the Hittites who, unlike the Mesopotamians, were eager to acquire this new means of making war.

The Mittani sold horses to the Hittites and also a new type of chariot with spoked wheels on revolving hubs, and the horses had better harnesses so that they could gallop wherever the ground permitted. These early chariots were much in advance of their time. During the next two thousand years, chariotry represented the *corps d'élite* of innumerable successful armies, but throughout this period few improvements or modifications were made to the chariot. The number of spokes was increased and the distance between the wheels was widened to 4 feet 8½ inches—which became the standard width of carts and carriages, to the present day, and eventually the standard gauge for railways in many parts of the world. Otherwise, the chariots from which the ancient Britons defied Julius Caesar, about two thousand years ago, were virtually identical with those the Mittani had sold to the Hittites about two thousand years before.

Records found in the old Hittite capital describe how a Mittanian horse dealer named Kikkuli left precise descriptions for "training and acclimatization of horses" in Turkey.[2] Kikkuli's notes make it clear that the Mittani were thoroughly accustomed to chariot racing as well as to breaking and training horses. Unfortunately, other Mittani records (if they left any) have yet to be found and deciphered.

It seems that acclimatization was a recognized problem in introducing horses into Turkey; a century later a Hittite king wrote to an ally farther north asking for "young horses . . . because the cold of the Anatolian plateau . . . would kill off old horses".[3]

[1] Professor Stuart Piggott: *Ancient Europe: A Survey* (University Press, Edinburgh, 1965), p. 142.
[2] O. R. Gurney: *The Hittites* (Penguin Books, London), pp. 104 *et seq.*
[3] J. K. Anderson: *Ancient Greek Horsemanship* (University of California Press, Berkely, 1961), p. 5.

About 3700 years ago Egypt was invaded. "Something incredible and frightful befell the Nile country. . . . Suddenly, like a bolt from the blue, warriors in chariots drove into [Egypt]. . . . Even before the Egyptians realized it . . . their country was taken by surprise, overrun, and vanquished."[1] Shortly after this, a brigade of Hittite charioteers surprised and captured the supposedly invincible Babylon. About a century later, other chariot-borne warriors overthrew the third great centre of civilization in the Indus valley. In less than three hundred years, illiterate barbarians destroyed all the greatest civilizations of that period, and in every case they owed their victory to the mobility which their horses gave them.

The Earliest Recorded Horse Breeders

The Aryan nations, including the Mittani, who were breeding horses on a large scale about four thousand years ago, left no records, and the earliest horse breeders of which we have any detailed information were the Assyrians. Their horses appear to have lacked stamina at first, as each mounted warrior had to lead a spare one (see Fig. 6). Gradually, bigger and more powerful horses appeared which could not only carry a man all day but his weapons and armour also.

Fig. 6　Assyrian Warrior with two Horses, *c*. 2800 years ago

Originally, all the principal horse-breeding nations were east of Europe and of the Mediterranean. Three thousand years ago armour was beginning to be used in the Middle East, as also were missile weapons such as bows and arrows, so that if horsemen were to operate within bow-shot of enemy infantry it was necessary that they, and if possible their horses, should be protected by a light form of armour. I am indebted to Mr H. Russell Robinson, Assistant to the Master of the Armouries (Her Majesty's Tower of London) for the information that eastern horse armour of about 2500 years ago weighed up to 50 pounds, and that of the rider rather less, to which must be added the weight of his weapons. This means that if the warrior 'rode' at 11 stone when not armed, his charger must have carried nearly 18 stone on the battlefield.

The first recorded successful breeders of weight-carrying chargers were Persians, who also produced high-class race horses which may have been among the ancestors of the present-day Arabian Horse. Their magnificent heavyweight Nisaean chargers

Fig. 7　Persian Weight-carrying Chargers, *c*. 2400 years ago

[1] Warner Keller: *The Bible as History* (Hodder and Stoughton, London, 1956), trans. by William Neil, M.A.; p. 101.

[18]

(see Fig. 7) were said to have had "feet that shake the earth". Anderson calculates that they stood just over 14 hands.[1] Two thousand four hundred years ago these chargers were the pride of the invincible Persian King, Darius I, who chose for his epitaph: "I was an excellent horseman and an excellent hunter. Nothing was impossible to me."

At this time, southern European horse breeders seem to have been making speed their first priority and to have produced lightly built animals, not up to much weight, but with promise of quality, as illustrated in Fig. 9, which shows Etruscan mounted infantry of approximately this period. Prominent horse-breeding nations in the Mediterranean area about 2000 years ago are listed by Anderson[2] who quotes contemporary authors, praising horses from different regions. Mention is made of horses bred in Egypt, Greece, North Africa, Parthia, and Spain. Oppian is quoted as stating that the Spanish were the fastest horses then known, though lacking in stamina, and that "for long distances the dappled Moorish are best".

In considering these ancient writers, it must be remembered that breeds of horses in the true sense could only be established in areas not regularly overrun by horse-borne conquerors whose chargers (invariably stallions) would have left their mark on the horses of every conquered country.

By about 1750 years ago, two north-European nations had produced heavyweight chargers, bred no doubt from the heavy Forest horses of Scandinavia and North Germany (see p. 15). The first to appear were the Goths, who fought their way from their Baltic home to southern Russia where they perfected their cavalry tactics, and where their horses flourished, and perhaps received an injection of Eastern blood. Then from North Germany came the Vandals whose heavy chargers carried them across Europe and over the Strait of Gibraltar into North Africa, where, during the century of their occupation, their cold-blooded horses left a long-enduring imprint on the native breeds. Some two centuries later, a third Teutonic nation, the Lombards, emerged, also mounted on heavy chargers. By this time stirrups had been introduced from the East and, aided by these, the Lombard Cavaliers were able to wield a huge lance called the *contus*. A contemporary writer, Paul the Deacon, recorded the feat of a Lombard champion who not only unhorsed his opponent, but "bore him aloft, wriggling" on his lance point.[3]

Fig. 8 Earliest Representation of a Rider, *c.* 3500 years ago

The Lombards eventually rode south into Italy, where their massive stallions gave substance to the local horses. As the centuries went by, the armour of both men and horses was made progressively heavier, and weight-carrying chargers began to appear in many parts of Europe.

By about 1300 years ago, excellent riding horses were being produced in Syria and Palestine. In the wars between the eastern Roman Empire and the Moslems, the Romans often relied on "auxiliary cavalry recruited from the Tributary Arabs".[4] These Tributary Arabs came from Syria and from what is now Jordan, where good-quality horses had been bred for centuries. Later, these Arabs were converted to Islam

[1] Anderson, *op. cit.*, p. 27 and the description to Plate 8a.

[2] *Ibid.*, pp. 17 *et seq.*

[3] Quoted by Charles Oman, M.A., F.S.A.: *A History of the Art of War* (Methuen, London, 1905; second edition), p. 48.

[4] Bernard Lewis: *The Arabs in History* (Hutchinson's University Library, London, 1958; Arrow edition), p. 53.

and formed an important part of the Moslem armies.

Eight hundred years ago, when Christians and Moslems clashed in the Crusades, captured Eastern stallions were brought back to Europe, where the nations gradually came to recognize that success in war depended to a considerable extent on the quality of the chargers available. From then on, horse-breeding was practised systematically in almost every country, often under royal patronage.

Riding Becomes General

The development of riding in civilized countries was retarded by a number of factors. The first horses to be tamed lacked the stamina to carry a grown man for any length of time. Moreover, riding was considered vulgar. Kings, chieftains, and even fairly junior officials always travelled by chariot, which was the status symbol of the age. Sir Leonard Woolley wrote: "The Mittani might ride on horseback—*i.e.*, on stallions—but in the eyes of the native Mesopotamian that was an unseemly habit."[1] This may explain why the earliest known reproduction of a rider, carved about 3500 years ago, shows an Egyptian groom out exercising his master's horse (see Fig. 8). Zeuner, referring to this carving, described riding as "a practice almost unknown"[2] at that date.

Fig. 9   Etruscan Mounted Infantry, *c.* 2300 years ago

Nearly one thousand years after this statuette was carved, an Egyptian army was besieging Memphis. The ruler of the city fled. "He sate himself upon a horse, he asked not for his chariot, he went downstream in fear."[3] The Egyptian scribe scorned his defeated enemy, not for flying by night nor for abandoning his subjects, but for the more disgraceful fact that he fled on horseback.

The early riders had many problems to overcome. Stirrups were unknown until about 2000 years ago (and in Europe for centuries after this), and saddles and bridles were still being developed. The Roman Grattius Faliscus, writing about 2000 years ago, recorded that the Nasomones of North Africa rode without bridles, controlling their horses "with a light rod". The African writer Nemesianus, some 250 years later, stated that the North African horse wore no bridle, but was controlled by light blows of a stick which caused him "to start, to turn, to run directly on"[4] (see Fig. 10). Anderson states that in those days saddles (when used at all) had no saddle-tree but usually consisted of a quilted saddle cloth secured by a breast band, sometimes a girth,

[1] Sir Leonard Woolley: *The History of Mankind* (published for UNESCO by George Allen and Unwin, London, 1963), vol. ii, "The Beginning of Civilization", p. 521.
[2] Zeuner, *op. cit.*, p. 321.
[3] *Cambridge Ancient History*, *op. cit.*, p. 272.
[4] Anderson, *op. cit.*, pp. 20 *et seq.*

and, more rarely, a crupper. The reins were attached to a large tassel hanging below the horse's neck, which continued to provide some degree of check on the horse's mouth when the rider dropped his reins to use a bow and arrow.

**Fig. 10   North African riding without Reins,
c. 2200 years ago**

Most nations quickly mastered the art of riding astride, but Fig. 11 shows Spanish warriors of about 2250 years ago riding into battle sitting sideways on their horses.

The gradual improvement of bridles and bits took centuries, and bits have continued to be improved until the present day, but even today many Arabs ride on a nose-band without a bit at all (see p. 30).

Sir Leonard Woolley emphasized that the Mittani rode on stallions. It seems that this was invariably the custom, perhaps because, being larger, they were better suited to carry an armed man. However this may be, it became established at an early stage that stallions were the only possible mounts for warriors. This sentiment, which persisted until recently, was stressed by Richard Berenger only 200 years ago, when he said: "It was a custom rigorously observed that no knight of chivalry or other gentleman should ride upon a mare, it being thought dishonourable and vile. The mares were always devoted to the cart and all the ignoble services."[1]

Berenger quotes the Venerable Bede, a Northumbrian monk who wrote about 1250 years ago, as stating that in his day prelates and other churchmen were accustomed to travelling on foot, "but if upon urgent occasion they were obliged to ride, they used mares only". Berenger gives the opinion that this was "as a mark of humility, the mare not being so full of pride and spirit as the horse".

Whatever the reason, only stallions were ever used as war-horses. Some four and a half centuries after Bede wrote, a Scandinavian princess organized the production of a magnificent tapestry, portraying her Lord on his charger, fully equipped for battle. She directed that the masculinity of his steed should be emphasized by an alteration in colour on the tapestry, which had the effect of demonstrating not only the sex of the animal but the unfamiliarity of the royal ladies with the details of equine anatomy.

Before this tapestry was commenced, and indeed before Bede wrote, stirrups had been introduced from the East and had come into general use in Europe. They solved the last technical problem of men riding astride. No thought was given to female riders.

The earliest indication of the use of the side saddle appears—astonishingly—on a Pictish tombstone of about A.D. 750.[2] This monument shows a Pictish princess riding

Fig. 11   Spanish Cavaliers seated sideways, *c*. 2150 years ago

[1] Richard Bergenger, Esq., Gentleman of the Horse to His Majesty, King George III of Britain: *The History and Art of Horsemanship* (printed for T. Davies and T. Cadell, London, 1771), vol. i, p. 168.

[2] Stuart Cruden: *The Early Christian and Pictish Monuments of Scotland* (H.M. Stationery Office, Ministry of Public Buildings and Works).

apparently on a side saddle. The Picts occupied parts of Scotland and Ireland. Their origin is obscure and there is no indication as to when or how they developed side saddles, which began to be used in Eastern Europe some centuries after the princess. Their use rapidly became general and they were first introduced into Britain by the retinue of Anne of Bohemia, who came as a young bride to the unfortunate Richard II in 1382. Her father had ruled Bohemia; he and his family were related or connected by marriage to most of the royal families of Europe, so it is clear that by 1380, or thereabouts, the use of the side saddle was general in the courts of Europe.

It was widely appreciated in Britain where, up to that time, women had ridden, in Berenger's words, "with their legs indecently astride".[1] Even with the aid of a side saddle, ladies were considered to be incapable of managing stallions and rode mares, like the prelates. Spirited ladies who objected to being restricted to mares could only sit sideways on a pad behind the male rider of a stallion. Thus in 1579, Queen Elizabeth I "rode behind her Master of the Horse when she went in State to St Paul's".[2] The following year coaches were introduced to Britain, which ended this practice.

The Horse in History—War

The history of domesticated horses obviously includes a proportion of the history of their owners, and horse-masters have done much to shape the course of human history. At first, the horse was regarded mainly as an instrument of war. "With one single exception . . . the horse is never mentioned in the Old Testament but in a military connection. It was the animal of war, as the ass was of peace."[3]

As we have seen, the horse burst upon the ancient world drawing a fast-moving chariot, but as soon as an adequate number of riding horses became available, the greater flexibility of cavalry made the chariot obsolete on the battlefield, though it was long retained for racing, hunting, and for ceremonial purposes. As recently as 2500 years ago there still existed in the Mediterranean area horses which were said to be "not strong enough to bear men on their backs; but when yoked to chariots they are among the swiftest known".[4]

When Julius Caesar was expanding the Roman Empire 2100 years ago he met chariots only in Britain. Throughout the mainland of Europe they had been superceded by cavalry several hundred years before.

The earliest detailed records of warriors on horseback come from Assyria, which comprised eastern Persia and western Iraq. Assyrian bronze reliefs of about 2900 years ago show mounted spearmen each leading a spare horse (see Fig. 6). No doubt they changed horses from time to time. These spearmen may well have fought on foot and have really been mounted infantry. Other contemporary reliefs show mounted archers in action. Assyrian records make it clear that they were short of riding horses. Their total army numbered over 60,000, of whom a mere 2000 were mounted.

Some indication of the distribution of horses in the Middle East at that time is given by a monument erected by an Assyrian monarch 2825 years ago. This gives details of the armies of a dozen kings who had opposed him. The rulers of two City States in what is now Syria contributed between them nearly 2000 horsemen, the same number of chariots, and 30,000 infantry; no other king produced any horsemen. King Ahab of Israel (which then included much of present-day Jordan)contributed no horsemen, 2000 chariots, and 10,000 infantry. Five rulers had nothing but infantry, while three produced infantry plus a few dozen chariots. One sheikh, described as "Ginzibu the Arab", produced 1000 men on camels and nothing else.

[1] Berenger, *op. cit.*, vol. i, p. 105.   [2] *Ibid.*, p. 184.
[3] *Illustrated Bible Treasury*, annexed to King James' Edition of the Holy Bible (Eyre and Spottiswoode, London), p. 284.
[4] *The History of Herodotus* (The Tudor Publication Co., New York, 1947), trans. by George Rawlinson, ed. by Manuel Komroff; pp. 267 and 268.

As time went on, almost every nation began to rely on cavalry, which was, for example, the key to the remarkable series of victories achieved by Alexander the Great. The most notable exception was Rome, who relied principally on her legions of heavily armoured infantry and employed mounted mercenaries for cavalry purposes. Rome's most successful general, Julius Caesar, was in an embarrassing predicament when he needed to parley with an enemy general who, well knowing that Caesar had no reliable cavalry, refused to meet unless it was agreed that each leader would be escorted only by horsemen. Caesar was forced to dismount some of his mercenaries. He then "mounted the Tenth Legion on their horses and proceeded to the meeting place".[1] History does not relate what the faithful Tenth Legion (or the horses) thought of this procedure.

Julius Caesar was fortunate never to have been opposed by first-class cavalry; his second-in-command, Curio, was defeated and killed by Numidian cavalry in North Africa, while the balance of power in the Roman world was changed when Caesar's partner, Crassus, was killed and his army virtually destroyed by Parthian cavalry.[2]

Some three hundred years after Caesar's day, the army of Imperial Rome was opposed by a force of Persian heavy cavalry which completely defeated it and captured the Roman Emperor Valerian, who paid homage to his conqueror (see Fig. 12).

After this, the Roman Empire was divided into two parts, east and west, and in the century after Valerian's capture, the Goths, on their massive cold-blooded horses, launched a full-scale invasion of the eastern part of the Roman Empire. The Emperor Valens marched innumerable legions to oppose them; they met at Adrianople. In the ensuing battle, the Gothic cavalry rode through and over the Roman army. The Emperor and all his principal officers were left among the dead.

Field Marshal Montgomery wrote: "The battle of Adrianople is . . . of great significance. From then on, until the English archers and the Swiss pikemen challenged them in the fourteenth century, heavy cavalry were to be supreme in Europe."

He goes on to state that "the heavily armoured knight with his lance, his retainers, and the characteristic features of his warfare (chivalry and heraldry) derived from" the Goths and similar illiterate horsemen, and not from the more "civilized" Romans.[3]

After this victory, part of the Gothic nation known as the Visigoths rode into Italy where they defeated the armies of the western Roman Empire and sacked Rome itself.

Fig. 12   Roman Emperor surrenders to Persian King, A.D. 260

[1] Major-General J. F. C. Fuller: *Julius Caesar, Man, Soldier, and Tyrant* (Eyre and Spottiswoode, London, 1965), p. 108.
[2] *Ibid.*, p. 171.
[3] Field Marshal Viscount Montgomery: *A History of Warfare* (Collins, London, 1968), p. 127.

[23]

When in A.D. 409 they quitted the Peninsula "it was by their own choice, for there were no troops left in the world who could have expelled them by force".[1]

A generation after the Visigoths had left Italy, Europe was menaced by teeming thousands of pagan horsemen led by the dreaded Attila, the self-named "Scourge of God". The Visigoths, under their King, Theodoric, joined the Roman General Aetius and defeated the Huns in the battle of Châlons. "The victory was won . . . by sheer hard fighting, the decisive point having been the riding down of the native Huns by Theodoric's heavier Visigothic horsemen."[2]

From then on for centuries heavy cavalry was invincible when it charged directly at its objective. The last example of a decisive battle where infantry remained unbroken for a number of hours when opposed by heavy cavalry was at Hastings, where it seems that the Norman horsemen never quite charged home: "sometimes they cast [their lances] through the air like javelins. This shows that [the Norman lance] was a light weapon unlike the stouter lance of the later Middle Ages",[3] or the much earlier *contus* of the Lombards.

Armour became increasingly cumbersome and heavy until an acute observer remarked that "It protects the wearer and prevents him from injuring others."[4] The improvement of firearms gradually rendered heavy armour obsolete, and about four hundred years ago, the combination of light armour with a fast, handy horse began to prove more effective than the traditional combination of heavy armour with a ponderous charger. War-horses began to be bred lighter and faster, to the dismay of some heavily built warriors of the old school (see p. 123).

The Horse in History—Peace

All the great civilizations arose among horse-owning, horse-breeding, and horse-using nations; those in which the horse was either unknown or in the untamed state were backward and no great forward movement of mankind was made without the use of the horse.[5]

As horse breeders gradually produced bigger and stronger horses, and as the practice of riding became common, kings and rulers began to communicate by mounted couriers in a way which previously had been impossible.

It was the introduction of the horse from the East which, perhaps more than any other factor, changed the face of international politics—the beginning of the second millennium [B.C.] shows an extraordinary quickening of political conversation between Asia Minor, Egypt, and Mesopotamia.[6]

Innumerable examples could be given. After the early death of the celebrated Pharaoh, Tutankhamen, about 3300 years ago, his widowed queen, still in her early twenties, feared that she might be forced into marriage with one of her subjects. In desperation she sent messengers galloping over a thousand miles as the crow flies to the Hittite capital, bearing this message to the king: "My husband has died and I have no son, but of you it is said that you have many sons. If you would send me one of your sons, he could become my husband." Unfortunately, the Hittite king delayed while he made sure that this remarkable offer was genuine. By the time his son reached

[1] Oman, *op. cit.*, pp. 20 and 21.

[2] *Ibid.*

[3] Sir James Mann, K.C.V.O., Master of Armouries, Her Majesty's Tower of London, "Arms and Armour" in *The Bayeux Tapestry* (Phaidon Press, London, 1957), pp. 66 and 67.

[4] Colonel G. T. Denison: *A History of Cavalry* (Macmillan and Co., London, 1913), p. 135.

[5] *Encyclopaedia Britannica*, 1968 edition, vol. xiii, p. 701.

[6] *Cambridge Ancient History*, *op. cit.*, vol. ii, p. 227.

Egypt, the queen's supporters had lost control, the Hittite prince was murdered, and the queen was forcibly married to an Egyptian.[1]

Fig. 13   Lion-hunting from a Chariot, c. 2600 years ago

About a century later, Rameses II of Egypt wooed and won a Hittite princess by missives and presents carried by relays of galloping envoys. Contemporary accounts describe how she travelled to the frontier in a royal chariot escorted by a glittering array of Hittite cavalry, to be received by a similar escort of Egyptian horsemen: "And they brought the daughter of the great [Hittite] Prince before His Majesty, and His Majesty saw that she was fair of countenance like a goddess . . . and he loved her more than anything else."[2]

The Assyrians were great hunters as well as great warriors. Apart from hunting in the ordinary way their kings delighted in slaughtering lions and other wild animals much as gladiators did in the Roman circuses. The Assyrians caught and kept quantities of wild animals, which were released in a selected strip of desert surrounded by the Assyrian army. Assyrian monarchs slaughtered these captured lions, literally by the dozen, sometimes from chariots, with bows and arrows, sometimes on horseback, with lance and sword—in either case accepting a considerable degree of risk (see Fig. 13).

Although the Romans preferred to fight on foot and not as cavalry, they recognized the importance of horse transport and organized a courier service along their excellent roads. This consisted of relays of horse teams which drew a light four-wheeled vehicle called a *reda* at a considerable speed. Roman couriers regularly covered 80 miles a day; Julius Caesar is said to have travelled 100 miles a day by *reda*.[3] In an emergency 130 or 150 miles could be achieved in a day.

The Romans took less interest in horsemanship than the majority of their less civilized contemporaries who delighted in fast horses of good quality. These were particularly valued for hunting big game which, in those days, was found by hounds, pursued on horseback, and brought down by a javelin thrown by a galloping rider:

> The white-skinned, fair-haired, blue-eyed barbarians who, out of the wreck of the Roman Empire, carved the states from which sprang modern Europe, were passionately devoted to hunting. . . . The kings, the nobles, and the freemen of the regions which now make France and Germany, followed not only the wolf, boar, and the stag . . . but the bear, the bison, and the Aurochs, the huge wild ox; one of the early Burgundian kings was killed while hunting the bison; and Charlemagne was not only passionately devoted to the chase of these huge wild cattle, but is said to have prized the prowess shown therein by one of his stalwart daughters.[4]

[1] Gurney, *op. cit.*, p. 31.   [2] Keller, *op. cit.*, p. 116.   [3] Fuller, *op. cit.*, p. 73.

[4] W. A. and F. Baillie-Grohman (eds.): *The Master of Game* (Chatto and Windus, London, 1909; second edition), foreword by President Theodore Roosevelt, p. xxi.

Originally all ploughing and heavy draught work was done by oxen, but after the invention of the hard horse-collar in China about 2000 years ago horses began to be used for dragging the ponderous heavy carts of those days. The introduction of metal horseshoes increased their efficiency.

The light wheels that had carried chariots so effectively over the level plains and deserts of the Middle East and North Africa were useless in the undrained tracks which passed for roads in post-Roman Europe. Enormous vehicles with huge ponderous wheels were dragged slowly with innumerable jolts by teams of five to ten horses, generally harnessed in tandem (see Fig. 14).

Since mares were thought unfit to carry warriors (see p. 21) the development of weight-carrying chargers for heavily armed knights resulted, as a by-product, in the development of powerful mares capable of heavy draught work, which covered the ground much faster than oxen. The fast-moving stage-coach of the last century only became feasible when roads of a modern type were constructed to equal, but hardly to surpass, the Roman roads of 1500 years before. In the intervening centuries, there was little or no demand for fast-moving draught horses.

This section would not be complete without a reference to the history of trick riding. The feats performed in the modern circus are, in some cases, of great antiquity. The well-known expert Mr M. Wilson Disher claims that "performing animals were part of everyday life long before the Romans"[1] and, on page 24, he refers to a Roman term meaning "a performer who leapt from horse to horse". Contemporary writers make it clear that trick riding and performing horses were quite common in the Middle Ages (see Fig. 15).

Medieval Horses

Medieval riders seem to have taken little interest in the finer points of horsemanship, and to have had equally little consideration for their unfortunate mounts, which were urged along with whip and spur until the destination was reached or a change of horse became available. If the horse survived to be ridden again, so much the better. If not, there were always plenty more.

Possibly for this reason, medieval writers give extraordinarily little accurate information about the type or breed of horses then in use. For example, the famous Chronicler Sir John Froissart, familiar as he was with all the Courts of Europe, left a detailed description of innumerable wars and tournaments between about 1320 and 1399, but he describes horses by breed only on one occasion, and then uses two names for the same type of horse.

Fig. 14 Medieval Carriage, c. A.D. 1300

[1] M. Wilson Disher: *Fairs, Circuses, and Music Halls* (Collins, London, 1942), pp. 17 *et seq.*

The Scots are bold and hardy and much inured to war. When they make their invasions into England, they march from twenty to four and twenty leagues, without halting, as well by day as by night, for they are all on horseback—the Knights and the Squires are mounted on large bay horses, the common people on little Galloways.

A little farther on, he states that the less wealthy Scottish soldiers were "mounted upon little Hackneys that were never tied up . . . but turned, immediately after the day's march, to pasture on heath or in the fields".[1] Froissart recognized the strategic importance of the mobility of the Scottish army, but he describes the majority of their horses alternately as "Galloways" and as "Hackneys", using the terms as though they were synonymous.

Clear evidence of the lack of knowledge concerning horses and their management is given, a century later, in the *Boke of St Albans*, first published in 1479 by Wynkyn de Worde. This famous compendium of medieval learning gives remarkably full details of hawking and hunting, and even of fishing, together with details of heraldry, coats of arms, and other courtly matters. It also purports to give information about horses, for the printer's 'blurb' states: "This present boke showeth the manere of hawkynge and huntynge. ... . It showeth also a good matere belonginge to horses: wyth other commendable treatyses."

The "good matere belonginge to horses" consists of precisely nine surprising lines which, converted into present-day language, run as follows:

A good horse should have fifteen properties and conditions. That is to wit three of the man, three of the woman, three of the fox, three of the hare, and three of the ass. Of a man: bold, proud, and hardy. Of a woman: good chested, with good hair, and easy to leap upon. Of a fox: a good tail, short ears, with good action. Of a hare: a large eye, a head with no loose skin, and able to go fast. Of an ass: a big chin, a flat leg, and a good hoof.

The passage ends with the following assertion: "Well-travelled woman, nor well-travelled horse were never good." That this rigmarole, probably traditional and possibly handed down from previous centuries, should have been included in a book showing expert knowledge of hunting and hawking—and even of dogs, of which a number of separate breeds and types are listed—reveals the extraordinary lack of knowledge of horses which prevailed at that time, and which makes it so difficult to investigate the origins of our present-day breeds.

It seems probable that 'breeds' in the modern sense were not contemplated at this period, each horse being assessed for the task to which it was most suitable, without

[1] Thomas Johnes, trans. from the French: *Sir John Froissart's Chronicles* (printed at the Haford Press, 1803), vol. i, pp. 31 and 32.

regard to its origin. Berenger quotes a fascinating "Chequir Roul" of the horses kept in the London stables of the Duke of Northumberland in 1512.[1] The horses were divided into "gentil hors, palfreys, hobys, naggis, cloth-sek hors, and male hors". There were four palfreys, "One for my Lady and 2 for her gentil-women and one for her Chamberlain". Four "hobys and naggis" for his Lordship, one to be ridden, one to lead, one for the groom, and one "to stay at home for my Lorde".

Also, there were "7 great trottynge hors" to draw "my Lorde's" chariot, and a nag for the chariot man to ride. For Lord Percy, the heir, a "great doble trottynge hors" and a similar, called a "curtail", for his Lordship "to ride on out of towns". When his Lordship came to a town he entered it on a "trottynge gambaldynge" horse. There were also ambling horses for daily use.

Berenger explains these terms. The "gentil" horse was "of a superior and distinguished breed"—no indication was given of what breed this might be. "Palfreys" were "elegant" horses with "easy paces" used by knights "on common occasions" and by ladies. "Hobys" were "strong, active horses of rather a small size. They are reported to have been originally natives of Ireland."

A "cloth-sek" horse "was a cloak-bag horse, as the 'male' horse is one who carried the portmanteaux". A "grete doble trottynge hors" was a "tall, broad, well spread horse whose best pace was the trot, being too unwieldy . . . to be able to gallop". A "curtail" was a horse with a docked tail. A "gambaldynge" horse was "one of show and parade—a maneged horse", and so on. These descriptions seem to confirm that breeding as we understand it was not dreamed of in those days.

Some fifty years later, Thomas Blundevill produced his "Arte of Riding",[2] in which he lists the breeds of horses known in those days. He divides them almost entirely by their countries of origin—the Sardinian, the Hungarian, and the "Highe Alamagne" are considered to be breeds regardless of their size or type or the duties they performed. This appears to be the earliest comprehensive list of 'breeds' in Britain. It is further discussed on page 123.

Horsemanship becomes an Art

The Greeks, and possibly some of their contemporaries, made considerable strides in the art of horsemanship, as is proved by Zenophon's works "Hippike" and the less well-known treatise "The Cavalry Commander",[3] written 2300 years ago. Numerous commentators have pointed out that many of Xenophon's principles still make sense today. For example, he knew the importance of gaining a horse's confidence and of training by encouragement and by the offer of reward rather than by punishing mistakes.

After the eclipse of Greece, Xenophon's principles were neglected and no European author contributed any work of importance on horses or horse management for some eight hundred years. After the introduction of stirrups from Asia, some 1500 years ago, riding in European countries went ahead and developed on several different lines— for example, there was a cross-country style for hunting and hawking, where any and every sort of going had to be negotiated as fast as possible, and a more formal style for warfare and tournaments. Richard Berenger recorded that the horses used for the latter purposes were known as "Dextrarii", "Magni Equi", or "Great Horses because they were required to be of the largest size, and were always intended to serve in war or in the exercises of the Tournament".[4]

[1] Berenger, *op. cit.*, vol. i, pp. 178 *et seq.*

[2] Thomas Blundevill: *The Fower Chiefyst Offices belonging to Horsmanshippe* (printed by Wyllyam Serres at the Signe of the Hedgehogge, London, *c.* 1565), Folio 6 *et seq.*

[3] Xenophon: *Scripta minora* (Loeb Classical Library).

[4] Berenger, *op. cit.*, vol. i, p. 169.

Berenger adds that "these Great Horses were all required to be dressed or taught, that they might perform their task with more readiness and fidelity". The term "dressed" came from a French word which survives in our word "dressage". Their riders were obliged to learn the art of "maneging their horses in conformity to certain rules and principles". War horses were said to be "maneged" or schooled, although it appears that their training was limited to certain rather rudimentary manoeuvres. The Great Horses, and their continental equivalents, were controlled by extraordinarily powerful curb bits, augmented by sharp spurs which were sometimes over a foot in length. (See Plates 17 and 18.)

About 450 years ago there was a sudden upsurge of interest in horses and horsemanship in northern Italy. Leonardo da Vinci published a pamphlet, *The Proportions of a Horse*, and is said to have been the first to use the 'hand' to measure a horse's height. This was followed, in about 1550, by a book, *L'Ecurie de Sieur Grison*, which soon became famous, and led to the formation of what became known as the Neapolitan School of Riding. Grison's book was founded largely on Xenophon's works, but, unfortunately, he advocated the use of the heavy curb bits which had been developed in the Tilt Yard. His influence, and the new method of measuring horses, soon spread across the length and breadth of Europe. For example, King Henry VIII of England decreed that all substantial land-owners must keep a number of breeding mares of "the altitude or height of 13 handfuls at the least".[1]

A dozen years later, Thomas Blundevill, afterwards famous as the author of *The Fower Chiefyst Offices belongyng to Horsmanshippe*, was commissioned by the Earl of Leicester to translate Sieur Grison's book into English. Sidney Felton relates that eventually Blundevill abandoned the work of translation and produced his own book "though expressing Grison's ideas".[2]

Italian riding masters were introduced to the English Court at about this time. Their methods and their writings had a marked effect on the system of horsemanship then in vogue, but inevitably there were disagreements between those horsemen who wished to train their horses only for the fairly simple manoeuvres required for war and those who wished to school them for the finer arts of equitation. Blome deals with this conflict at some length in Chapter 9 of *The Gentleman's Recreation* where he contrasts the "Manege which is proper for the Cheval d'Escole" (*sic*) with that "which is proper for the Cheval de Guerre" and concludes that the

Fig. 15 Medieval Performing Horse, *c*. A.D. 1340

confounding of these two . . . makes a great many talk very ignorantly about maneg'd horses, some disputing the whole art of riding the Great Horse, because for want of Education they know nothing of it, while others are such formal Academists that they pretend every lesson is as necessary in action [*i.e.*, in war] as Stopping, Turning, and the like.[3]

In spite of all opposition, informed and otherwise, Grison's ideas spread fast. Soon after his first book was published, a Riding School was evolved in Spain, based partly on the methods of riding developed by the Spanish Cavaliers, modified by the principles taught by Grison and his successors at the Neapolitan School. The Spanish Riding School was later transferred to Vienna where, even today, it still operates in its full glory (see p. 52). Meanwhile, the Neapolitan Riding School was going from strength

[1] Henry VIII, Statutes of England 27, Chapter 6.
[2] W. Sidney Felton: *Masters of Equitation* (J. A. Allen and Co., London, 1962), pp. 28–43.
[3] Richard Blome: *The Gentleman's Recreation* (printed by S. Rycroft, London, 1686), Part II, p. 4.

to strength. Pignatelli, who succeeded Grison as Director of the Riding School at Naples, had a wide influence on European riding; the future riding masters of both Louis XIII and Louis XV of France were among his better known pupils. Both of these French riding masters wrote important books and spread the Neapolitan doctrine far and wide. Their successor, the famous De La Guerinière, wrote one of the best known books on riding of all times, which is the foundation of the doctrine taught in modern times at the Spanish Riding School. It has had a considerable effect on the teaching of military equitation, both in Eastern Europe and in Germany, and its influence has continued long after the original Neapolitan School and its other offshoots have disappeared—often as a result of being occupied (and their horses requisitioned) by Napoleon's victorious armies about 160 years ago.

In recent years a 'new' style of 'western riding' has become increasingly popular for pleasure riding on both sides of the Atlantic. It has been developed from the style of riding of the North American cowboy, but although classical riders tend to disparage this sytem, it is certainly by no means new. It was brought to Mexico by the Spaniards when they re-introduced horses into North America. They had acquired it centuries before from the Moors, who in turn had learnt it from the Moslems some 1200 years ago.

The style of riding without a bit and by neck reining is still common in some Arab countries. General Sir John Glubb comments: "Those who have only ridden with our English impedimenta of snaffles and curbs and reins may find it difficult to believe that 'hands' are as necessary and equally effective when galloping a well-bred horse with only a rope to hold her."[1]

In America, in the numerous competitions for 'Western Riders', one of the standard tests requires that "The horse shall, on command, come promptly and without resistance from a hand gallop to a free relaxed walk on a completely loose rein. The better trained horses accomplish this in 100 ft or less."[2] Felton remarks on page 53:

When our modern cowboy rides in his Mexican saddle, using a single rein attached to a high port bit . . . carrying a high bridle hand and guiding his horse by neck reining, he is practising a method of riding which . . . with some modification, has come to him . . . from those very Saracens who were the foes of Richard Cœur de Lion.

Horse Racing and Race Horses

The earliest recorded horse race formed part of an Olympiad about 2600 years ago. Thereafter, horse racing became a regular feature of these original Olympic Games and was known throughout the Greek and Roman world. The rules were then distinctly different from those of today. For example, on one occasion a famous mare threw her jockey at the start of the race, galloped round the course, and came into the straight among the leaders: "On hearing the trumpet, [she] quickened her pace, reached the umpires [judges] first, knew that she had won, and stopped." The mare was not only declared the winner but was honoured by a monument recording her achievement.[3]

Outside Europe horses were raced in Persia, Arabia, and Egypt but such records as remain give no details of the horses or of the distance run. Horses were raced in North Germany, and in Britain during the Roman occupation, but throughout most of the Roman world the more dramatic chariot racing seems to have been the favourite.

[1] General Sir John Glubb: *The War in the Desert* (Hodder & Stoughton, London, 1960), p. 127 *et seq.*
[2] Felton, *op. cit.*, p. 58.
[3] Anderson, *op. cit.*, p. 14.

The early Christians were entirely opposed to racing of any sort, and at the first Council of Arles in A.D. 353 all persons concerned with racing in any form were severely censured, while those who raced chariots were made liable to excommunication unless they renounced this ungodly activity. In spite of this threat, racing seems to have persisted for some generations, but there are few definite references to horse racing for six hundred years after the fall of the Roman Empire.

The earliest account of horses being raced regularly is in A.D. 1170, when Fitzstephen referred to "Horse Fairs" where horses of all kinds were sold every Friday on a *campus planus* or "smooth field" situated just outside one of London's city gates. Sometimes the horses were raced. Unfortunately, Fitzstephen, like all medieval writers, gives only the most superficial description of the horses. He states that they consisted of "strong steeds wel limmed", and he also refers to geldings "whom the buyers do specially regard for pace and swiftness". He adds, "the boyes which ride the horses . . . do runne races for wagers, with a desire for praise or hope of victorie".[1]

A fuller account, attributed to Stephanides,[2] states that on Fridays "except some greater festival intervene" horses were brought to the Smoothfield to be sold and that every Sunday during Lent mounted games took place on this Smoothfield (believed to be the present-day Smithfield) which sometimes included races.

> Two or three boys are set on horseback to ride a race. The signal being given, they set off and push their horses to their utmost speed, sparing neither whip nor spur, urging them on at the same time with loud shouts and clamours to animate their endeavours and call forth all their powers.

After this date, horse racing took place all over Britain at fairs and on holidays, but curiously there are no such records of horse racing on the Continent. Froissart, the famous Chronicler, records only one contest in the nature of a horse race, and this was more of a match than a race. The King of France and his brother, the Duke of Touraine, agreed to race from Montpellier to Paris for a wager of 500 francs, a considerable sum in those days. Froissart states that they "rode on, night and day, frequently changing horses, or had themselves conveyed in carts when they wished to take any repose". The King reached Paris in four and a half days, to find that the Duke, "who would at all times exert himself to get money", had beaten him by about four hours. Froissart adds that the Duke "made himself be paid the wager in ready money".[3] There is some doubt as to the distance actually covered. Froissart claims they travelled 150 leagues, but the map suggests a shorter distance. In any case, both competitors would have been beaten by a Roman courier in a hurry, 1200 years before.

As racing in Britain became increasingly well established and the honours to be won became more sought after, greater attention was paid to the horses which were raced though, unfortunately, contemporary writers give us but little definite information about them. It appears that they were generally known as "running horses" or "Galloways". They were selected for breeding solely on their performances in races, the most successful stallions being mated to the most successful mares.

The first British monarch to own race horses and to run them seems to have been King James I, who obtained an Arab stallion, the Markham Arabian, originally bought in Constantinople. This horse failed both as a sire and on the race course, and James's second Arabian stallion fared little better. Nevertheless, James did much to promote racing in Britain. "Public races were now established, and such horses as had given proof of superior abilities became famous and their breed was cultivated."[4]

---

[1] Fitzstephen quoted in *A Survey of London* by John Stow (printed by John Wolfe of London, 1598), p. 61.
[2] Quoted by Berenger, *op. cit.*, vol. i, pp. 164 *et seq.*
[3] Johnes, *op. cit.*, vol. ii, pp. 125 *et seq.*
[4] Berenger, *op. cit.*, vol. i, p. 188.

James's successor, King Charles I, was a great patron of racing and maintained a Royal Stud. After his defeat in the Civil War and subsequent execution, horse racing was forbidden and almost died out, though Oliver Cromwell (more broadminded than other rebels) preserved some of the late king's brood mares. Royalist officers attempted to introduce horse racing to the Continent during their period of exile, but without success.

After the Restoration in 1660, King Charles II re-established racing in Britain on an increasing scale, and made Newmarket the principal centre. The "Round Course" was created in 1666. The king not only owned and bred race horses, he himself rode in races and sometimes won. He also imported breeding stock. This was the period when the Thoroughbred was in the process of being created, and it has been pointed out that every Thoroughbred existing in any part of the world today can be traced back in male line to one of three foundation sires, and in the female line to one or more of about thirty 'tap-root' mares.[1]

In 1752 the Jockey Club leased land at Newmarket and built a Coffee Room for the convenience of its members. This is the first recorded action of the Club, whose origin is wrapped in mystery, but soon after this it began to influence racing at Newmarket, the most important course then in existence. Fifty-six years later the Club purchased the whole of Newmarket Heath and took control of all race meetings held there. In 1832 other British race courses were "recommended" to adopt the Jockey Club's rules, and in 1870 the Club formally recognized other race meetings held under the "Rules of Racing" previously laid down for Newmarket.[2]

The great burst of interest in racing and race horses extinguished that in ambling or pacing horses, formerly very popular in Britain. Many of the best of these went to North America, where they helped to found strains of pacers and trotters which became famous. This led to the pacing and trotting races which have since become so popular in many parts of the world, but never in Britain, where the public are interested only in horse racing in its classic form.

For the first 150 years or so after the Restoration, most races were run in heats over distances of two to four miles, the horses carrying relatively heavy weights—up to twelve stone and sometimes more. Horses of that period might have to race anything from eight to sixteen miles in one day, and for this reason were seldom raced before they were four years old. Towards the end of the eighteenth century, shorter races for three-year-olds became popular, and some races, including the original Derby, were run over one mile.

The earliest example of a two-year-old being raced was in 1769, but by ninety years later over one-third of all horses raced in Britain were two-year-olds, and in the year 1890 nearly half were two-year-olds. The Jockey Club tried to check this tendency by limiting the number of races for two-year-olds at each meeting.[3] Nevertheless, this emphasis on short races led some British breeders to concentrate on speed without sufficient regard to staying power, a tendency less evident in countries such as France, where different circumstances prevailed.

During the last half-century, Thoroughbred breeding has become increasingly an international affair. Stallions had crossed national frontiers by purchase or capture from a very early date; more recently, high-quality mares and fillies have been purchased from their country of origin for breeding purposes.

The greatly increased facilities for air travel now enable race horses to compete wherever their owners prefer, and Mr Schapiro's International Race at Washington D.C. has attracted competitors from many countries. The racing public usually considers horses to belong to the country in which they have raced most regularly or most

---

[1] See article on "The Thoroughbred Horse", p. 50.

[2] Eric Rickman, "Robin Goodfellow" of the *Daily Mail*, 1929–49: *Come Racing With Me* (Chatto and Windus, London, 1951), pp. 30 *et seq.*

[3] *Ibid.*, pp. 54 *et seq.*

17 *The Great Italian War-horse represented in one of the famous battle-pieces of the Renaissance. The sturdy armour-bearing animal, almost cubistically realized, is seen in this detail of a painting by Paolo Uccello, commissioned by Piero de Medici to commemorate the skirmish of San Romano in April 1432.*

18 *Through the eyes of Albrecht Dürer the German war-horse becomes less abstract, every tuft and nail is shown. This famous copper engraving, dated 1505, is in the British Museum, and is known as "The Great Horse" (see pp. 28–29).*

Two plates from Johannes Stradanus's collection of notable breeds, dated 19
1570. above: *the Flanders stallion, already showing the characteristic great
neck and small head later to be familiar in the paintings of van Dyck and
Rubens.* below: *the Spanish horse, equally famous in the Middle Ages and
often the gift of kings* (see p. 88).

20 *While in exile in Antwerp, William Cavendish, Marquis, later Duke of Newcastle, published in 1657 a famous book on equestrianism, La Methode et Invention Nouvelle de Dresser les Chevaux, with illustrations by Abraham van Diepenbeke. The plate Caprioles par le Droite shows the Marquis carrying out a manoeuvre nowadays associated with the Spanish Riding School in Vienna (see p. 52). One of the ducal seats, Bolsover*

Another plate from "the Duke of Newcastle's book" depicts the author 21
standing in the centre directing galloping, trotting, and walking to left and
right. Note how the horses have been trained to hold their heads.

A Friesian horse ridden by Pieter Schout in the cavalcade greeting Prince William of Orange at Amsterdam in 1660. A comparatively rare equestrian portrait in Dutch painting by Thomas de Keyser, recording the finery Schout wore on that occasion. 22

23   *The Byerley Turk, the earliest of the three Eastern sires from whom all bloodstock is descended (their influence is discussed on pp. 50 and 124). The first recorded mention is when he was ridden by Captain Byerley at the Battle of the Boyne, 1690. A print from the painting by John Wootton.*

An Arabian Horse, belonging to JOHN BREWSTER DARLEY Esq. of ALDBY.

The Darley Arabian was the second of the renowned trio 24
of Thoroughbred ancestors and perhaps the best known.
He was imported from Aleppo by John Brewster Darley
of Buttercombe, near York, in 1705. He was a bay of
fifteen hands, with a large forehead flash and three white
fetlocks, clearly seen in this print after a painting by
John Wootton.

25   *The Godolphin Arabian, also known as the Godolphin Barb, was brought to England in 1730 by Edward Coke, who discovered him pulling a cart in Paris, and is reputed to have been stolen from a royal stud in Barbary. He was afterwards purchased by the second Earl of Godolphin and was one of the most successful progenitors imported into England before or since. George Stubbs was employed in 1790 to paint this adaption of Wootton's original contemporary portrait.*

Flying Childers, celebrated son of the Darley Arabian and the most popular 26
horse of his day. He was foaled in 1715, his dam being Betty Leedes and
his owner Leonard Childers of Carr House, near Doncaster. He was never
beaten, although it must be said that he only ran five times. Painting by
John Wootton.

27 *Although Eclipse was painted by Francis Sartorius more often than by any other painter this fine picture is by George Stubbs. Eclipse was bred by the Duke of Cumberland and foaled during the eclipse of 1764. He did not run in public till he was five years old. He was never beaten, and none disputed the claim that he was the fastest horse in England since Flying Childers.*

A striking painting of an unknown grey stallion, with his harness and   28
saddle-cloth clearly delineated, being held by a groom in royal livery. The
picture is dated 1786 and is by Francis Sartorius, one of the most prolific
painters of horse portraits.

29 *Grey Diomed beating Traveller at Newmarket in 1798;*
a good example of how artists saw the galloping horse
before photography revealed the familiar 'rocking-horse'
posture to be impossible in nature. Grey Diomed was bred
by Sir Charles Bunbury, Bart, in 1785. Painting by
Francis Sartorius.

Cross-country races by 'young bloods' from one church tower to another by
moonlight were the origin of steeplechasing. Here Henry Alken shows them
"screaming, whooping, like devil-rid maniacs" dressed in nightgowns and
caps clattering through the quiet village street at Nacton, much to the alarm
of the "affrighted villagers". A print published in 1839.

30

31   *Merry Tom, a Clydesdale foaled in May 1848 near Carlisle and strikingly portrayed by R. Harrington. Issued as a coloured aquatint by C. Hunt in 1856.*

32 *A contrast in harness and vehicles.* above: *Maud S. "The Queen of the Turf" and "fastest trotter the world has ever known". Foaled in Kentucky in 1874 and owned by Robert Bonner of New York. Hand-coloured lithograph. below: Krasa, an Orlov Trotter and winner of the Emperor's Prize. Painting of 1870 by N. Sverchkov in the Moscow Museum of Horse-breeding.*

recently, as opposed to that in which they were bred. For example, when Sir Ivor won the International Race at Washington in 1968 he was regarded by the American public as a British horse, though he had been bred in America and trained in Ireland, while the second horse, Czar Alexander, was regarded as an American horse though he was pure Irish-bred and had been raced in Britain, France, and Germany before being exported to the U.S.A.

Riding becomes Competitive

From very early times, skill in riding has been considered a desirable social accomplishment as well as a necessity for cavalry and for all mounted officers. Nearly three hundred years ago, Richard Blome wrote: "There is certainly no exercise more Noble and Manly than this of the *Manège*—it makes a man firm and easy on Horseback, and vigorous and adroit in Action."[1] He adds that skill in riding "gives a man a graceful and Martial Air, which one may perceive in some fine Horsemen (even when they are on foot)".

After jousting and similar medieval pastimes had been eclipsed by racing, some of the earliest forms of mounted competition were developed from cavalry training and, in more recent times, were sponsored by the War Departments of the nations concerned. For example, about a hundred years ago the British War Office was sponsoring an annual competition known as the "Lloyd Lindsay", which is of particular interest as it was probably one of the first competitions to involve team jumping, and is almost certainly the first competition in Britain to include an element of jumping 'against the clock'.

In this competition, each team of four riders had to cover a course of six furlongs, which involved clearing a flight of hurdles, dismounting to fire five rounds at targets, remounting to jump a second flight of hurdles, dismounting to engage further targets, and remounting to take a final flight of hurdles before making a dash to the finishing post. A time limit, initially of twelve minutes, was set, each team's score on the targets being increased by five points for every half minute below the time limit, and reduced by one penalty point for every six seconds above it.

The winning team secured the "All England" prize of £50, a considerable sum in those days, and the competition, held on Wimbledon Common, attracted great public interest. The spectators often included members of the Royal Family.

The event was open to all mounted units, including the Regular Cavalry and the Yeomanry (predecessors of the British Territorial Army), and was almost always won by Yeomanry regiments who normally secured the first three places. One Yeomanry regiment[2] won the 'All England' prize in 1876 in the record time of 7 minutes 25 seconds, achieving the highest score ever obtained with the carbine then in use. This regiment was second in 1877 and first again in 1878. Three years later, at the Royal Military Tournament, they won five first, seven second, and three third prizes. Contemporary reports suggest that their successes were largely attributable to the superiority of their horses which, being accustomed to galloping across country with the Blackmore Vale and Portman Hunts, were more suited to competitive work than the chargers of the Regular Cavalry.

Apart from military competitions, many exhibitions of various kinds included classes for horses of different breeds and types, but for some reason jumping classes seem to have been a novelty, even one hundred years ago. For example, they were featured

[1] Blome, *op. cit.*
[2] The Queen's Own Dorset Yeomanry.

[33]

at the International Horse Show at Manchester in May 1874, but were omitted at the much bigger International Horse Show sponsored by the Société Hippique at Paris in April 1875, though the latter included a "Carousel" consisting of "Feats of Horsemanship such as Tilting at the Ring, Throwing the Javelin, et cetera".[1]

Twelve years later, at the Great London Horse Show at Olympia, prizes of over £1200 were offered for Hunters, Hacks, Four-in-Hands, Tandem, and Jumping, and in 1907 the first International Horse Show at the same venue offered 124 classes for riding, harness, and agricultural horses of all kinds. These classes included one for the "Wide Jump" and one for the "Champion High Jump"; the latter attracted three French, nine Belgian, and ten British entrants. The top rail started at 5 feet 6 inches and was raised to 6 feet and to 6 feet 6 inches, after which it was to be raised by 3 inches at a time. The judges were required, in making their awards, to consider "the form in which the horses had taken their jumps". There was also a jumping competition "Over the whole Course, open to the World" which attracted Belgian, British, Canadian, Dutch, French, and Spanish entrants, to a total of seventy-five. Jumping was also a feature of some of the Hunter classes.

This was one of the first really international shows; the directors included four Americans, seven Britons, and three Canadians, as well as representatives of Belgium, France, Germany, Holland, and Italy. The vice-presidents included eight Dukes, nine Marquesses, fifty-three Earls, and innumerable other members of the British aristocracy.

The modern series of Olympic Games was revived in 1896, but it was not until 1908 that these included any form of equestrian competition. In this year Polo was introduced, and at the next Olympic Games, in 1912, there was a number of equestrian events.

At this time, all international competitions were the prerogative of military teams, civilian entries being unknown. In almost every country, inter-unit competitions were organized through the cavalry schools which flourished throughout the last century, and which continued until the mechanization of cavalry regiments some thirty years ago. Some cavalry schools survive today.

Early this century, the Italian Cavalry School at Pinerolo and its 'University' at Tor di Quinto had eclipsed all rivals due to the revolutionary system of the "forward seat" invented by Lieutenant Frederico Caprillo. Based on non-interference with the horse, the forward seat was first a military system and second a method of going across country. The weakness lay in the fact that it incorporated neither collection nor control of stride, both of which are essential to success in modern showjumping over big, spread fences, and over double and treble combination fences set at difficult distances. But these obstacles were then undreamt of, and the new system was enormously successful. News of it spread like wildfire and pupils came from all over the world to learn the new forward seat. Among many famous riders who came as students was Paul Rodzianko, who returned in 1907 to the Russian Imperial Cavalry School where he organized the show team which in 1914 became the sensation of Olympia (London) and Madison Square Garden (New York). Later, he taught equitation in Britain, where his pupils included Colonel Sir Mike Ansell (as he now is); then he served as official instructor to the Irish Free State Cavalry School in Dublin during the 1930s when the Irish team won important competitions on both sides of the Atlantic. In later years, students at the Italian School who were of international importance included Generals Chamberlain and West who later "returned to the United States to revolutionize the U.S. Cavalry instruction at Fort Riley".[2]

After 1912, continental instructors in the art of horsemanship began to develop methods of teaching dressage concerning which the Fédération Equestre Internationale, generally known as the F.E.I., claims that "it makes the horse calm, supple, and keen,

[1] The London *Times* (April 19th, 1875), p. 7.
[2] Felton, *op. cit.*, p. 68.

thus achieving perfect understanding with his rider . . . the horse thus gives the impression of doing, of his own accord, what is required of him". Different methods for teaching dressage were evolved in continental countries, and tests regulated by the F.E.I. became increasingly popular on the Continent, though in those days dressage was almost entirely ignored in Britain.

Meanwhile, showjumping had become firmly established on both sides of the Atlantic, but here again Britain preferred to ignore the new style fences which were becoming fashionable elsewhere, and resolutely refused to jump 'against the clock' as was being done overseas, though just before the Second World War, Colonel Sir Mike Ansell took part in an international competition at Nice, where, over the new-style fences, he succeeded in being 'placed' every day. On his return to Britain he organized for his regiment, the 5th Royal Inniskilling Dragoon Guards, a horse show at Colchester, with jumps of the new continental type. Despite scepticism from older riders, this show proved an immense success and laid the foundation for a reversal of the traditional British showjumping practices, and brought these nearer the style adopted by the rest of the world.

Horses and Riders in Post-War Europe

The greatest impact of the Second World War was felt in Europe, where war-time privations were endured for over four years, followed by a hangover of austerity for about as long again. Indeed, there must have been many who supposed that the Second World War would not only see the end of competitive horse sports in Europe but also the total eclipse of the horse as a means of recreation. Few people in 1940 would have believed that, within a quarter of a century, there would have been greater public interest in, and support for, European equestrianism than there had ever been before.

During the War itself, while the rest of the world was relatively unaffected, Europe's shortage of petrol and oil led to a curtailing of motor transport, and, especially in country districts, horse transport increased rather than diminished. This was particularly so in occupied countries where horses, discarded by the armies, became available for civilian use. As most continental armies had used a great deal of horse-drawn transport, a large number of horses were set free in this way.

As the tension of war bit more deeply, the greater became the need for some form of escapism. There was an urge to get back to pastimes and activities associated with pre-War conditions. For example, when the British Government permitted limited entertainment organized locally in what were known as "holidays at home", most rural districts hastened to organize gymkhanas and showjumping competitions. When the War ended there was a natural desire to return as quickly as possible to everything associated with peace and security, and for many people this included competitive riding; so, throughout Europe, enthusiasts began to revive the pre-War equestrian competitions.

In 1942, in a German prison camp, Colonel Sir Mike Ansell had joined with other British riding enthusiasts, including Colonel Nat Kindersley, in planning a revival and improvement of showjumping in Britain, making use of the continental style fences and of the new technique which had been tried out so successfully at Colchester in 1939 (see above). At the end of the War, despite the fact that he had lost his sight, Colonel Ansell and his friends succeeded in persuading the older generation, and the first post-War major event in Britain, the Victory Championship at the end of 1945, was held over a new style course of the type planned by the officer prisoners in 1942. The event was a triumph for Colonel Ansell's theories and a personal triumph for Colonel Nat Kindersley.

[35]

The next problem was to persuade all concerned to dramatize British showjumping by introducing a time limit and deciding between competitors with equal points by a jump-off against the clock. This principle was new to British riders, and to British horses, but eventually it was accepted and practised, and in the 1948 Olympic Games in London, the British team secured the bronze medal, coming behind Mexico and Spain, and thus leading all the countries which had been involved in the recent war.

At these Olympic Games, the Three-day Event attracted great interest, though the British riders made a poor showing. Later in the year, the Duke of Beaufort, Master of the Horse to Her Majesty The Queen, offered Badminton Park as a site for an annual British Three-day Event. This has become extremely popular and is regularly patronized by Royalty. It undoubtedly has played a great part in Britain's subsequent success in this event.

Before the War, international competition had been the prerogative of military teams, but since the War, with cavalry regiments disbanded and military stables empty, international showjumping and combined training became open to civilians. Although countries such as France, Eire, Spain, and Portugal still field military teams, most of the world has gradually succumbed to infiltration of non-military riders of both sexes. Such cavalry schools as survived have in most cases opened their doors to civilians. In countries such as Britain, where there are no longer cavalry schools, there are civilian schools like the National Equestrian Centre at Stoneleigh in Warwickshire.

Thus the old military principles are still being handed down to new generations of horsemen and horsewomen, who make use in competitions of the knowledge accumulated by their ancestors, whose survival in battle depended on the training of their horses and on their own skill in the saddle.

As years went by, more and more nations began to compete in international riding competitions; by the early 1950s West Germany was back among the leading contestants, as also was Italy and in the last ten years these two nations have shared with Britain the principal honours in European equestrianism.

The successes achieved by each of these three nations are due to rather different factors. The principal asset of the German teams, in addition to their excellent standard of riding, lies in their magnificent home-bred horses. Their successes in the international field have led to enormous public support. For instance, the great show at Aachen attracts thousands of non-riders every day, just as in other countries ball games attract thousands of non-players.

In Britain, on the other hand, the reaction to her successes has been a desire to participate. Showjumping and the spectacular and fascinating Horse of the Year Show attract big audiences, as does the unique Three-day Event at Badminton, but competitive riding otherwise does not attract substantial crowds. On the other hand, entries for shows, big and small, have become almost unmanageable. There are nearly seven thousand registered Jumpers in Britain, against five hundred in Spain.

In Italy, as in Britain, competitive jumping is not a popular attraction. In Rome, it is only on the fashionable Sunday that the crowd becomes substantial, but here again, their international team relies on excellent horses in the hands of a relatively small number of very experienced riders.

In most European countries, interest in horses is confined to those for competitive work. Draught horses are being replaced by mechanization, but the loss is largely balanced by the increasing number of horses bred for riding either for pleasure, racing, or competitive events. In nearly every country there is a growing interest in children's ponies, which indicates that the younger generation is keen to ride.

Against all the odds, an interest in riding and in the art of horsemanship has survived throughout Europe, the skills being divided among many nations; the majority of countries have some contribution to make, so that in riding, unlike so many other sports, Europe can still claim superiority over the rest of the world.

[36]

THE BRITISH ISLES

(Comprising the United Kingdom and Eire)

The tide of mechanization which has surged over Britain during the last forty years has inevitably had far-reaching effects upon the status of the British horse. Once a necessity, both in town and country, it has now moved into the luxury category. As far as the light horse is concerned, it has possibly benefited from the change: certainly it works far shorter hours, though equally certainly it does not always receive the knowledgeable care which was the stock-in-trade of the old-fashioned groom.

It is the working horses who have been dealt the hardest blow by the march of progress. For agricultural purposes the heavy horse has been largely replaced by the tractor, while the light vanner has virtually disappeared from the towns. Although a few people continue to employ the horse for commercial purposes, more often than not their reasons for doing so are purely sentimental. There are still a few holdings, and certain types of land, on which tractors are not a practical proposition, but in nearly every case the horse has been replaced by mechanization, not only because the tractor works faster and reduces the quota of essential labourers to a minimum, but also because it requires no attention at week-ends. The old days when the carters used to return to the stables to feed their horses on Saturday afternoons and three times on Sundays have gone for ever.

In Ireland, where progress is slower, the horse is still in use to a far greater extent. The more massive breeds are, however, not indigenous to that country, and, apart from a small concentration of imported Clydesdales, the bulk of the heavier horse population is confined to the Irish Draught Horse, a clean-legged and very active dual-purpose animal. Perhaps its greatest value is as a foundation mare for the breeding of high-class Hunters. Irish horses are famed all over the world, and in every case they are descended, sometimes only one generation away, from the Irish Draught Horse. England has always imported a great many of its Hunters from Ireland, while of the English-bred Hunters some of the best were to be found in Wales, the progeny of the Welsh Cob mares. With the decline of the heavy-horse population, and with the disappearance of Welsh Cobs in their hundreds, there was a very real threat to the British-bred Hunter too. Ten years ago the horses bred in Britain seemed to be getting lighter and lighter, with a frightening diminution in bone and substance, but in recent years, thanks to the constant vigilance of the Hunters' Improvement and Light Horse Breeding Society, the trend appears to have been halted, though there is still a great shortage of heavyweight brood mares.

In Britain riding of every kind is on the increase, and is now officially recognized as a 'growth sport'. The Riding Club movement has spread like wildfire through the towns and cities, and in many suburban districts too. Members come from most of the trades as well as from the professions, and all matters concerning equestrianism are treated very seriously, with instruction in stable management, dressage, and cross-country riding.

[37]

Longer established, and firmly entrenched in the life of thousands of country-bred children, is the Pony Club, whose work in encouraging the care of horses and ponies, and in improving the standard of horsemanship in the young, has without doubt done much to assure the future of the horse in this country.

Pony trekking on native ponies and cobs has also made great headway during the last ten years in the wilder parts of Britain, such as Dartmoor and Exmoor, and in the Welsh mountains and the Lake District. The urge to explore the countryside from the back of a horse is seldom matched by any great prowess in the saddle, but the combination of enthusiasm and a quiet animal is sufficient to ensure that the trekker enjoys his holiday and his horse is none the worse for the experience. More ambitious is the devotee of the newly incepted long-distance rides. Competitors are required to cover fifty miles of fairly difficult country within a specified time limit, at an average speed of some seven miles an hour. Before the days of motor horse-boxes practically every Hunter covered as much ground in a good day's hunting, and the old brigade may well regard the title 'long-distance ride' as a misnomer. Nevertheless the exercise appeals to increasing numbers of people who might not otherwise have much experience in getting a horse fit, and the pursuit is unobjectionable provided that there is adequate veterinary inspection available at every check-point.

For the more experienced rider there is, of course, the hunting field, which in Britain is the source from which almost every other equestrian activity springs. Fox-hunting is more than holding its own, and there are more packs of hounds registered now than there were before the First World War. There are new recruits to the ranks of fox-hunters every year, from all walks of life: one of the more recently registered packs is that of the Banwen miners, in South Wales, whose team of Pony Club children have twice won through to the final of the Prince Philip Cup at the Horse of the Year Show at Wembley. The Banwen have a coloured Master and huntsman, who has earned a great reputation in this field.

Showjumping is probably the best supported of all the non-professional horse sports, and with its large television audience is certainly the one which receives the most publicity. Hundreds of young riders are inspired with the ambition to jump for their country, emulating the Pat Smythes, David Broomes, and Harvey Smiths who have occupied the limelight for so many years by winning prizes for Britain with a succession of horses whose names have become household words.

Countrymen are perhaps more concerned with point-to-point racing, particularly those who farm and are unable to spend much time away from home. The really up-and-coming horse sport, however, is Horse Trials, or Combined Training, known on the Continent (where it originated) as the *concours complet*—the complet test of horse and rider. It had its inception in this country at Aldershot in 1948 as the Olympic Three-day Event, and a year later the first national Three-day Event ever held in this country took place at Badminton. The Royal Family took an active interest in this function, which they have since maintained, and the sport has grown from that of a small and somewhat esoteric circle of enthusiasts to one whose entries have increased to staggering proportions in less than twenty years.

The idea of the Three-day Event—a test of dressage or training, a speed and endurance cross-country and steeplechase phase of considerable severity, and, finally, a showjumping test—has been taken up by the Pony Club, whose individual branches provide the young entry with an excellent introduction to the real thing. Combined training is, on the whole, even more popular with young riders than showjumping. Both sports have been well served by British victories over the years—for example, the Olympic gold medal for showjumping won by our team at Helsinki in 1952 and the Olympic Three-day Event gold medal won by our team at Stockholm in 1956. More recently, in 1965 and 1967, the British showjumping team won the President's Cup, while the British Three-day Event team won the European Championship at Punchestown, Ireland, in 1967, and the gold (plus the individual silver) medal at the Mexico

Olympics in 1968, when the British riders also won the individual silver and bronze medals for showjumping.

Polo is only a shadow of its pre-War self, largely due to the mechanization of the cavalry regiments, which provided so many of our best players. Even so, the game continues to flourish. The Duke of Edinburgh's support brings in the crowds at Windsor, and once again the Pony Club has ensured that there will be at least a nucleus of players in twenty years' time.

With all those outlets for horses and ponies, there is a constant and growing demand for all types of light horse and pony, and every breeder is now assured of a ready market for his young stock. The greatest increase has been in the number of ponies bred, both of the recognized nine native breeds and of the 'improved', or Show Pony, type. Dutch and German buyers are regular visitors to the Welsh Pony sales, held each autumn in Wales and the Border Counties, and a Mountain Pony stallion recently made the record price of £1000. There is also a tremendous demand for mares and the trade in ponies may be said to be booming.

Government regulations require stallions to be licensed at the age of two years, and records show that the number licensed increased by about 30 per cent between 1965 and 1967, when it totalled just under 2000, of which a quarter were non-pedigree —mostly pony and cob. Of the 1460 or so pedigree stallions, 473 were Welsh Mountain ponies, while 270 were Thoroughbred, and 168 Arabian. Next in popularity came the Hackney (87), the Welsh Cob (69), and the Shire (52). One solitary representative each of Haflingers, Karabakhs, and Lipizzaners was licensed, but the only Knabstrup dropped out of the register in 1965, and was replaced by a solitary Quarter Horse.

Considering the small number of Thoroughbred and Arabian stallions in Britain, it is astonishing how much influence they have, and have had, on horse-breeding throughout the world.

The Arabian Horse (See Plate 1)

The Arabian Horse is accepted throughout the world as the purest of all breeds. It is claimed that the breed was in existence at the time of Mohammed, and flourished at the Courts of the Hashemite Princes in the seventh century.

With the onset of mechanization following the First World War, the pure-bred desert Arabian declined almost to extinction, apart from a few Royal Studs. However, today there are many countries outside the desert areas where the breed is widespread. The British Isles, the western part of the United States, and Poland are probably the countries with the biggest interest; Arabian Stud Books are kept in the following countries: Argentina, Australia, Bulgaria, Canada, Egypt, France, Holland, Hungary, Japan, Pakistan, Poland, Rumania, South Africa, Spain, Turkey, the U.S.A., the U.S.S.R., and the United Kingdom.

The infusion of Arab blood into breeds of horses throughout the world is abundant. The British Thoroughbred is descended from Eastern stallions mated with the native Galloways, followed by subsequent crossings of Arab and Barb stallions and mares imported from different parts of the Ottoman Empire. Many people take the view that the more important sires were Arabian.

The different strains of Arabians in existence today may raise some controversial points, but basically a strain is a female line descended through the generations from a particular foundation mare owned by a sheikh or a tribe. The average size is between 14 and 15 hands, but there are pure-bred Arabs in this country both over and under these heights. There are no height restrictions within the breed. The most usual colours today are greys, in varying degrees from nearly black, through shades of dapples and flea-bites, to pure white; also chestnuts of all shades and bays, although bays appear to be in the minority in this country at the present time. Bright and distinct colours are looked upon with the greatest favour.

The Arabian Horse has many outstanding characteristics which cannot be confused with any other breed, the outward and visible ones being the gay, high carriage of the head and tail, the dancing and quick action at all paces, and the outstanding beauty of the head. Small and wedge-shaped, with broad cheekbones, the profile is concave, the large, prominent eyes being set rather low in the head and between a broad forehead, which goes down to a small delicate muzzle with large, curving nostrils. The ears are small and alert, the coat and the skin are as of fine silk, and the legs have little or no feather.

In Arabia today Kehailan is the name used for the principal strain. A colloquial translation of this is "nice eyes". The Bedouin looks for eyes which are more egg-shaped, in the form of a blunted oval, than triangular, as in the common horse. The skin round them and the eyelids should be dark.

Less visible characteristics, but equally important, are the dense quality of the bone, the hardness of the feet, great strength of muscle, and acute eyesight and hearing.

Besides these structural characteristics, Arabian horses are renowned for their powers of endurance, ability to carry heavy weights over long distances, courage and intelligence, gaiety blended with docility of temperament, ability to thrive under conditions where other breeds would perish, and longevity.

When crossed with Thoroughbred and Hunter mares Arabian horses can produce horses of great size and agility. Alternatively, when crossed with the native mountain and moorland ponies of these islands they produce, in almost all sizes, the ideal pony for any child. Horses and ponies possessing Arabian blood have been at or near the top of all the major competitions for conformation and performance in this and other countries over the past quarter of a century.

The English Arab Horse Society, formed in 1918, now has a membership of nearly 1500, with 190 Studs in operation. Arabian horses are exported all over the world.

The Children's Riding Pony (See Plate 10)

The Children's Riding Pony, at its highest level of excellence, is principally a British phenomenon. This is due to the fact that the British Isles are blessed with a unique heritage of nine distinct breeds of native pony. Not only are most of them admirable children's mounts in their natural state, but, more important still, they are superlative foundation stock for breeding the top-quality show ponies—either Thoroughbreds or Hunters in miniature—which set a standard for the rest of the world.

There has been a prodigious improvement in the standard of children's ponies since the War, and it has been achieved by the use of small Thoroughbred stallions of the Polo-pony type and of Arab sires. The first-cross pony will have few pretensions to championship status, though there have been exceptions, but the second and subsequent crosses have produced superlative ponies, full of quality and yet retaining their pony characteristic, and with it the hardiness, sure-footedness, and intelligence of the mountain and moorland breeds.

The best-looking and most successful ponies have been bred up from Welsh mares, the most notable foundation mare in the last twenty years being the Welsh Gypsy Gold. Covered by the Arab stallion Naseel, who stood in Ireland, she produced, among five or six winning progeny, the now legendary Pretty Polly and My Pretty Maid. Not only did they win every big championship in England for some four seasons, but, retired to stud, they produced more champions in their turn. One of them, Pollyanna, was sold to the United States for £6000.

Pony-breeding is a thriving industry in Britain, and countless small Studs have grown up during the last twenty years. Now every horse show of any stature stages a full classification for Children's Riding Ponies to be shown in hand, in addition to the saddle classes. They are almost embarrassingly well filled for each age-group, from yearlings to three-year-olds, in addition to the classes for brood mares, who are shown with their foals at foot. At the bigger shows each age-group is divided into different sections for each height of pony—not to exceed 12·2 hands, 13·2 hands, and 14·2 hands respectively—and an entry of from thirty to forty in each class is by no means uncommon.

There is a ready home market for these products, and breeders are fortified by the knowledge that those young ponies who fail to make the grade as show ponies under saddle will always find a market as hunting or general-utility ponies. For the better-made ponies there are big rewards: a yearling colt was sold for £1000 in 1966.

The Cleveland Bay (See Plate 8)

The Cleveland Bay is one of the oldest British breeds. Its origin is obscure, but it has been recognized as a distinct breed in the Cleveland district of North-east Yorkshire for more than two hundred years. Apart from an infusion of Thoroughbred blood about the end of the eighteenth century, it appears to have maintained itself free from outside influences.

The typical Cleveland Bay is a powerful, active, clean-legged horse, between 16 and 16·2 hands, with from 8½ to 10 inches of hard, flat bone equal in quality to that of the Thoroughbred. His colour is invariably bay with black points, white, except for a very small white star on the forehead, being unacceptable. In spite of their size, good specimens of the breed are short-legged, and at maturity (which, at six to seven years, is later than in the Thoroughbred) will measure as much or more from the top of the wither to the point of the elbow as from the elbow to the ground. Other characteristics of the breed are longevity, fertility (provided that the animals are not allowed to get too fat), and a natural jumping ability which has been a feature of the breed for over a century, ever since the 'leapers' began to appear at Agricultural Shows in the North.

The breed's greatest asset, however, and the one which has ensured its survival for so long, is its prepotency when used for crossing with other breeds, especially those smaller and lighter than itself, to which it transmits much of its own size, hardiness, and magnificent bone. This has led to its being exported all over the world. As long ago as the 1850s the Cleveland Bay stallion Champion (54) was exported to Germany, and was at stud in Hanover till he died at the age of twenty-eight years. The United States, which has its own Cleveland Bay Horse Society, has always been a good customer, and since the last War horses have often been sent to Canada, South Africa, Japan, Pakistan, Czechoslovakia, and Australia.

The Cleveland Bay Horse Society was formed in 1884, when the demand for faster and lighter carriage horses, too easily supplied by crossing the Cleveland with Thoroughbred or part Thoroughbred horses, threatened the old breed with extinction. The breed was saved by publishing a Stud Book, from which animals known to have any trace of "blood or black" (either Thoroughbred or carting blood) were rigorously excluded, and by encouraging farmers in and around the Cleveland district to maintain pure-bred stock. Again, in the 1950s, when tractors had displaced horses on the farms and horse-breeding was at its lowest ebb, farmers sold their mares or put them to Thoroughbreds for Hunter breeding, and numbers again fell below danger-point. This time the Society decided to abandon its old policy of discouraging the use of the breed for crossing, and to recognize that this was in fact its main function in the modern world (though the breed still proudly provides the Bay carriage horses for the Royal Mews). Coming at a time when there is a shortage of the right type of horse for crossing with the Thoroughbred, this has brought about a revival of the breed, and numbers are again rising steadily. The first cross produces heavy and middleweight hunters, showjumpers, and brood mares, which can be put back to the Thoroughbred sire to produce the rather faster animal needed for Trials and Three-day Events.

The Clydesdale (See Plate 36)

Scotland has long been noted for its contribution to the breeds of farm livestock, and to the draught-horse world it has given the Clydesdale, that noble animal so popular at home and abroad. In the beginning horses were bred for carrying rather than for draught purposes. With the coming of the Industrial Revolution two centuries ago, demand favoured animals of more weight and substance, and breeders in that part of the country then known as Clydesdale (now Lanarkshire) strove by selective mating within the native breed to perfect a better type of heavy horse, which became known as the Clydesdale.

The Clydesdale has been developed into a handsome, weighty, and powerful animal, with ample gaiety of carriage and outlook. Among its outstanding characteristics is a combination of weight, size, strength, and activity with exceptional wearing qualities in respect of the feet and legs. These characteristics have been consistently aimed at throughout the history of the breed. The old saying "No foot—no horse" is as true today as it was when first spoken, and the successful efforts made to perfect the feet and legs of the Clydesdale have helped to maintain the breed's reputation.

The Clydesdale has an exceptionally quiet disposition. For an animal of its size and weight it is astonishing how easily it is controlled. Properly handled when young, and broken to work with care, it is obedient and docile at all times, and it has proved itself ideally suited to work on the land or haulage duties on the streets.

The Clydesdale is a very active horse. It must have 'action', which means high lifting of the feet, so that when viewed from behind the foot at every step is lifted clean off the ground. Action for the Clydesdale judge also means close movement. The forelegs must be planted well under the shoulders, and the legs must be plumb and, so to speak, hang straight from the shoulder to the fetlock joint. There must be no openness at the knees and no inclination to knock the knees together. Similarly, the hind legs must be planted closely together, with the points of the hocks turned inwards rather than outwards; the thighs must come well down to the hocks, and the shanks from the hock joint to the fetlock joint must be plumb and straight.

As already mentioned, the formation of the feet is of the greatest importance. They must be open and round like a mason's mallet. The hoof heads must be wide and springy, with no suspicion of hardness such as may lead to the formation of sidebone or ringbone. Pasterns must be long and set at an angle of forty-five degrees from the hoof head to the fetlock joint.

A Clydesdale should have a nice open forehead, broad between the eyes, a flat profile, a wide muzzle, large nostrils, a bright, clear, intelligent eye, big ears, and a well-arched, long neck springing out of an oblique shoulder with high withers. Its back should be short, and its ribs well sprung from the backbone, like the hoops of a barrel Its quarters should be long and its thighs well packed with muscle and sinew. It should have broad, clean, sharply developed hocks and big knees, broad in front. The impression created by a thoroughly well-built typical Clydesdale is that of strength and activity, with a minimum of superfluous tissue.

From their beginning Clydesdales have been exported regularly throughout the British Commonwealth, and to many foreign countries where horses are required for haulage purposes. Their popularity has been maintained throughout the years, and in 1966 forty-eight in all were shipped abroad. In 1911 the breed established a British record for heavy horses when the stallion Baron of Buchlyvie was sold by public auction for £9500.

The Cob (See Plate 4)

The qualifying adjective for the Cob is 'weight-carrying', and when the animal in question has had a height limit of 15·1 hands imposed upon it the requisite make and shape become readily apparent. The Cob is a short-legged, butty little animal with the bone and substance of a heavyweight Hunter—a real *multum in parvo*. Although all its many virtues are confined in so small a space, ideally it is beautifully proportioned, and with its gay carriage and ability to gallop, plus the jumping ability inherent in every good and active Cob, it is at its best a most attractive and useful animal.

Traditionally an old gentleman's horse, because it is easier to mount than a big heavyweight Hunter, and generally easier to ride, it is also an ideal animal for a youth who has outgrown the pony stage and is still too young to require a full size Hunter. It is most often to be found in Ireland, Wales, and the West Country, where its lack of inches and cat-like agility make it invaluable for scrambling over hairy banks and awkward places and for the heavily wooded areas where forestry is practised only in fits and starts and overhanging branches are a hazard to bigger horses.

The vanner type is purely a harness horse, high-actioned, straight of shoulder and with a coarse, underbred head. The true riding Cob has the low, straight movement of the blood horse and, according to the old adage, "a head like a lady's maid and a farewell like a cook". The rounded quarters of the cob are one of its most distinctive features, and in the past they were well set off by a close-docked tail which gave them a very jaunty appearance. Since the docking and nicking Bill became law—and for animals turned out at grass it is possibly just as well that it did—Cobs have been shown with full tails. But, apart from the humanitarian aspect of the case, there is no doubt that they have lost some of their unique character in retaining their tails.

The Connemara Pony (See Plate 15)

The Connemara Pony is indigenous to the western seaboard of Ireland and, owing to the remoteness of the area and the fact that the ponies run in droves in the most inaccessible parts of the mountains, the breed has remained uncontaminated.

The existing Stud Book was started in 1923 under the auspices of the local Pony Society and the Department of Agriculture. All stallions in Ireland have to be licensed by the Government.

No animal is accepted for the Stud Book until it is two years old and has been passed by the Society's Inspection Committee, which attends various centres in Connemara every year, thus ensuring that the animal accepted is sound and true to type, and not, as in the case of other breeds, accepted on its breeding alone. The type selected has to be short-legged, about 13·2 hands. (Anything over 14 hands is not accepted.) It should have good shoulders, with a true and easy movement. The head and neck should be well balanced and the bone hard and flat, measuring approximately seven to eight inches below the knee. The colours are grey, black, brown, and dun, with an occasional roan or chestnut. One of the most popular colours is dun with a black streak down the back. As a number of the mares are still worked, it is essential that they should have a good temperament. This is borne out by the very large export trade to the U.S.A., where the Americans are far more particular about the temperament of a child's pony than anything else.

The main demand for export to America has been for the smaller type of Connemara, as the Americans have plenty of big ponies of their own. Large numbers are exported to Great Britain, and in recent years to Sweden, Germany, France, Belgium, and Holland.

In order to improve the pace and riding shoulders of the breed, two small Thoroughbred stallions and one part-Arab stallion were purchased by the Society and used on native mares. Such of the male progeny of these matings as were considered suitable were kept by the Society, and in their turn used as stallions. One of the Thoroughbreds, Little Heaven, was at stud for a number of years, and produced the international showjumper Dundrum out of a Connemara mare. Although he is only 14·3 hands, he has won competitions in which he has had to jump nearly seven feet.

One of the chief difficulties which breeders outside Connemara have experienced is that, when fed on better land, the animals tend to get too big and do not remain true to type. A high-class showjumping pony has been known to grow four inches when it was six years old!

The Dales Pony (See Plate 12)

The Dales Pony is a native of the eastern side of the Pennine Ridge, and is closely related and similar in appearance to the Fell Pony, as both breeds undoubtedly sprang from the same root stock.

The Dales Pony is today the largest and heaviest of the English native pony breeds, standing 14 to 14·2 hands, with 8 to 8½ inches of bone, and capable of carrying a sixteen-stone man on the fell or of pulling up to a ton in weight on the streets.

These ponies have been bred on the farms of Northumberland, County Durham, and the North Yorkshire Dales for many generations. They have been used for general farm work, as tradesmen's ponies, and in the mines. A certain amount of outcrossing has occurred to get a more useful animal for the work required.

About a century ago a famous Welsh Cob stallion, Comet, came to Westmorland to compete in the trotting matches, which were a local sport. Comet left behind him many good colts, and every Dales Pony today traces back to this great Welsh Cob, who could trot ten miles in thirty-three minutes carrying twelve stone on his back.

With the introduction of the motor-car on the roads, the tractor on the farms, the electric float on the streets, and the mechanization of the mines, the Dales Pony breeders struck a bad patch. Quite literally hundreds of good ponies were slaughtered for meat, and in the early 1950s it looked as if the Dales Pony would become extinct.

One or two dedicated breeders remained, and with the interest in pony trekking a new market was found for the Dales Pony, which is ideal for the job, being quiet to handle, hardy, and surefooted. Today there is a flourishing Breed Society, and the demand for ponies, both as riding ponies and for harness, far exceeds the supply.

Dales Pony mares crossed with Thoroughbred horses make good foundation mares for breeding Hunters, showjumpers, and Event horses, as they are active, good movers, and have plenty of bone.

A Dales Pony should not exceed 14·2 hands. Colours are black, dark brown, which is locally known as heckberry, and a very occasional grey; there are no chestnuts or odd colours. Dales are smart and stalwart in appearance, very active, with profuse manes and tails and silky feathers on their heels. They have great bone and good, open feet, which should be blue-black in colour. There should be no white markings on a Dales Pony, other than a small star or snip on the forehead. A white face, or white hoof, denotes a Clydesdale cross somewhere in the pony's ancestry, but a white heel or coronet on the hind leg is accepted, though there must be no white above the fetlock joint.

The Dartmoor Pony (See Plate 34)

In the south-west of England lies a vast area of wild moorland known as Dartmoor, a place of rugged granite tors and bleak, windswept slopes mostly over 1000 feet high. From the earliest times a race of small, hardy ponies of riding type has lived here.

Until the end of the nineteenth century the ponies were not registered and type varied considerably. Then, in 1899, a Dartmoor Section of the Polo Pony Society's (now the National Pony Society) Stud Book was opened. A standard of points was produced, and it is particularly interesting to see that the standard of the Dartmoor Pony has remained virtually unaltered from that drawn up in 1899, most of the original wording being incorporated in the Official Description of the Dartmoor Pony of today.

Interest in the breed gradually rose to a peak about 1927, when registrations reached a total of 103 in vol. xix. The Second World War hit the breed very hard, as Dartmoor became a battle-training area, and in 1945 the Stud Book was opened to ponies either passed by inspection or placed at selected shows. In 1957 the Stud Book was closed to all except the progeny of registered ponies, though later, in 1961, a grading-up Register (the Supplementary Register) was opened with more stringent regulations than previously. The first grade (SR1) was closed in 1966 with 280 entries, but the second grade (SR2) will remain open indefinitely. All SR ponies are branded with the Dartmoor Pony Society's triangle on the neck.

Dartmoors are ideal first ponies, sure-footed, kind, and sensible. Because of its good front and excellent head carriage children feel really safe riding a Dartmoor, for there is plenty in front of the saddle. Dartmoors are fascinated by children and keenly interested by all they do. The Dartmoor is also the best possible foundation for producing larger ponies for the older child to show, hunt, or just enjoy.

Dartmoor ponies can now be found in Canada, the U.S.A., Denmark, Holland, Belgium, and Germany. France is also showing great interest in the breed.

The Exmoor Pony (See Plate 35)

Exmoor is that wild expanse of country in the north-east corner of Devon and the tongue of West Somerset, where the two counties join. It is bounded on the North by the Bristol Channel. It is a wild and solitary place, and the creatures living on it need to be extremely hardy in order to survive the winter. This has been the home of the Exmoor Pony, which it has shared with the wild Red Deer, and where it has been preserved in its natural state since earliest times.

The Exmoor is one of the hardiest of ponies. For this reason it is of the greatest importance to horse breeders, and this has also been recognized in other parts of the world, particularly in Canada and Denmark, to which countries the pony has been exported.

Exmoors provide the finest foundation stock. They have great powers of endurance, are agile and quick-witted, and can thus avoid all kinds of trouble in awkward situations. When crossed with a Thoroughbred the foals inherit the characteristics of both sides. They can carry extraordinary weights much beyond the capacity of many others. It is quite usual for farmers, and heavy ones at that, to use them for shepherding and hunting on the Moor.

The pure-bred Exmoor is at once recognized by its mealy muzzle, which is, in fact, the colour of oatmeal. These mealy markings are also to be found round the eyes, inside the ears, inside the legs, and under the belly. Seen from the front, the forehead should look wide, with prominent and quite unmistakable eyes, known locally as 'frog' or 'toad' eyes. Nevertheless they are very beautiful, with the lids slightly hooded like a hawk's. The general effect is kindly. The ears should be short, thick, and pointed and set on a wide forehead. The nostrils should be wide and of generous proportions. The body should have a deep, wide chest, with a back of medium length and very powerful loins. The shoulder should be well set back, making the pony very sure-footed. The legs should be clean and with neat, very hard feet. The colour may be bay, dun, or brown, but no white markings or white hairs may be carried anywhere. The coat has a texture different from that of any other breed. It is harsh and springy, and in winter it carries no bloom. In summer the coat is close, hard, and shines like brass. The tail hangs down close to the quarters, and has a fan-like spread of hairs at the root.

The foals have a thick woolly undercoat, with a top coat of very long, harsh hairs which protect it from the wet. The mares must not stand higher than 12·2 and the stallions 12·3 hands.

Exmoors make splendid children's ponies provided they are properly handled and broken, but the first purpose they serve is as foundation stock to provide sturdy and intelligent horses.

The Fell Pony (See Plate 13)

As the name implies, the Fell Pony is indigenous to the British Lake District and the northern end of the Pennine Range. In olden times the Fell Pony was the 'maid of all work' on the farms, besides being the trap pony for the family and the riding pony for shepherding on the fell. Great numbers of ponies were bred on the wild fells of Northern England, and those not used by farmers were sold at the local fairs—Appleby, Brough Hill, Kirkby Stephen—and became pack ponies for the carriage of lead from the mines in Allendale, Weardale, and the surrounding district to the ships at Newcastle and the industrial area of the north-east coast.

In the days before the motor age sport was local, and the pony men made their own fun by organizing trotting matches. To quote from the Stud card of Mountain King, foaled in 1901, his great-grandsire was by Little John, who was out of Dolly, a mare who trotted 2 miles 120 yards within seven minutes. Dolly was also dam of Heather Bell, the fastest trotting pony of her day.

The Fell Pony of today is a direct descendant of those active, weight-carrying ponies, and, fortunately, when the Fell Pony Society was formed about 1900 the National Pony Society opened a section in its Stud Book for the Fell. The Fell Pony Society has always had strict rules regarding entries in the Stud Book; very little alien blood has been introduced for seventy years.

The quality and standard of the Fell Pony have been improved greatly over this period by careful selection and by line breeding to the best strains within the breed. For crossing purposes, or as foundation stock, the Fell Pony has much to commend it, and excellent results have come from a Fell Pony stallion and a Hunter or Thoroughbred mare. The success of this type of breeding is in direct proportion to the purity of the pony stallion, as in all breeds of British native pony.

The only accepted colours are black, dark brown, dark bay, and an occasional grey. The height limit accepted by the Stud Book is 14 hands, and the average height is 13·2 hands. Legs and feet are exceptionally strong and sound, knees are prominent, and hocks wide, large, and clean. Head carriage is high, due to very good sloping shoulders. The body is compact, with great depth of girth. Strength, activity, alertness, these are the characteristics of the breed, coupled with a delightful pony temperament.

Fell ponies, particularly stallions, have been exported to Canada, Spain, Tripoli, Germany, Pakistan, and many other countries of the world for upgrading and an infusion of substance.

[44]

The Hack (See Plate 3)

The Show Hack, as it is known in England, is easy enough to define on paper, but in practice it is a nebulous animal because it conforms to no specific standards, and 'Hack type' is one of the most controversial of all ringside topics. On only one aspect of this vexed question are all the experts agreed—that they know the right article when they see it.

Many years ago, before the advent of the internal-combustion engine, there were two different types of Hack in Britain. First, there was the Covert Hack, the animal on which its owner rode to the meet, where he changed over on to the first of the two Hunters detailed to carry him behind hounds throughout the day. Then there was the Park Hack, a far more elegant animal, on which a rider, exquisitely attired in the height of fashion, might disport himself, at the same time indulging in a little gentle exercise, in, for example, Hyde Park's Rotten Row.

The modern Show Hack comes more properly into the latter category. He is—or should be—above all a horse of excellent conformation, imposing presence, and superlative movement, with the longest stride possible, lighter and more elegant than the Hunter. Not only must he be possessed of impeccable manners, but he must also be able to boast a high standard of training. Unlike a Hunter, a Hack is required to give an individual show, during which he demonstrates his schooling by such movements as a simple change of legs, a change of rein, perhaps a half-pass to right and left, and finally a rein-back and halt with complete immobility. There are individual variations on the formula, but the more esoteric equestrian extravagances are not encouraged, lest the whole devolve into a circus act.

There are two classes of Hack at the principal Horse Shows—the small Hack, which does not exceed 15 hands in height, and the large Hack, with an upper limit of 15·3 hands. The small Hacks are generally not of so high a standard, nor of so even a type, as their cousins, and it is only the exceptional small Hack which can beat a large one in a championship. They are very often bred up from pony mares by a Thoroughbred sire, and often from part-bred Arabs or Anglo-Arabs. It is by no means unusual for a 14·2 hands children's pony which has grown and been measured out of the pony classes to reappear in the show ring as a small Hack.

Although elegance in a Hack is of primary importance, blood weeds with insufficient bone and depth are certainly not encouraged. Substance is every bit as desirable in the Hack as in the Hunter, and a fine outlook and length of rein—in other words, a good front—are essentials.

The training, production, and presentation of the Show Hack is a very considerable art, and one, moreover, which only a handful of present-day exhibitors can achieve. Nor is a knowledge of dressage of particular assistance to its possessor, for judges penalize Hacks who go like dressage horses. But the ranks of Hack exhibitors are becoming fuller each year, and there is no doubt that a really well-trained Hack, produced to the hilt by an expert, is one of the most attractive sights in the show ring.

The Hackney Horse (See Plate 6)

The name Hackney, from the Norman *haquenée*, was in use in England for many centuries to describe a horse for general riding purposes, as distinct from a war-horse, before it was chosen as the breed appellation when a Society was formed at Norwich in 1883 to compile a Stud Book for English Trotting horses. These Trotters had been a recognized variety for many years before this date, and were chiefly found in East Anglia, parts of Lincolnshire, and East Yorkshire. They were known as Norfolk Cobs, Roadsters, or nag-horses. The best traced their descent from Shales, a son of the Thoroughbred Blaze by Flying Childers.

From the middle of the nineteenth century Hackney stallions were in great demand as improvers of the native stock in many countries, and for producing military and carriage horses.

About the turn of the century the growing popularity of horse shows led to a demand for stylish high-stepping carriage horses, and in this rôle, with its natural lofty gait, the Hackney was supreme. The advent of the motor-car reduced the demand until, after the First World War, only the best show horses could find a worth-while market.

The modern Hackney is a horse of from 14·3 to 15·2 hands, bay, brown, black, or chestnut in colour, usually having some white markings. Its head is straight or convex in profile, and its eyes and ears express a vigorous and alert personality. Its head should be well hung on a neck of average length, with some crest, and it is generally more muscular than the Thoroughbred. The throat and jaw should be clean-cut to allow free breathing when the horse is 'bridled'. The shoulder should be flat and laid well back to give great scope for the action of the forelegs, and the withers, while they are usually less prominent and a little thicker than those of the Thoroughbred, must not be excessively fleshy. The back should be of average length, with well-sprung ribs and a good depth of body, standing on good limbs, flat and clean of bone, with short cannons and nicely sloped pasterns. The feet should be round and fairly upright, with good strength of horn, not flat and spreading. The walk of the Hackney is important, and it should be brisk and springing, denoting muscular tone and activity. The trot should be lofty, true, smooth, and progressive, with hind legs propelled well forward under the body.

Most English Hackneys are now descended from the brown stallion Mathias, foaled in 1895, through his son, Buckley Courage, and the latter's sons, Mersey Searchlight and Solituce. Some other strains survive in other parts of the world. There are active Breed Societies in Great Britain, Canada, Holland, South Africa, and the United States.

The Hackney Pony has been evolved from the horse variety during the past eighty years, and it is now generally regarded as a separate breed. It is distinguished by its extreme action at the trot, and ranges in height from 12 to 14 hands. The best specimens have abounding quality and pony character. Hackney Ponies are bred in considerable numbers in North America, and they are becoming popular in Australia and South Africa.

The Highland Pony (See Plate 16)

One often sees the Highland Pony described as the largest of the British ponies. This is erroneous, as the best type of Highland Pony usually stands 13·2 to 14 hands, but it can certainly be described as the strongest pony. The stallions should have 9 to 10 inches of bone and the mares 8 to 8½ inches. The breed varies in size from 12·3 to 14·2 hands, and is usually one of the various dun colours, the golden dun being the most characteristic. It is also seen as black, brown, and grey, and occasionally dun or fox colour, with a silver mane and tail. The dorsal stripe is almost invariably present in all pure-bred Highland Ponies, except on the blacks, browns, and black/greys.

The Highland is a strong, compact pony with a finely arched neck, a small, shapely head, and a wide forehead between the eyes. The muzzle should be soft and velvety, with wide, open nostrils, large, expressive eyes, small, neat ears, a flowing mane, and tail of soft hairs, carried high and gaily. The legs should be strong with short cannons and flat bone, rather sloping pasterns, well let down, clean hocks, clean heels, and just a tuft of silken hair at the fetlock joint, the hooves open, round, and of dark, hard horn. The general appearance should be of strength, but combined with great beauty and true pony character.

Today the Pony is to be found chiefly on the farms on the Scottish mainland and in Studs north and south of the border, although there are still a few in the Western Isles. It is not exactly known how the breed originated, but it is assumed from its colour and other characteristics that it has descended from the Northern European horse. In any case the Highland Pony of today is the result of the introduction of much foreign blood throughout the ages. The ponies originally found on the Western Islands had a good deal of Arab. Among others the MacNeils of Barra crossed their little native mares with Arab stallions. This inspired some native bard to describe one of their ponies as "MacNeil's milk-white steed with flowing mane and tail surpassing in fleetness the stag of the forest".

Arab blood was introduced into the ponies of Mull by a prominent breeder at the close of the last century. The ponies of the mainland had been similarly improved by the use of stallions of the best French breeds sent by Louis XII of France to James IV of Scotland.

The Highland Pony has a delightful temperament, although it is rather suspicious of strange folk and places. Once it is acquainted with a new owner it has a wonderful trust very akin to that of the Arab Horse. It has always been closely associated with the crofter and stalker, just as the Arab Horse has with the Bedouin. Because of the Highland Pony's stocky appearance, people assume it is without temperament; the reverse is the case. It is a very intelligent and sensitive animal and responds readily to kindness and understanding and is quickly soured by rough handling.

Highland ponies may be seen competing in most of the principal horse and pony shows both in Scotland and England, and many fine specimens of the breed have been successful in winning supreme championships over all other native breeds both in hand and under saddle.

The Hunter (See Plate 5)

The Hunter is British—and Irish—in origin, largely because these islands are at once the birthplace and the spiritual home of European fox-hunting. It has perhaps the toughest assignment of any riding horse in the Western World, in that possibly for as much as two days during every week of the hunting season, from November to the end of April, it may be out of its stable for anything up to eight hours, a considerable part of which time may be spent in galloping over and jumping out of wet and heavy ground. It may, moreover—though with motorized horse transport this is no longer an inevitable requirement—be asked to cover a distance of 40 to 50 miles in a day.

If the Hunter is deficient in stamina it will not 'stay' until the end of a hard day. If its limbs are not of the best they will not stand up to the work, and it will break down, put up curbs and spavins, and generally fall prey to the multitudinous leg troubles to which horses are prone. Thus it must be bred to achieve the best conformation possible to gallop and jump, and at the same time to carry weight for long periods.

Hunter sires are almost invariably Thoroughbred, and the Hunters' Improvement Society annually offers premiums to the owners of the best available stallions who are calculated to produce up-to-weight Hunters. Most of them have already proved themselves on the race course, and a horse that has withstood several seasons in training is unlikely to be deficient in stamina.

Really good Hunter brood mares are increasingly difficult to find, owing to the virtual disappearance of the Irish Draught mare, whose daughters, by a Thoroughbred, were such valuable foundation stock. The Yorkshire Coach Horse, the old-type Cleveland Bay, and most other clean-legged mares with bone and substance are also lost to us. But there are still countless good young Hunters being bred from the deep, short-legged, roomy mares which are still to be found, while modern methods of feeding vitamins and mineral additives have undoubtedly improved the structure and circumference of the bone below the knee and hock, which is so vitally important.

The Hunter showing classes, producing as they do the prototype of animal, have a profound influence upon the breeding of Hunters and, indeed, of all light horses. A champion Hunter, moreover, must not merely be as nearly perfect as possible standing still. It must cover the ground when it moves, and it must be able to gallop at the head of a hunt.

There is an ever-increasing tendency, with the constant infiltration of Thoroughbred blood, for the quality weight-carrying horse to disappear. When it does emerge it sweeps all before it and commands a very high price.

Conformation, movement, ride, and manners are all assessed by the Hunter judge, who also wants to find quality and substance in the right proportions. Well-shaped, open feet, short cannon bones, big flat knees and hocks, depths of girth, well-sprung ribs, a nicely sloping shoulder, a shortish back, and strong loins, culminating in powerful quarters, are his guiding principles. The perfect horse has never been foaled, and the laws of compensation have to prevail, but the best type of Hunter fills the eye and has a majesty and distinction all its own.

The Irish Draught Horse (See Plate 9)

The Irish Draught, also known as the Irish Light Draught Horse, was the indigenous breed of working horses in Ireland, prior to the importation of the Shire and the Clydesdale. It is thought that quite a number of them originated from Connemara and grew bigger and stronger on the better land in other parts of Ireland. They should have good shoulders, good neck and head carriage, free, easy and true action, and no hair at all on their legs, except perhaps at the fetlocks.

They are capable of doing all agricultural work on a farm as well as being good fast travellers on the road; they are natural jumpers. The average height of a mare is 15·1 hands and of a sire 16·2 hands. The colours are grey, bay, brown, and chestnut.

The mares are ideal for crossing with a Thoroughbred stallion to produce weight-carrying Hunters and showjumpers. Work of Art, Supreme Champion, and Teneriffe, a well-known show winner, were both out of the same Irish Draught mare.

The Irish Draught Horse Book was established in 1917 by the Department of Agriculture and Fisheries. One thousand one hundred and eighty mares and 270 stallions were inspected, of which 374 mares and 44 stallions were accepted. The entries to date are 6464 mares and 577 stallions. About 150 mares are registered annually. Mares and colts have to be inspected before acceptance.

Free nominations are awarded by the Department to Irish Draught stallions, as well as prizes in the Irish Draught mare classes at shows. A number of yearling colts likely to make stallions are selected by the Department, who pay a subsidy to the owners to retain them. The suitable ones are subsequently purchased by the Department for allocation as sires.

The breed was very much depleted during the 1914–18 War as large numbers of the best mares went away, being requisitioned by the Army in the R.H.A. and R.F.A. as 'Gunners'. Having no hair on their legs they did not develop 'greasy heels', etc., in the Flanders mud. They were also hardy enough to live on the Army ration. Some of them left Kilkenny in the Gun Teams in 1914, and were still there to march into Brussels in the Ceremonial Parade in 1918.

The breed suffered its most serious depletion in the last two decades from the unrestricted export of mares to the Continent for slaughter. Work of Art's dam was exported for meat before her owner realized that she had produced a champion. However, during recent years the country was fortunate enough to have a Minister of Agriculture and Fisheries who was an enthusiastic hunting man, as well as being a breeder of bloodstock. He assembled a Committee of Farmer-Breeders to make a survey of the whole horse- and pony-breeding industry.

Since December 1964 the export of horses to the Continent for working purposes has been prohibited, and a similar prohibition in regard to horses for slaughter has been in operation since March 1965. Exports of horses to the Continent now consist only of Thoroughbreds, Army and Police Remounts, and horses for sport, recreation, and similar purposes.

The New Forest Pony (See Plate 14)

The origin of the New Forest Pony is difficult to trace. There have been wild ponies in Great Britain from time immemorial, and there were certainly ponies in that part of Hampshire declared a Royal Hunting Forest 900 years ago by King William Rufus, and known ever since as the "New Forest".

In the year 1893, an observer in the New Forest was struck by the excellence of the mares, but found the stallions sadly lacking in quality. Shortly afterwards the late Lord Arthur Cecil decided to introduce stallions of kindred mountain and moorland breeds, such as Highland, Fell, Exmoor, Dartmoor, and Welsh. As most native British ponies spring from a common origin this apparently drastic step was not so revolutionary as it sounds. Unfortunately, the scheme was extended a few years later to include such alien blood as Arab, Hackney, and Polo-bred stallions. This was not a success as it introduced more 'horse' than 'pony' type into the breed, and the resulting progeny found it difficult to live adequately on the sparse winter forest keep.

The first New Forest Pony Stud Book was published in the year 1910. This included stallions of many different breeds. Only two volumes were published, and from 1915 till 1958 all registrations were done through the British National Pony Society and were printed in their Stud Books.

This mixture of outside blood explains why the New Forest Pony still varies so much in type, from the small 12·2 child's pony to the larger animal of 14·2 hands and under. For the last thirty years no such outcrosses have taken place, and since 1938, when the present New Forest Pony Breeding and Cattle Society was formed by the amalgamation of the two original Societies, all new registrations are carefully scrutinized before an animal is accepted into the Stud Book. Since 1959 the Society has printed its own Stud Book every year.

The height limit for a New Forest Pony is 14·2 hands. Any colour is accepted except piebald and skewbald. The ponies should have plenty of bone, and those of 13 hands and over should be capable of carrying adults as well as children. In temperament New Forest ponies are ideal. They are intelligent, very easy to break, and quick to learn. They are almost all traffic proof, and are the best of family ponies for all purposes. Hunting, jumping, long-distance riding, polo, and harness-work are some of the many activities in which the New Forest Pony has proved its worth and held its own with all breeds. A 13·2 stallion has, in recent years, won numerous cups and championships in open mountain and moorland riding classes. A pair of 12·2 ponies have beaten all comers in private Driving Marathons, having been first at the Royal International Horse Show at the White City, at Richmond, and at numerous other shows up and down the country. In the U.S.A. a New Forest stallion is used by an M.F.H. to hunt hounds from a sleigh in winter.

New Forest ponies are in great demand abroad. Both Holland and Denmark have imported several hundred in the last seven or eight years, and both countries have their own New Forest Stud Book. Sweden is now finding the ponies ideal for its children, and others have been exported to Canada, France, and the U.S.A.

The pony population of the New Forest numbers between 2000 and 2500, of which some 150 are stallions. Only registered stallions are allowed to run in the Forest. These are inspected each spring, and those which do not attain a specified standard are rejected and may not run in the Forest again.

In addition to the ponies bred in the Forest there are numerous private Studs, both in the Forest and in other parts of Great Britain, where New Forest stallions and mares are kept.

The Shetland Pony (See Plate 33)

The Shetland Pony is the smallest of the British native breeds, varying in height from 26 inches to the Stud Book limit of 42 inches; the average is probably 38 inches. Even when bred on more favourable land and in milder climatic conditions than in their native islands, the height of these ponies does not usually increase.

Any colour is acceptable, black and dark brown being generally the most common, but chestnut and grey have become more popular again in recent years. At one time there were considerable numbers of roan, dun, and cream, but these are now scarce. Skewbald and piebald are still fairly prevalent in the Islands.

The Shetland Islands, lying about one hundred miles to the north of Scotland, are the home of the breed. Exposed as they are to the fiercest of Atlantic weather, only the hardiest of the animals can prosper and breed; no point is more than four miles from the sea, and during the all too prevalent gales salt spray is driven to all parts. Consequently, there are no trees, and the only shelter is in small valleys or on the lee side of hills. The land varies from deep peat to bare rock-strewn expanses, with a few scattered areas of good soil.

The earliest remains of the Shetland Pony found in the Islands are of those which were apparently domesticated during the Bronze Age (some 2500 years ago). It is probable that the

33 *SHETLAND PONY*

34 *DARTMOOR PONY*

35 *EXMOOR PONY*

36 *CLYDESDALE*

37 *SUFFOLK PUNCH*

38 *SHIRE*

39 *KLADRUBER*

40 *LIPIZZANER*

41 *MURAKOSI*

42 *FURIOSO*

43 *NONIUS*

44 *SHAGYA ARAB*

45 *POLISH ARAB*

46 *HUCUL*

47 *KONIK*

48 *POLISH ANGLO-ARAB*

original ponies were 13·2 hands high, of Tundra origin, which reached the British Isles before the retreat of the ice-fields; during the isolation of the following centuries the size became reduced. Apart from some infusion of blood from stallions brought in by the early Norse settlers a thousand years ago, these ponies have remained pure-bred.

Until 1850 there were virtually no roads in Shetland and all transport was by boat or pony. Essentially, this pony is a general-purpose animal for pack or saddle, capable of carrying heavy loads, or humans, over rough and difficult ground, with sure-footed alertness. It was not until about 1860, when the huge demand arose for underground work in the coal mines of north-east England, that they were developed for draught work, and the thick heavy type was sought after and bred for this purpose. Now, owing to mechanization there is no demand for this type.

Shetland ponies have an extremely docile and gentle temperament, are easy to train, have great courage and character, and are adaptable for all work commensurate with their size. They make ideal first ponies and companions for children, and are excellent for driving or light carting.

Almost every country in the world has at one time or another imported these ponies, who adapt themselves and become acclimatized without undue difficulty to wide variations of climate, from the Falkland Islands to the Arctic Circle. The U.S.A. and Canada imported large numbers in the latter half of the nineteenth and early years of this century, and also in the 1950s. At present European countries are the chief importers. Holland, Sweden, Denmark, Belgium, and France have Stud Books for this breed.

The Shire Horse (See Plate 38)

The origin of the Shire Horse dates far beyond existing records. We are, however, indebted to those enthusiastic writers who have delved deeply into the history of British horses for much that is of interest to all who regard the Shire as the greatest of our heavy horses.

The Shire is probably the direct descendant of the medieval Great Horse (see pp. 28–29). Undoubtedly the breed was originally developed for military purposes, but the desire for quicker and more thorough cultivation of the land, together with the need for transport horses able to move great weights, caused breeders to turn their attention to producing horses to fulfil these requirements. The desire of breeders, even in those days, was to establish uniformity of type, character, and appearance, and to keep authentic records, and in 1878 the Shire Horse Society was formed.

A Shire stallion should stand from 16·2 to 17·2 hands, weighing from one ton to 22 cwt when matured without being overdone in condition, and with good feet and joints.

A Shire mare should be on the quality side, long and deep with free action, and of a feminine and matronly appearance, standing from 16 to 16·2 hands on short legs and having plenty of room to carry her foal. Shire geldings range from 16·1 to 17·2 hands, with weights from 17 cwt to over one ton; they are thick, well balanced, very active, and gay movers. Shire colouring is black, bay, or grey.

The Shire has all the qualities looked for in a draught animal—strength, constitution, stamina, and adaptability—and has nobly played its part on farms and in our towns and cities. With great muscular forearms and immense power in its frame, the Shire has moved weights which would surprise those who have not actual experience of its potential.

At a Shire Horse Society's London Show three weight-pulling tests were arranged. First, on granite setts in wet and slippery conditions, two Shire geldings, yoked to a springless dock wagon and in tandem fashion, moved off pulling 18½ tons. The shaft horse took the whole weight on the turn for the return journey. Then, on wooden blocks, 16½ tons was the load, and here again the shaft horse moved the whole weight before the trace horse had got going.

The Shire breed has enjoyed a considerable measure of export trade, the United States of America, Canada, and South America being the chief customers, with Australia, Germany, and Russia also receiving periodical consignments.

The Suffolk Punch (See Plate 37)

It is indeed sad that the development of mechanized farming has meant the decline in numbers of Suffolk horses, which, with their rich chestnut colour, are surely among the most beautiful, intelligent, honest, and good tempered of our domestic animals.

The Suffolk Horse can be traced back to 1506 and must be one of the purest breeds, having retained its lovely chestnut colour and clean legs, and having been famed through the ages for compactness and its hardy constitution. Suffolk horses have been exported to all parts of the world, including Russia, Australia, Africa, and the Americas, and they are still being exported.

As their name implies they originated in the County of Suffolk, but for many generations they have been regarded as natives of all East Anglia. Longevity is a particular feature of the breed, due no doubt to their docile disposition—one Suffolk gelding owned by a London coal merchant was shown at the London Cart Horse Parade for seventeen years in succession until he was twenty-one years old. There are many records of mares breeding regularly in their twenties. The average height is about 16·2 hands and many Suffolks weigh over one ton. They have a girth of over 8 feet, and some stallions have over eleven inches of bone below the knee. This great weight on sound clean legs, coupled with their wonderful temperament and ability to thrive on very small rations, has led to their popularity all over the world.

The success of the breed is due in no small measure to careful selective breeding over many years by the East Anglian breeders, assisted by the rigid rules adopted by the Breed Society for registration, and at the Breed Society's Sales. No animal could be shown at any of the leading Agricultural Shows, or sold at the Breed Society's Sales, without a Veterinary Certificate of soundness. This policy has led to the development of the magnificent Suffolk Punches which we see at present-day agricultural shows. They are still being worked for specialized jobs in agriculture and by breweries for short haulage, etc.

The Thoroughbred Horse (See Plate 2)

The Thoroughbred is a horse entered in or eligible for entry in the General Stud Book. Any animal claiming admission must be able either to be traced at all points of its pedigree to strains already appearing in pedigrees in earlier volumes of the General Stud Book, or to prove satisfactorily some eight or nine generations of pure blood, to trace back for at least a century, and to show such performance of its immediate family on the Turf as to warrant the belief in the purity of its blood.

The publication of the first volume of Messrs Weatherby's Stud Book was in 1793, but the origin of the Thoroughbred dates to much earlier times. Inevitably it is tied up with the history of racing. The first race of which details were recorded took place in 1377 between horses belonging to the Prince of Wales (afterwards Richard II) and the Earl of Arundel. But it was in the days of the Tudors and Stuarts that real progress began. There was a serious setback when, under Cromwell, racing was among the many banned sports, so it can be said that Charles II was the true founder of the prosperous bloodstock breeding industry we know today.

So greatly superior were the horses of this period that all modern Thoroughbred horses descend from three stallions and some thirty mares living in the seventeenth and early eighteenth century. The three stallions were, first, the Darley Arabian (imported in 1705), from whom descend in direct line Eclipse (1764) and St Simon (1883), the two sires to have the greatest influence ever on the modern Thoroughbred; second, the Byerly Turk, whose greatest descendants were The Tetrach (1911) and Tourbillon (1928); and third, the Godolphin Arabian, responsible for Hurry On (1913) and Man O' War, the greatest American horse. The influence of these three horses can be demonstrated by extending the pedigree of any modern racehorse. As an example, in the pedigree of Bahram (winner of the 2000 Guineas, Derby, and St Leger) the name of the Godolphin Arabian appears 28,232 times, that of the Darley Arabian 44,079 times, and the Byerly Turk 64,032 times. These three famous sires are illustrated on Plates 23, 24, and 25.

There was a steady increase in the number of Thoroughbred mares in the British Isles up to 1960 when there were 7980 registered mares. The numbers have shown a tremendous increase in the last ten years.

Whereas the three foundation stallions were of Eastern origin, there is very strong evidence to show that there was a distinct breed of race horses in this country before the importation of Eastern sires began and from which some of the foundation mares originate. Without this stock it would not have been possible to develop the Thoroughbred in the short space of two hundred years to the supreme animal we know today.

At present there is no horse in the world which can compare with the Thoroughbred as far as speed is concerned. The five-furlong course at Epsom has been covered in 53·6 seconds (i.e., 42 m.p.h.). As a result, the Thoroughbred is used to improve the native breeds in nearly every country in the world and is acknowledged as by far the best source for such improvement.

The average height of a Thoroughbred is about 16·1 hands, and a good representative should measure over 8 inches of bone below the knee. Horses of 17 hands and over are rare, but occur occasionally.

All colours, except multi-colours such as piebald, are found, the commonest being chestnut and bay or brown.

The Welsh Cob and the Welsh Pony of Cob Type (See Plate 7)

The exact origin of the Welsh Cob is lost in the mists of time, but it was well established as a breed by the fifteenth century. Tudur Aled, the famous Welsh poet of the early sixteenth century, gives a description of a Cob very similar to that laid down today, and he goes on to describe its ability to carry weight, gallop, jump, and swim.

Until the advent of the motor-car and the tractor, the Welsh Cob was an indispensable part of the rural life of Wales. It did all the light work on the farm, took the farmer and his wife to market, and on Sundays to Chapel, after which it took part in trotting races. Renowned for its courage, speed, and soundness, having the best of feet and hard flinty bone, the Cob was the farmer's most prized possession and its pedigree was handed down from one generation to another.

There were two major Cob-breeding areas. Cardiganshire and Pembrokeshire produced the larger Cob, which owed something to the blood of the Pembrokeshire Packhorse. Those from Breconshire and Radnorshire were smaller, with more pony character.

This distinction was recognized when the first volume of the Welsh Pony and Cob Society Stud Book was published in 1902. Two sections were set aside for Cobs; Section D was, and still is, for the Welsh Cob; Section C is for what is now known as the Welsh Pony of Cob Type. The introduction to Volume I says: "The only practical difference between those entered in each of these sections of the Stud Book being the height and proportionate strength and power of the larger Cob entered in Section D."

During the two World Wars many Welsh Cobs were bought by the British Government for use as Packhorses and Remounts, and many of the best mares were thus lost to the breed. In between the Wars the Cob, crossed with the Thoroughbred, was the foundation of many good Hunters. These were short-legged horses of quality, capable of carrying a big man across country.

Today the true Welsh Cob retains the activity, dash, and intelligence of its ancestors. A natural jumper, with an equable temperament, it is the ideal family horse, being strong enough to carry a man and gentle enough to carry a girl. In hilly or rough country its unique qualities and natural sense make it the ideal Hunter. Courageous yet docile, it takes readily to harness and as a general-purpose ride-and-drive animal is supreme.

The same may be said of the smaller Welsh Pony of Cob Type. As a trekking pony it is unsurpassed, and, as this form of recreation increases, demand far outstrips supply. Both have a strong constitution and are very hardy. They combine quality with strength and the utmost freedom of action in all paces.

The predominant colours are bay, black, brown, chestnut, and roan, but any colour is permitted except piebald and skewbald.

The Welsh Pony of Cob Type does not exceed 13·2 hands. For the Welsh Cob there is no height limit. The majority are between 14·2 and 15·1 hands.

The Welsh Mountain Pony and the Welsh Pony (See Plate 11)

The Welsh Mountain Pony of today is basically the same as its remote ancestor which roamed the Welsh hills before History began. Environment and climatic conditions have a great bearing on type, and the Principality of Wales, with its mountains, hills, and deep green valleys, has produced one of the most beautiful ponies in the world. The hallmark of a Welsh Mountain Pony is a small, quality head with a bold eye and a small, prick ear. Their action, characteristic of a pony bred to live on rough, steep ground, is quick and active, with ample flexion of knees and hocks, and moving with the utmost freedom in all paces.

Agile and sure-footed, they are natural jumpers, and with their inherited intelligence, soundness of limb, and hard constitution have always been one of the best possible foundations from which to breed larger ponies and horses.

There is a high percentage of Welsh blood in the majority of all British Children's hunting and show ponies of the present day. It is most predominant in the smaller ponies under 13·2 hands.

The old indigenous colours were bay, brown, black, roan, dun, and cream, with a few chestnuts and greys, more or less in that order. Now, however, bright chestnuts are becoming more plentiful.

As in most British native pony breeds outside blood has occasionally been used, but the Welsh Mountain Pony has had no out-cross for many years.

This very old breed is universally in demand, because, apart from their very attractive appearance and adaptability, they are a mixture of gentleness and courage, which makes them most excellent ponies for children, and they are equally at home either ridden or in harness.

There are today still many herds of Mountain ponies on the Welsh hills, and numerous Studs outside Wales. However, breeders like to go back to Wales from time to time for fresh blood in order to keep the type and vigour of the pony bred on their native hills.

The Welsh Mountain Pony (Section A in the Welsh Stud Book) does not exceed 12 hands. The Welsh Pony (Section B in the Welsh Stud Book) does not exceed 13·2 hands and inherits many of the characteristics of the Mountain Pony, the foundation of the breed, of which it is a larger and stronger edition. It was originally produced by crossing the small Welsh Cob with the Welsh Mountain Pony.

Extensively used for shepherding and hunting on the Welsh hills, they are now bred for the most part as children's ponies, both to hunt and to show.

CENTRAL EUROPE

AUSTRIA, for centuries before 1918, was the keystone of an Empire which embraced much of Eastern Europe. In those days race horses were bred at a number of important Studs, and Austrian Thoroughbreds had a considerable effect on the breeding of Czechoslovakian, Hungarian, and Polish race horses.

A relic of this Imperial past is the Spanish Riding School, imported centuries ago from Madrid, which still flourishes as a unique institution. Two hundred years ago there were many such riding schools, but the others on the Continent of Europe were destroyed, and their horses appropriated, during the Napoleonic Wars. Fortunately the Spanish School, with its world-famous Lipizzaner horses, survived to have a marked effect on Eastern European styles of horsemanship. (See Plate 70.)

Nowadays, although Austrians are still keenly interested in horse racing—both galloping and trotting—only just over 700 warm-blooded stallions were registered at the last census against more than three times that number of Noric Draught horses.

Nearly a quarter of Austrian farm land consists of Alpine pastures, so a fast-moving, sure-footed pony, such as the Haflinger, is a necessity. There is so great a shortage of draught animals, however, that in some districts milking cows have to be harnessed for traction purposes.

A separate variety of the Noric Horse—spotted somewhat like a Knabstrup, and known as a Pinzgauer—used to be considered a separate breed, as also did the Oberlander from Bavaria, but both these sub-varieties are now merged in the Noric Horse which is also known as the South German Cold Blood.

Other breeds to be found in Austria include the Oldenburg and the Nonius.

The Haflinger Pony (See Plate 55)

The brand of the Haflinger ponies is the national flower of Austria, an Edelweiss, with an 'H' in the centre. The Etschländer Mountains near Meran (the mountain district of Hafling) is the chief area for these hardy, popular, chestnut or palomino mountain ponies with their distinguishing flaxen manes and tails. The breeding centre is the village of Jenesien, but the breed is also very much at home in Bavaria.

This pony is extremely strong and has a great capacity for work, although it only stands about 13·3 hands. The Haflinger is generally reckoned to belong to the cold-blooded type.

Opinions differ as to the origin of the breed: one is that the pony is a descendant of the Alpine Heavy Horse, adapted to mountain heights; others consider that the Haflinger belongs to an ancient breed of European ponies and that it was evolved by selective crossing.

Both Oriental and Noric blood, together with the mountain climate (1500 to 2000 metres), helped to develop the Haflinger into a fixed breed. An especial contribution to their hardiness is the raising of young stock on Alpine pastures—*Alpung* (Alping) as it is locally known. On the steep slopes they have full opportunities to develop their hearts and lungs and to prove the soundness of feet and legs.

The original Arab stallion El Bedavi, through his half-bred great grandson El Bedavi XXII, is regarded as the founder of the modern breed. All true-bred Haflinger ponies are descended from this stallion.

The district of Hafling was lost to Austria after the First World War, and the breed was reorganized in the Austrian Tyrol; Hucul, Bosnian, Koniks, and small Noric horses were used to keep the breed intact.

The ponies are not used until they are four years old and are said sometimes to be still at work at forty years old! One of the special characteristics is the length of back and the strength of the loins and freedom of shoulder and leg action.

Modern Haflingers are in great demand and are exported to many parts of the world. Their ability to work hard in difficult conditions and on a sparse diet, combined with their attractive chestnut or Palomino colouring, have ensured them world-wide popularity. Of late years over one hundred stallions have been registered annually.

The Noric Horse (See Plate 54)

The kingdom of Noricum was a vassal state of the Roman Empire. Its borders were much the same as those of Austria today, and it was well served with serviceable roads and passes, which implies that there must have been considerable traffic for those times—and traffic across mountains meant horse-drawn or pack transport.

Just across the southern borders of Noricum lived the Venetii, who were established there for nearly 900 years B.C. These people were famous for their horse-breeding. Subsequently this became the native land of the Haflinger, and most probably the Noric Horse owes its descent, at any rate in part, to these ancient mountain ponies.

Early on the Noric Horse was bred in Juvavum near Salzburg, and, in the Middle Ages, the best type was found in the Gross Glockner mountain region. From 1565 onwards the breed was under the jurisdiction of the Monasteries, and later of the Imperial Court. Spanish, Neapolitan, and Burgundian stallions were used to improve the breed.

Today a hard, medium-sized working horse is required. It is deep through the heart, and short on the leg with long, sure action. The colour is generally chestnut or brown. The stallions have to undergo the normal test to prove willingness in harness—the ability to pull a heavy load and to walk 500 metres and trot 1000 metres in a given time.

Stallions are required to be tested before being used at stud, to prove their suitability. Certain breed societies have also instituted tests for mares carrying their first foals.

As has been mentioned, the Noric is also bred throughout Bavaria and South Germany, so much so that it is often known as the South German Cold Blood.

CZECHOSLOVAKIA has a long tradition of breeding quality horses. The Stud at Kladruby near Pardubice on the Labe is said to be the oldest operative Stud Farm in the world. It was founded in 1572 by the Emperor Rudolph II, with horses imported from Spain. He also used Spanish foundation stock for his second Imperial Stud Farm which he founded in 1580 at Lipizza. Both Studs flourished, and by 1729 the Kladruber Stud maintained thirty stallions and three hundred mares, while the Lipizza Stud had about half this number. Unfortunately, the Stud Farm at Kladruby and its archives, including the Stud Books, was destroyed in 1759 after a battle in the neighbourhood, though some of the horses were saved by being moved into Hungary. The Stud was revived six years later, still with horses of Spanish blood, but in some cases with a cross of Neapolitan.

In 1765 another Imperial Stud Farm was founded at Kopcany in Slovakia and stallions were interchanged between these three Imperial Stud Farms and others owned by the Church, which also promoted horse-breeding. For example, the stallions Maestoso and Favory, each of whom founded famous strains of Lipizzaners, were foaled at Kladruby, as were many foundation mares of the Lipizzaner breed.

The successes achieved by British Thoroughbreds in the eighteenth century made a considerable impact on Czechoslovakian breeders, and by 1813 there were only eighty-four mares of the old Spanish breed left at Kladruby, where British Thorough-breds were bred with considerable success, though Anglo-Normans and Cleveland Bays proved to be less successful.

Less than twenty miles from Kladruby at Pardubice is the famous steeplechase course where the longest steeplechase in continental Europe (6900 metres—nearly $4\frac{1}{2}$ miles), with thirty obstacles, was run every October from 1874 until 1968.

The Stud at Kladruby was controlled by the Imperial Court until 1918, since when it has been administered by the Czechoslovak State. The State has encouraged the production of young stallions suitable for improving working horses for agricultural purposes, though the Stud still maintains its herd of white Kladruber horses.

In addition to the breeds described below English Thoroughbreds are bred on a considerable scale: 280 Thoroughbred mares were registered in 1967. The main Stud is at Napajedla in Southern Moravia where there are four stallions and sixty-five mares. There are also a large number of English half-breds distributed all over Czechoslovakia.

Shagya Arabs are also bred, as are Gidran and Furioso horses, while at Novy Tekov there are pure-bred Nonius. There are also a number of Trotters and Haflingers and some Huculs and Fjords. The latter two breeds are being crossed at Topolcianky to add substance to the Hucul.

Heavy agricultural horses now make up less than half the total horse population and are tending to decline. Work is being done to produce a general-purpose horse for agriculture and for riding; this is based on the Oldenburg crossed with Thoroughbreds and half-breds.

Czechoslovakia exports horses all over Europe and some Shagya Arabs have gone to America. In most years the demand for Czechoslovak horses is greater than the country can supply.

The Kladruber (See Plate 39)

The Kladruber breed takes its name from the famous Kladruby Stud and stems from foundation stock originally imported from Spain. At first the horses were of various colours, but since the beginning of the nineteenth century only black and white horses have been bred. The Imperial stables never had less than eighteen stallions of each colour. These magnificent animals stood 18 hands or over, and drew the Imperial coaches in teams of six or eight, until the end of the Empire in 1918. Only the emperors themselves ever used the teams of white stallions, which were associated with festive occasions, the black stallions being used for funerals. The emperors used to ride Kladruber stallions from time to time.

Black and white Kladrubers were interbred to a considerable degree, and the original Spanish blood was refreshed with Neapolitan. For example, two of the surviving families of white Kladrubers (Generale and Generalissimus) stem from a grey stallion born in 1775 at the Kopcany Stud, where he had been sired by an imported black Neapolitan stallion.

From the foundation of the Stud in 1572, the breed of Kladrubers consisted of the descendants of Spanish foundation stock which had received further injections of Spanish blood, and of Neapolitan stallions of Spanish ancestry, but had no other cross, though stallions were regularly exchanged with other Imperial Studs where the same old Spanish strain had been maintained.

About 150 years ago attempts were made to find a successful outcross. For many years these invariably failed, but in 1921 crossing with a Shagya Arabian proved very successful. Since 1918 the size of the typical Kladruber has been reduced, and today they stand between 16·2 and 17·2 hands. The Old Kladrubers (as they are now described) stood 18 hands or over. These smaller Kladruber stallions are now being used to improve agricultural horses, and also to produce useful cross-breds for riding. They have been particularly successful at dressage, but are less successful at jumping or steeplechasing.

Since 1938 black Kladrubers have been bred at a separate establishment some twenty miles from the main Stud.

The Lipizzaner (See Plate 40)

This ancient breed takes its name from the Stud founded by the Emperor Rudolph II at Lipizza in what was then part of the Austrian Empire. The foundation stock of this Stud was entirely of Spanish origin, as at Kladruby. Another Stud was founded at Piber in Austria by Grand Duke Karl, with six principal foundation stallions: two were Kladrubers, Maestoso and Favory, both of which founded prominent strains of Lipizzaners; two others were Conversano and Neapolitano, imported from Italy but said to have been bred from Spanish ancestors; then Pluto, who is believed to have carried Danish Fredericksborg blood; and, finally, Siglavy, who is believed to have been an Arabian. The foundation mares were in most cases of Spanish origin.

Over the years stallions were frequently exchanged between the Lipizza, Piber, Kladruby, and other Studs (see the preceding article), and it was not until the opening of the famous Spanish Riding School at Vienna in 1738 "for the education of the nobility in the art of horsemanship" that horses from the Lipizza Stud were found more amenable to training in High School Airs, and began to be regarded as a separate breed.

For the last two centuries the horses used at the Spanish Riding School have increasingly been Lipizzaners. Only stallions have been trained in the Airs; it has been found that a stallion may become expert in only one or two of these complicated movements, and selected bloodlines tend to produce the most talented offspring. Lipizzaners are shown in action on Plate 70.

Only grey Lipizzaners are used for the famous Quadrille, and perhaps for this reason artists almost always choose the greys for their pictures. Thus the impression has grown that all Lipizzaners are grey, though in fact they may also be brown or black. Originally chestnuts and duns also appeared, but these seem to have been bred out.

Years ago Lipizzaners were used to improve many of the Central-European breeds. One of the oldest warm-blooded breeds in Europe, their particularly gentle temperament and willingness to submit to training makes them a valuable cross for other breeds which are less amenable, but which possess other desirable qualities.

Lipizzaners are bred in many countries in Eastern Europe: in Czechoslovakia the main Stud is at Topolcianky where, in August 1968, there were ninety-three Lipizzaners, including four stallions and twenty-eight brood mares. In addition to these, there were over thirty stallions and several hundred brood mares scattered throughout the country. Apart from the stallions required for Riding School purposes, the breed was often used for agriculture, but now it is regarded almost entirely as a riding horse. Many appear in circuses and the breed is regularly exported, often for circus purposes.

HUNGARY enjoys a favourable climate, good-quality vegetation nourished by soil with the requisite mineral content, and, in short, has all the factors necessary for producing the outstanding horses for which the country has been noted for over one thousand years. Hungarian horses were in such demand nine hundred years ago that King László was forced to ban the exportation of horses from Hungary.

During the century and a half of Turkish Occupation, the horse population was greatly influenced by the Arabian and Syrian stallions of the Turkish Cavalry. The first modern Stud in Hungary was founded in 1784 at Mezöhegyes some fifty miles north-east of Szeged. By 1810 this Stud included 4000 mares. Another important Stud was founded at Bábolna in 1789 and is now the headquarters of pure-bred Arabians in Hungary.

To promote the breeding of quality horses, successive Hungarian governments have established stallion depots throughout the country, largely equipped with imported horses. Between 1780 and 1790 the Hungarian Government imported over five hundred stallions for this purpose, for the most part British Thoroughbreds or pure-bred Arabians.

A surprising proportion of Hungarian horses, even those used for draught and agricultural purposes, have the hallmark of quality that denotes a warm-blood ancestor not many generations away. Most Hungarian horse breeders run their mares in herds of a score or so, each with a stallion, often a Thoroughbred. This system accounts for the hardiness of Hungarian horses and for their ability to thrive in difficult conditions.

In addition to the breeds described below, Hungary is noted for its Arabians; some have founded dynasties which have become famous throughout Eastern Europe as, for example, the well-known Shagya purchased in Syria in 1836. The Shagya strain has spread widely and is still thriving in Hungary and the neighbouring countries (see Plate 44).

Probably the best-known Hungarian strain of Arab stems from O'Bajan, a black colt, bought about 1885, who was active at stud in Hungary for twenty-five years, producing over 300 foals, of which 112 qualified as stallions. O'Bajan was buried in the courtyard of the Bábolna Stud, where his tombstone is still shown to visitors.

Another **Arabian** whose descendants constitute a definite type was Siglavy-Gidran, imported from Arabia in 1816. He was a chestnut and described as "very tempestuous". Gidran Arabians are now numerous throughout Eastern Europe and are regularly crossed with local mares. Today the breed is in two types, the Middle European being the heavier and more substantial, while the Southern and Eastern type shows more evidence of its Arabian origin. Usually chestnut, occasionally bay, and very rarely grey or black, they are used for sporting purposes and as Event horses. The heavier ones are sometimes driven.

Lipizzaners (called Lipizzans in Hungary) are bred in several regions. Since 1961 the principal Stud has been at Szilvásvárad in the Bükk mountains, which has sixty-six pure-bred mares.

English Thoroughbreds have played an important part in improving many Hungarian breeds; they have been bred pure in Hungary for over a century. The famous Kisbér, bred at the Hungarian Stud which still bears his name, won many races throughout Europe, including the Derby in 1876. The Kisbér Stud is now the headquarters of the so-called "Kisbér Type" of half-bred horses sired mainly by English Thoroughbred stallions. After the Second World War this Stud came under the management of Bábolna and some Hungarian stallions have been used there in recent years.

Over one hundred years ago Hungarian breeders began to specialize in Racing Trotters, and the present-day Hungarian Trotter can claim ancestors from every part of the world. The first recognized Trotting stallion was Cupido, who is said to have performed in an American circus in 1883, since when American Trotters, Russian Orlovs, French Trotters, English Thoroughbreds, and many others have been used to improve the Hungarian Trotter. The interest in trotting was greatly increased in 1933 when a grand new trotting track was opened, and since 1945 Hungarian Trotters have carried off major prizes at many international contests.

The Furioso—North Star (See Plate 42)

This is one of the most important families of English half-bred horses in Central Europe. The original Furioso was imported from Britain in about 1840, and from 1841 to 1851 he produced ninety-five stallions which were distributed to Studs throughout the old Austrian Empire. The Furioso breed was reinforced by many other British stallions, the most famous of which is North Star, got by a son of Touchstone out of a grand-daughter of Waxy, and who is sometimes said to have had Norfolk Roadster blood. He was described as a very compact dark-brown horse, short on the leg, with a beautiful well-bred head. Many of North Star's descendants achieved fame on Hungarian trotting tracks. The Furioso and North Star families are now so closely interwoven that they are sometimes regarded as one breed. They are found throughout Austria, Hungary, Czechoslovakia, Poland, and Rumania. Covering such an area, they naturally vary in both size and colour, but the best of them are excellent saddle horses and have won honours in every kind of competition—in jumping and dressage as well as racing, steeplechasing, and Three-day Events. A few of the heavier type are used for light draught and even for light agricultural work.

The Murakosi (See Plate 41)

The Murakosi is a comparatively new breed which has been developed in the last fifty years, principally in the south of Hungary in the neighbourhood of the river Mura, from which it takes its name. The foundation stock consisted of native mares of a type which extended over the frontier into what is now Yugoslavia and were originally sometimes known as Mur-Insulan. These were improved by imported Percheron and Belgian Ardennes stallions, as well as by good quality Hungarian stallions and, it is said, by Norics from Austria.

As arable farming became intensified after the First World War there was great demand for a good-quality, fast-moving horse capable of heavy agricultural work, and the Murakosi exactly fitted this requirement. By 1925 more than 20 per cent of all the horses in Hungary were Murakosis, and the breed continued from strength to strenth until the last War, by the end of which the breeding stock had been greatly depleted.

Huntsman and hounds of the Ottawa Valley Hunt Club   49

51   *A Tachanka, a four-horse team of Don horses, near Rostov*

52 *The horse as a circus performer*

Between 1947 and 1949, seventeen Belgian Ardennes stallions were imported from France and fifty-nine from Belgium, and the breed was soon re-established. This injection of Ardennes blood, coupled with traces of Oriental inheritance from far-distant ancestors, distinguishes the present-day Murakosi from the many other heavy draught horses of Central Europe. The breed is classed as cold blood, but many of these animals are of excellent quality and even distinction. They are noted for their good constitution and even temperament, and are particularly efficient converters of fodder into energy.

The breed now has two types: one heavier, at 16 hands or more, the other lighter and smaller but more active. The most usual colours are chestnut, bay, and black, but grey and roan are sometimes to be seen.

Murakosis are also bred in Poland and Yugoslavia.

The Nonius (See Plate 43)

Nonius Senior, the founder of the breed, was foaled at Calvados, France, in 1810. He is said to have been by an English half-bred stallion out of a Norman mare. During the Napoleonic Wars he was captured by Hungarian cavalry from the Rosières Stud in France and taken to the Mezöhegyes Stud. There he produced fifteen outstanding stallions out of mares which included Anglo-Norman, Arabian, Circassian, Holstein, Lipizzaner, Spanish, and Turkish. His son Nonius IX seems to have been more prepotent than his father. Many of the best Nonius stallions and mares were said to be the result of fairly close interbreeding, but whatever the truth of this they were certainly extremely popular. By 1890 the registered descendants of Nonius included over 2800 stallions and over 3200 mares. By this time the breed had established its present tendency to mature late and to live a correspondingly long time.

The present-day Nonius is an excellent dual-purpose horse, widely used for all purposes from sporting to light agricultural tasks. Many Nonius stallions have been exported to other countries to improve the native breeds. Mated to English Thoroughbred stallions, Nonius mares produce excellent hunters and showjumpers, some of which excel at dressage. The usual colours are black or brown, and the height varies from about 16 hands to 14·2, the smaller variety (often bay in colour) being preferred in some parts of the country.

YUGOSLAVIA is largely dependant on agriculture, while forestry is beginning to be of importance. About 30 per cent of the country consists of forest, while of the ground fit for agriculture about half is arable and the rest is pasture and meadow.

The Yugoslav Government has encouraged modernization of farming, which has resulted in a considerable degree of mechanization on the larger arable farms, but this has, as yet, had little impact on the thousands of small family farms, many in the mountainous regions, all of which still rely on horses to a considerable extent.

Stock breeding is being stimulated by the Government, and improved breeding methods, both of horses and of other domestic animals, are playing an important part in the economy. Nevertheless, the lack of modern transport in the upland areas, and the severity of the mountain trails and passes, restricts commerce to pack-horse transport, especially in bad weather.

Besides the Bosnian Pony described below, Yugoslav Studs produce a number of Nonius horses and also Belgian and Noric Heavy Draught horses. Of the lighter breeds, the Arabian and the Lipizzaner are the most popular, followed by English half-breds.

The Bosnian Pony

The Bosnian Pony is generally brown or chestnut, black, or grey. It is bred in Bosnia, Herzegovina, Montenegro, Macedonia, and in part of Serbia. The main Stud is at Borike, while others are at Pale, Banja, Luka, and Livno.

This pony is regarded as one of the most important breeds in the Balkan States. Out of Yugoslavia's estimated 1·3 million horses, the Bosnian Pony counts for over 30 per cent. Mountain ponies have been bred from time immemorial in Central Europe, principally for pack-transport purposes, for which they are still used in isolated districts. Because breeding conditions are more suitable in the better-cultivated north-west Yugoslavia, and because breeders in this area have been, on the whole, more careful in selecting breeding stock, a better type of pony known as the Posavac is found in this area. In spite of a similar genetic origin to the southern ponies, this is a bigger, stronger, and more valuable animal.

The basic origin of the native Bosnian Pony is believed to be the Tarpan, crossed with the Steppe-bred ponies similar to the wild Prjevalski. When the Turks conquered this area they introduced Eastern blood, which has considerably refined what otherwise might have been merely a heavy mountain pony. Eventually, too much Eastern blood was introduced, resulting in a light spindle-legged pony which proved to be of little practical use. Then breeders reverted to the traditional blood lines and achieved better results.

In 1933 three stallions were selected which were the founders of those first-class ponies which are today in extensive demand. These stallions, which remained at stud until the end of the Second World War, were Misko, a small and very compact pony of the Tarpan type, which had tremendous influence on all subsequent breeding, Barut, and Agan, both of whom were bigger and heavier than Misko; the blood of Agan is today found only in the pedigree mare lines.

Nowadays all stallions are tested for pack-transport purposes, having to carry 2 cwt over a distance of 10 miles, and this has been achieved in 1 hour 11 minutes.

A number of stories are told illustrating the remarkable intelligence of the Bosnian Pony. Dr Vucan Sala, former Director of the State Stud for Bosnian ponies, relates how a peasant had had a favourite pony seized by the Croatian Army. Ten years later he was awakened by persistent neighing outside his house, where he found to his astonishment his pony, alone, but carrying a pack of wine bags. It turned out that the pony, recognizing even at night that he was near his old home, had managed to escape, and to return to his master.

POLAND has been a country of horse breeders and horse lovers for as far back as its history can be traced. In the ancient days, successive Polish monarchs instituted Royal Studs which helped to improve the chargers of the famous Polish Cavalry.

Unhappily, there have been a number of occasions when Poland has been occupied and her Studs plundered of the best breeding stock, but after Poland recovered her independence in 1918, horse-breeding was revived on a national scale and between the two World Wars Polish riders on Polish horses won innumerable prizes in international events, particularly at the Olympic Games at Paris, Amsterdam, and Berlin.

Since the last War, Polish breeders have concentrated on high-class warm-blood horses for sporting purposes, and on producing a good quality all-purpose utility breed. To achieve the latter object breeding has been organized and re-organized to an extent which has caused some confusion. For example, in 1947 the Polish Ministry of Agriculture founded a new Stud at Liski in the Masury district; a Masuren breed was developed which was most successful in international competitions, but now both the Masuren and the older Poznan breeds are merged in the new Wielkopolski.

United Nations statistics show Poland as having about 2½ million horses, the largest horse population in Europe. The Polish Government takes an active interest in horse-breeding, and comprehensive records are kept for every recognized breed; Stud book entries must conform to current Government regulations.

In addition to the breeds described in detail, Poland has many English Thoroughbreds, mostly in the Government-owned Studs. These are sometimes used to improve other breeds, but English Thoroughbreds have been bred pure in Poland for many years, and often represent the country in international races.

Another breed, now well established, is the Norwegian Fjord Pony, first imported in 1946, which is bred pure at Nowielice and is used to improve native-bred ponies.

A little-known variety which is beginning to be regarded as a separate breed is the Kopczyk, a small cold-blood horse which stems from a prepotent stallion got by an unknown sire out of a half-bred mare. Short, with powerful legs, this good-looking horse has tremendous endurance and cheerfully achieves an amazing amount of heavy work on a minimum ration of low-grade fodder. Another useful cold-blood horse for agricultural work is the Mur-Insulan, originally from Yugoslavia. This was one of the ancestors of the Hungarian Murakosi (see p. 56). The draught horses of the Sadecki district of southern Poland are in the process of being recognized as a separate breed under the name Sadecki. This variety contains Furioso blood, and the more lightly built animals make excellent riding horses. The Government Stud at Stubno is seeking to upgrade the variety by selective breeding.

Throughout Poland, heavy draught horses are being improved by imported stallions, often Swedish Ardennes. Well-established local types include the Sokolski Horse in north-east Poland and the Sztumski Horse from the neighbourhood of the Vistula Delta.

The Hucul (See Plate 46)

This powerful, though primitive, pony is of ancient lineage. Like the Konik, described in the next article, the Hucul is probably a direct descendant of the original Tarpan which dates back to the Stone Age (see p. 14). The immediate ancestors of the Hucul have flourished in the Carpathian Mountains, literally for thousands of years. Some experts believe that over the centuries there have been repeated injections of Eastern blood; whatever the truth of this theory, which is impossible either to prove or to disprove, the modern Hucul is a strong elegant pony with a medium-sized head, a short back, and sloping quarters.

For centuries they were used as pack animals on difficult mountain paths, over which they carried heavy burdens, whatever the weather, contending with snow and ice, and sometimes with thick fog. The present-day Hucul is used mainly in harness; it is the standard work-horse for thousands of highland farms in southern Poland and throughout the Carpathians. The larger ponies are sometimes ridden. The breed has a reputation for being sensible and extremely docile.

There was no systematic breeding until about a century ago, when a Stud was founded at Luczyna. The main Stud nowadays is at Siary near Gorlice. The most usual colours are bay or dun, but piebald Huculs are quite common.

The Konik (See Plate 47)

Konik means "small horse", and although it stands only about 13 hands, the Konik is more of a horse than pony. It can thrive and work hard on a meagre diet, which makes it popular with innumerable small farmers in Poland and throughout Eastern Europe. Like its smaller mountain cousin, the Hucul, the Konik is an 'improved' edition of the primitive Tarpan, and, again like the Hucul, the Konik shows a suggestion of Arab blood.

Konik horses have been bred in Poland for many centuries, and a uniform type is now universal. The breed is officially recognized by the Polish authorities because of its importance to small farmers and because of the demand for it in adjacent countries. It is bred systematically at Studs at Popielno and at Jezewice, and also is bred by a great number of small farmers.

Noted for its robust constitution and quiet temperament, the Konik has retained many of the characteristics of its wild Tarpan ancestors. A herd of Konik horses run, untended, in a reserve, and fend for themselves as they did centuries ago. Horses bred in this reserve are easily broken to harness and soon settle down to earn their keep.

The Malopolski

This dual-purpose horse of south-eastern Poland was produced by upgrading native mares with Arabian and Anglo-Arabian stallions. It is lighter than the Wielkopolski and has more quality, and with its elegant Oriental blood it is said to bear more resemblance to the original Polish Horse than any other breed of the present day.

Noted for their mild disposition, Malopolskis are sound and excellent movers and have tremendous stamina. Like most recently developed breeds the type varies in different parts of the region, the better quality being first-class riding horses. Among the more prominent local strains is the Sadecki, the largest and most powerful of all, and capable of draught work if required. This variety shows the influence of the Hungarian Furioso family and is now being systematically improved by selective breeding at the Government Stud at Stubno. Another important local type is the Dabrowsko-Tarnowski which shows the influence of Gidran blood.

The principal Studs now concentrating on the Malopolski are at Janów Podlaski and Walewic.

The Polish Anglo-Arab (See Plate 48)

The Poles have been breeding Arabians for many centuries and English Thoroughbreds for over two centuries, so it is difficult to discover when a Polish Stud first interbred the two to produce the first Polish Anglo-Arab, but undoubtedly this took place a very long time ago. Anglo-Arabs have for many years been an important factor in Polish horse-breeding, and have attained a standard of excellence in conformation, coupled with performance, which are hard to equal.

Polish Anglo-Arabs are frequently successful in every kind of equine competition from Three-day Events to hurdle races. In September 1958 the Polish-bred Anglo-Arab Aron won the international competition for riding horses in the Netherlands, and another, Blawat, is a well-known winner in international competitions all over Europe. Other Polish Anglo-Arabs have been prominent as Event horses in Belgium and Switzerland, and the Polish National Team, which has secured numerous successes in international competitions, includes a number of Polish-bred Anglo-Arabs among their regular mounts. The Government Stud at Janów regularly produces half-bred as well as pure-bred Arabs, and Equador, a half-bred Anglo-Arab, proved one of the most successful stallions produced by that famous Stud.

The Polish Arab (See Plate 45)

Arabian and Syrian stallions (Polish horse breeders differentiate between them) were brought back to Poland by returning Crusaders, and undoubtedly influenced the native horses. The earliest known reference to pure-bred Arabian horses in Poland is in 1570, when the king contrasted Arabian with Syrian and Turkish stallions at the Royal Stud at Knyszyn. For centuries, Eastern stallions of all varieties were captured from the Turks during a long series of wars, and the improvement they effected was such that Polish horse breeders came to depend on them. A limited number of pure-bred Arabian mares were captured also, and Arabians were bred pure in Poland from a very early date.

About 270 years ago, the Turkish wars came to an end and Polish envoys travelled to Asia Minor and beyond to purchase Eastern stallions and, where possible, mares. They bought a number of Arabian and Syrian stallions, particularly from Aleppo, Baghdad, and Damascus, and, in 1845, three pure-bred Arabian mares were imported by the owner of the Jarczowce Stud, each of which established a famous female line which still flourishes today.

Over the centuries, Poland has produced some of the best Arabian horses in the world, and these soon established an international reputation. Polish Arabians secured gold medals at the Paris Exhibitions in 1867 and 1900, while at the national Exhibition at Vienna in 1873, they secured innumerable prizes. Polish-bred Arabian stallions have been in demand throughout the world for over half a century. In 1912, the grey stallion, Skowronek, was exported to Britain where he won many prizes and, in 1920, was bought by the famous Crabbet Stud. His descendants are still prominent in Britain, South America, Spain, the U.S.A., and the U.S.S.R. At the present day, Polish-bred Arab stallions are regularly exported to Britain, Canada, Czechoslovakia, East Germany, Hungary, Italy, Rumania, and the U.S.S.R., and every year many go to the U.S.A.

In 1926 a Polish Arab Stud Book was introduced under the auspices of the Ministry of Agriculture. Previously pedigrees had been kept by every Stud. Many Polish Arabians have a pedigree that can be traced in full for ten generations, and sometimes as many as fourteen, extending back over 150 years.

In 1927 races restricted to Arabians were introduced and special courses were constructed at Lwow, Lublin, and Piotrków. The races are run at all distances from 1000 to 2250 yards. The Stud which specializes in colts for racing is at Michalow in the Kielce district, but the main Arab Stud is the Government owned establishment at Janów where horses have been bred since 1817.

The Slaski

Based in the district of Silesia in south-western Poland, this variety is in the process of gaining recognition, for although these horses have been bred systematically for many years, they are still a type rather than a genetical entity. They stem from the Oldenburg breed, and are claimed to be the heaviest and most powerful horses in existence which do not contain cold blood. There are now two types, the larger of which compares in size with a cold-blooded cart-horse, and a pair of big Slaski horses are said to do the work of four normal agricultural horses. They are much used for heavy draught in towns.

A smaller, brisker type is also found with good action and plenty of stamina. This type excels in harness and has a great future as a fast moving draught horse.

The necessary pedigree and other Stud documents are now being examined, and the State Studs are planning to reduce the size of the horse in an attempt to lessen its food consumption, with the minimum loss of power. Silesia has only about 8 per cent of the total horse population of Poland, but the Slaskis are by far the most popular horse in the region.

The Wielkopolski (See Plate 53)

The dual-purpose horses of Central and Western Poland, which together constitute the region of Greater Poland, are now regarded as one breed—the Wielkopolski. They include the much older Poznan Horse which had been in existence for nearly a century. This was the product of Arabian, Hanoverian, and British Thoroughbred blood, with a cross of Trakehner from what is now East Germany. The Poznan breed was officially recognized and stallion depots were provided. All this has now gone, and the Poznan Horse officially no longer exists, though the Wielkopolskis bred in the Poznan district are recognized as being of a distinct type. The same can be said of horses from the Masury District, formerly recognized as being of the Masuren breed. Polish experts are confident that these variations will not persist.

The Wielkopolski was produced by crossing native mares with Eastern and, to a lesser extent, with Trakehner stallions. They are big dual-purpose horses with excellent temperaments, equally suitable for riding and driving, while the heavier specimens can tackle any normal agricultural task. Full of courage for work and notably good movers, they are in great demand both in Poland and in the neighbouring countries.

SWITZERLAND still has nearly 60,000 horses, of which about three-quarters are light draught horses of the Franches-Montagnes breed described below. Horse-breeding throughout the country is controlled through ninety-one associations whose members own some 17 per cent of all the horses in Switzerland; that is, all except the least valuable cross-breds and working horses.

There is one Federal Stud at Avenches which controls about a hundred stallions; these are dispersed throughout the country during the breeding season. About the same number of stallions are owned privately, and, in 1967, 195 stallions at Stud achieved an average fertility rate of 61 per cent.

Apart from the Franches-Montagnes mentioned above, most of the breeding stock are either Einsiedlers, described below, or Swiss Holsteins. This latter breed constitutes nearly one-third of Swiss warm-blooded horses. It is strongest in the cantons of St Gallen, Thurgau, and Zürich. Breeders make every effort to ensure that the Holstein type is maintained and the utmost care is taken in the selection of breeding stock. The only other breed worthy of mention is the Haflinger (see p. 52) which is becoming increasingly popular in some regions. Thoroughbreds are regularly imported, but are not yet very strong numerically.

Horses have been bred in Switzerland from the earliest times, and the demand for general-purpose horses is still greater than Swiss breeders can supply, so that some 2000 horses of good quality are imported annually, many of which are required for the Cavalry or for mounted Volunteers. Horses for this purpose are regularly bought in France (see p. 72).

Swiss statistics show a steady increase in horses for riding and for competitive events at the expense of draught horses. The number of half-bred mares has doubled since 1960, while in the same time the number of draught horses has decreased by about 40 per cent.

The Swiss Government has been active in encouraging the breeding of suitable horses, partly through the Federal Stud mentioned above, and partly by organizing competitions between the breeders' associations and by paying bonuses for animals of good quality. Agencies of the Government also supervise sales of foals and young horses, and approved purchases are sometimes financed, which helps to support the market. The Government regularly buys suitable home-bred horses for the Cavalry and for the Infantry Supply Columns.

Switzerland is determined to maintain a horse population suited to her special circumstances. Her countryside is made up of innumerable small farms with steep slopes, some of which are inaccessible to motor vehicles, and the Swiss public taken an ever-increasing interest in riding and in mounted sport of every kind.

The Einsiedler (See Plate 56)

This breed takes its name from the Stud principally associated with it—at Kloster Einsiedel. It is also known as the Swiss Anglo-Norman. For centuries Anglo-Normans have been bred in the Alpine Valleys of Waadtländer and the Bernese Highlands. This most versatile breed shines as a good class riding horse, as an outstanding trotter, and as a light draught horse suitable for minor agricultural tasks.

Anglo-Norman breeding stock was first imported about 150 years ago and a number of stallions are maintained at the Federal Depot at Avenches.

The Einsiedler is widely distributed throughout Switzerland and is sustained by nine breeding societies. It is described as a horse *à deux mains*—an excellent riding or harness horse with a lively and obedient character.

This is a well-proportioned horse, with an expressive, alert head and a deep chest, and it moves with an easy, elegant action. The majority of Einsiedlers are home-bred, though mares are still imported, but only from recognized Anglo-Norman sources in appropriate districts of France. Horses of this breed are regularly purchased for the Swiss Army.

The Franches-Montagnes (See Plate 57)

This breed, also known as the Freiberger or Jura, originated nearly one hundred years ago. It was created by crossing native mares with Anglo-Norman stallions. Some experts believe that the blood of English half-bred Hunters and of Ardennes stallions was also introduced at this time, but the breed has now been kept pure for many years.

These horses proved invaluable for military purposes in both World Wars, and are still bought by the Swiss Army for draught purposes. They are also invaluable for agriculture and are especially popular on the numerous small family farms in inaccessible regions.

The increasing demand for all-purpose horses has led to experiments in crossing the Franches-Montagnes with warm-blooded stallions, but these have not been particularly successful, and the principal breeders are anxious to keep the breed as pure as possible in spite of the marked decrease in numbers. Consequently the type has changed but little.

The present-day Franches-Montagnes stands rather over 15 hands and weighs nearly half a ton. Immensely strong and compact, it is also extremely active, and remains the premier agricultural breed in Switzerland.

THE FEDERAL REPUBLIC OF GERMANY

A number of horse-breeding societies operate in each of the ten Federal States which together make up the Federal Republic of Germany. These societies were founded, in most cases in the second half of the last century, by groups of enthusiasts combining to improve the breed or breeds in which they were particularly interested. They are responsible for maintaining the Stud Books of each breed, and for controlling and directing breeding. They also organize local and general shows for breeding stock.

Under the German Animal Husbandry Act of July 1949 these societies can apply for official recognition as 'Breed Societies' to the Minister of Agriculture of the State in which each society operates. This recognition gives them the legal status of *Eingetragener Verein* (E.V.). The maintenance of each Stud Book is supervised by the German Agricultural Society, subject to the Animal Husbandry Act, which stipulates that no sire may be used for breeding unless it has been licensed and has a current service permit. These are granted only to stallions whose pedigrees are vouched for by a recognized Breed Society, and which have been certified by the relevant Licensing Committee to be likely to improve the general standard of the breed.

The Animal Husbandry Act lays down a standard of performance currently required from the dam of each young stallion presented for licensing, as well as a standard for the stallions themselves. The requirements vary according to the breed concerned. In the case of Thoroughbred and Trotter stallions a minimum racing requirement is laid down. All other breeds must qualify in a draught performance test which consists of pulling a sleigh burdened with a given weight.

Stallions may be kept privately, co-operatively, or by the State which may provide improver stallions from State-owned Studs (*Hauptgestüte*), as was formerly done at Trakehnen for the East Prussian Horse, and in Gräditz for the German Thoroughbred. At present there are two such Studs—one in Württemberg for the Württemberg Warm Blood Horse and for Arabians, and the other in Bavaria for South German Horses.

The State also provides Stallion Depots (*Landgestüte*) which distribute selected stallions to service centres in the region. Stallions are usually acquired for these Depots at the age of about two and a half, after the first licence has been obtained, but the Stallion Depot at Celle buys young colts freshly weaned, and rears them at a special centre. At three years old they go to the Stallion Testing Centre at Westercelle and are trained for one year, after which they are required to qualify at a higher level of performance than that laid down by the Animal Husbandry Act.

In addition to the horse-breeding societies, each State has various rider-and-driver societies which organize sporting events in accordance with the rules and regulations for testing horses' ability which are supervised by a Government-sponsored committee in each State. For testing horses' ability at international level, the standards of the *Fédération Equestre Internationale* are applied. In addition, there are special regulations for racing laid down by the Directorate of Thoroughbred Racing in Cologne, and for Trotting by the Society for Trotter Breeding and Racing in Bonn.

[63]

Each State provides special training centres for riding, riding instructors, and for horses. There is also a National Training Centre at Warendorf, which is also the headquarters of the National Olympic Games Committee.

The Society for Breeding and Testing German Horses (H.d.P.) at Bonn co-ordinates the work of the horse-breeding societies and of rider-driver societies throughout the Republic. The H.d.P. lays down general rules for the guidance of other societies and represents Breeding and Riding in the National Olympic Games Committee. It also provides the national representation in the *Fédération Equestre Internationale* and revises and confirms the regulations for testing the horses mentioned above and records results of all events. A score of horse-breeding societies are directly affiliated, with a private membership of over 5000.

The last livestock census, in December 1967, showed 283,000 horses in the Federal Republic, which included some 1200 Thoroughbred and 2400 Trotter mares, in addition to which nearly 40,000 horses were registered in the Stud Books of the Breed Societies. Of the latter, two-thirds belong to the breeds grouped under the heading of German Warm Blood—that is to say, Trakehners, Hanoverians, Holsteins, Olden-burgs, East Friesians, Württembergs, Bavarians, and Zweibrückers; 13 per cent are ponies or small horses (height at withers 120–147 centimetres); just over 10 per cent are German Cold Blood—*i.e.*, Rhenish-Germans and Schleswigers; and just under 10 per cent are Shetland ponies below 120 centimetres at the withers.[1]

Arabian horses have been bred in Germany for many years, formerly at the Royal Württemberg Stud in Weil, but were moved in 1932 to the Government Stud at Marbach-Lauter where the stock has been improved by systematic selective breeding.

There are a few private Studs in Germany which breed Arabians, all the breeders being members of the Society of the Breeders and Friends of the Arab Horse which is also responsible for the Stud Book. Arabians have been used from time to time for inter-breeding with the East Prussian, the Hanoverian, and the Holstein horses, and more recently, since the Second World War, with the East Friesian, but in recent times the Arabian has not been used to improve German Warm Blood horses, mainly because of its lack of size.

Another breed to be found in Germany is the Norwegian Fjord Horse which has become popular since 1950, especially in the north-western part of Germany and in the regions of Palatine and Hesse where it is replacing cows for draught purposes. The lighter type is used as a children's riding pony. Fjord breeding societies exist in every Federal State and there are now some 150 stallions and about 2000 registered mares.

Haflingers have been bred in Bavaria since 1935, when the army imported breeding stock from South Tyrol and established Stud Farms for military purposes. The Haflingers make excellent pack and draught horses in mountainous regions and are still bred in Upper Bavaria and Westphalia.

There are also about 650 Shetland Pony stallions and 3800 registered mares. Originally, many Shetlands were inter-bred with other small breeds, but a Stud Book was started in 1942 and pure-bred Shetlands are now more common. Pony-breeding societies exist in every Federal State and the Dulmen Pony is still popular, especially in the Meerfelder Brück region in Westphalia near the Dutch border. This ancient breed, the only native German pony, was first mentioned in 1316, but is now sadly reduced in numbers, there being only about a hundred brood mares.

The Bavarian Warm Blood

This new variety springs from the old Rottaler breed. The valley of the Rott is noted for its very good soil, excellent farming conditions, and splendid horses. By the time of the Crusades the Rottaler had won high esteeem as a charger, being considered at least the equal of the celebrated Friesian Heavy Horse.

[1] For note on metric measurement see "The U.S.S.R.", p. 107.

53 *WIELKOPOLSKI*

54 *NORIC*

55 *HAFLINGER PONY*

56 *EINSIEDLER*

57 *FRANCHES-MONTAGNES*

58 *SCHLESWIGER*

59 *EAST FRIESIAN*

60 *OLDENBURG*

61 *EAST PRUSSIAN OF TRAKEHNER ORIGIN*

62 *HOLSTEIN*

63 *HANOVERIAN*

64 *GERMAN TROTTER*

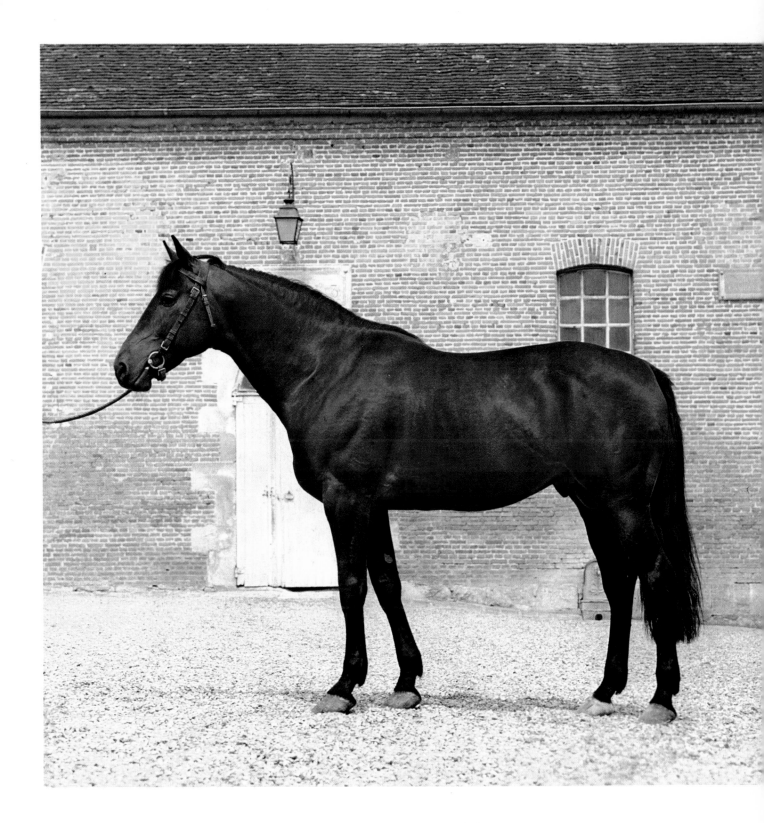

65 *FRENCH TROTTER*

66 *FRENCH THOROUGHBRED*

67 FRENCH ANGLO-ARAB

68 *BRETON*

Systematic breeding began in the sixteenth century under the influence of the monasteries, and in the eighteenth century British half-bred stallions were introduced, as also were Cleveland Bays and stallions from Zweibrücken and Normandy. By the end of the last century the demand for a heavily built warm-blood horse led to the introduction of Oldenburg stallions whose influence continued for some decades and gave increased substance to the Rottaler.

The present-day horse is of medium size, with great depth and width in proportion, and good bone. The breeders concentrate on producing horses with quiet temperaments. About ten years ago the traditional name of Rottaler was discontinued, and the improved horses from the region, mostly carrying Rottaler blood, are now officially known as Bavarian Warm Bloods. For the last five years these have been branded with a 'B' in a coat of arms surmounted by a stylized crown.

The East Friesian Horse (See Plate 59)

The breeding basis of the East Friesian was originally the same as that of the neighbouring Oldenburg Horse, and the principles applied to each show a great similarity. The first great promoter of the East Friesian breed was Georg Albrecht, under whose Regency in 1715 the first horse-licensing laws were laid down.

In the first breed register for which he was responsible, horses of English, Polish, Spanish, Turkish, Hungarian, Danish, Irish, East Prussian, and Oldenburg descent were entered, in addition to such breeds as the Siebenburger and the Senner.

High-quality stallions were often looked upon with disfavour by the farmer-breeders who were only interested in the utility type of horse, but stallions with Cleveland Bay and Norman blood, brought in from Oldenburg, were very successful.

Changes in type, made necessary by current demands and requiring alterations in the standard aimed at by the breeders, were at first very similar to those described in the Oldenburg but after the Second World War a further alteration was brought about with the use of Arab stallions from Marbach (Wind Ox, Jason Ox, and Halali Ox), while in recent years the homogenous grey Gazal from Bábolna, Hungary, has had a marked effect.

During the last few years Hanoverian stallions have also been used, and a very close co-operation in breeding and organization with the Hanoverian breed has now been planned in order to achieve as quickly as possible a type closer to the quality, multi-purpose horse which is required at present.

The East Prussian of Trakehner Origin (See Plate 61)

The province of East Prussia, the native heath of the noble Warm Blood Horse, used to be able to boast the highest density of horses in the whole of Germany. The foundation of the breed goes back to the Order of the German knights, which bred a lighter and heavier type to suit its various requirements.

The so-called "Schweiken", which goes back to the wild horse, had a great influence on the lighter types. In 1732 King Friedrich Wilhelm I founded the main Stud of Trakehnen, the most important improvement measure for the development of the East Prussian Horse. The herds of mares in this Stud had been segregated according to colour, and these various herds served through the utilization of specially selected stallions as foundation mares for various purposes. Trakehnen thus became the main producer of stallions for breeding requirements in East Prussia.

The type was developed at the beginning of the nineteenth century with an out-cross of Oriental horses (Arabs), but in later decades an increasing number of English Thoroughbreds was used. In 1913 no fewer than 84·3 per cent of all mares had been sired by Thoroughbred stallions.

The aim of the breeders was the production of a very noble horse, capable of being used for agricultural purposes, but in the main to serve as cavalry remounts. In order to guarantee the highest possible performance, only stallions who had been subjected to a year's training were used, and before going to Stud they had to be examined at the Stallion Testing Centre at Zwion.

By the end of the War the East Prussian Horse had proved itself throughout numerous treks to be capable of extraordinary performances. But of 25,000 horses registered in the East Prussian Stud Book in 1944, only some 1200 reached Western Germany for the continuation of their Stud duties.

The mares are now to be found throughout Germany, though there are four distinct breeding centres at Hunnesruck (Lower Saxony), Rantzau and Schmoel (Holstein), and Birkhausen (Palatinate). To continue and perpetuate this breed, as well as for the improvement of other warm-blood breeds, some 120 East Prussian stallions are at present available. There is thus every likelihood that the reputation of the breed as an excellent riding horse can be maintained.

Breeding is administered by the Society of Breeders and Friends of the Warm Blood Horse of Trakehner Origin in Hamburg.

The German Thoroughbred

Thoroughbred-breeding in Germany, based on importations from England, commenced at the beginning of the nineteenth century. The first Studs were established in the Mecklenburg and Pomeranian provinces of Northern Germany, where the ecological conditions varied considerably from those in England, and in Eastern Germany, more especially in Silesia, where Count Henckel and Count Renard played a prominent part in the establishment of the German Thoroughbred Horse.

Perhaps the greatest influence on the modern German Thoroughbred, however, was the foundation of two Studs in the west of the country towards the end of the last century—Schlenderhan, established in 1874, and Waldfried in 1895. These two Studs soon became independent of imported breeding stock and concentrated on developing their own blood lines. Waldfried was particularly successful with the progeny of the mare Festa, a daughter of St Simon. Other important private Studs of the present day are Erlenhof, Ebbesloh, Ravensburg, Mydlinghoven, Rottgen, Zoppenbroich, and Bad Harzburg, to name only a few.

The State of Prussia also started to breed Thoroughbreds in 1833, and from 1866 onwards based its activities on the Gräditz Stud near Torgau, with the special aim of promoting Thoroughbred stallions which, according to their performance and conformation, might be used for the improvement of the Warm Blood Horse.

The first race on record in Germany was run at Bad Doberan, Mecklenburg, in 1822—the same year in which the first German racing club was founded. Some years later racing started in Berlin, and 1869 the first German Derby was run, under the rules of the Directorate for Thoroughbred Breeding and Racing.

The German Jockey Club was founded in 1840, to be followed in 1867 by the Union Club. Until the end of the Second World War Hoppegarten, near Berlin, was the breeding and training centre for German Thoroughbreds. Since the end of the last war the Directorate has moved its premises to Cologne, where it is responsible for compiling the Stud Book which was opened in 1847.

There are still only about 1200 Thoroughbred mares in Germany. The most noted stallion since the war has been Ticino, by Ahanasius, bred by the Erlenhof Stud. Lesser-known Thoroughbred stallions are also used in nearly all the German warm-blood breeds in order to improve stamina, constitution, and quality.

The German Trotter (See Plate 64)

Trotting was developed in Germany during the closing decades of the last century, particularly in Hamburg, Berlin, and the west of Germany. In 1874 the first trotting club was formed in Hamburg—the Altona. Fourteen years later all the existing clubs amalgamated to form a special technical committee. After the Second World War regional organizations were operated in Berlin, Bonn, and Munich, but they were recently united to form the Society for Trotter-breeding and Racing in Bonn.

After the First World War the money penalty system was introduced and proved to be a very useful measure for the development of performance testing. The basis of the system lies in distance handicapping in accordance with stake money won, with time over a thousand metres as the yardstick. All Trotters who have covered this distance in less than 1 minute 30 seconds are included on the standard register. There is also an élite list for horses capable of covering the distance in 1 minute 20 seconds. Since 1927 there has been Register I for Trotter Thoroughbreds and Registers II and III for Trotter half-breds and Trotter crosses respectively.

The German Trotter was originally based upon the Orlov Trotters imported from Russia, but the quality of the German-bred products improved remarkably with the introduction of American blood. In recent years French Trotters have also been used.

The first German Stud of Trotters was founded in 1885 in Mariahall/Rhineland/Hesse. At the present time they are bred chiefly in the north, south, and west of the country, often on small farms with only one or two mares, as the Trotter has a well-deserved reputation for his equable temperament and tractability.

There are at present some 2400 Trotter mares in Germany—exactly double the number of Thoroughbreds. The most famous stallion was Epilog, who was French-bred on his dam's side and achieved a record time of 1 minute 18·6 seconds. His most illustrious son, Permit, holds the current record with 1 minute 17·3 seconds.

The Hanoverian (See Plate 63)

In common with many other breeds of horses, the Hanoverian was originally developed from a combination of indigenous horses with Oriental, Spanish, and Neapolitan stallions. The breeding of the Hanoverian has always been promoted by the ducal, and later royal, family of Hanover. The collaboration with British breeders, which already existed, became intensified in 1714 when George I inherited the British throne. On July 27th, 1735, George II founded, by order of his cabinet, the Stallion Depot at Celle. It commenced operations with fourteen black stallions of Holstein descent, and later English Thoroughbreds were widely used.

In the middle of the last century some 35 per cent of all the mares were served by Thoroughbred stallions, but the products were often criticized as being too light for agricultural use, so there followed a decline in the use of Thoroughbred blood and an attempt to consolidate and standardize the breed by giving preference to indigenous lines within the breed itself.

The declared aim was to breed a warm-blood horse that was as strong as possible, suitable for all types of agricultural work, but with sufficient blood, courage, and action for riding and driving purposes. In order to achieve this objective the use of Thoroughbreds, hitherto regarded as an essential safeguard for stamina and courage, was reduced to a minimal 2 to 3 per cent, and the breeding region of Hanover started to produce a multi-purpose warm-blood horse of high quality. When, however, at the end of the last War the rôle of the horse in agriculture declined steeply and rapidly, there was renewed scope for refinement of the breed, and the use of East Prussian and Thoroughbred stallions was increased to 7 or 8 per cent.

The field of warm-blood breeding in Germany is now dominated by the Hanoverian Horse. More than 7000 mares are served by selected stallions annually, and the type has become the guiding factor in warm-blood breeding. Thus many other breeding regions use Hanoverian stallions. For instance, the Westphalian horses which have been bred for many decades are, in effect, Hanoverians, although they are called "Westfalisches Pferd".

The breeding of the Hanoverian is conducted under the auspices of the Society of Hanoverian Warm-blood Breeders in Hanover and by the Westphalian Stud Book in Munster. The federal state of Niedersachsen is responsible for maintaining the stallion depot at Celle, with an affiliated stallion testing centre in Westercelle. The federal state of Northrhine-Westphalia serves the same purpose, by providing young stallions in the stallion depot at Warendorf (Westphalia).

The Holstein (See Plate 62)

The breeding of horses in Holstein, which was originally promoted by the monasteries, reaches far back into the mists of time. The indigenous breed of the area was crossed with Oriental, Neapolitan, and Spanish stallions. Then, following the Reformation, the promotion of horse-breeding became the responsibility of the Crown. At that time the Holstein Horse had already attracted buyers from Denmark, Spain, Italy, and France and had begun to influence the other German warm-blood breeds. In 1719 the first licensing regulations were laid down, and they were revised and tightened up in 1782.

Two factors have influenced the development of the Holstein Horse since that time. On the one hand was the use of English Thoroughbred stallions, imported since the beginning of the nineteenth century. Their favourable influence made the type more compact and shorter legged, while the then prevailing Roman nose became less frequent, and the galloping ability was improved. Of even greater importance was the importation of Yorkshire Coach Horse stallions, which brought the characteristic high and wide gait and a good temperament to the Holstein breed, so that its representatives earned a reputation as dual-purpose carriage and riding horses.

During the last decade, however, a complete change of the old breed type was brought about by using both German and English Thoroughbred stallions in vastly greater numbers than in the other German warm-blood breeding regions, to produce a multi-purpose riding horse who could gallop, jump, and be used for showjumping and Three-day Events.

When the stallion depot at Traventhal, run by the Schleswig-Holstein government, was closed down the Society of Breeders of the Holstein Horse in Elmshorn assumed responsibility for making the stallions available, as well as for compiling the customary Stud Book. Prospective stallions are sent at the age of three years, rising four, for performance testing at the Stallion Testing Centre at Westercelle. Originally the breeding area was limited to the coastal fringes, but later it expanded to cover the light soils of the peninsula.

The Holstein breed has produced a number of the very best German showjumping horses, among them Meteor and Tora. Fritz Thiedemann, the Olympic rider and former European champion, always rode Holsteins, which are also the favourite mounts of his pupil, Kurt Jarasinski.

The Oldenburg Horse (See Plate 60)

As early as the seventeenth century a strong type of horse, based on the Friesian, had been developed on the vast natural grasslands of Oldenburg. Count Anton Gunther, who lived from 1603 until 1667, was a most imaginative and far-sighted promoter of the breed, and his grey stallion, Kranich, became justly celebrated.

In the second part of the eighteenth century Spanish, Neapolitan, Barb, and English half-bred stallions were imported and the breed was then consolidated until, in the latter part of the following century, Thoroughbreds, Cleveland Bays, Hanoverians, and Norman horses were brought in. The resulting progeny produced a coach-horse type—very strong, deep, and wide with a marked tendency towards early maturity.

After the First World War the coach-horse type was superseded by a heavy warm-blood utility horse, and this type was favoured until, after the Second World War, increasing mechanization of agriculture forced the breeders to change their type yet again in order to produce a useful riding horse. The first step in this direction was the use of the Thoroughbred stallion, Lupus, and the Norman stallion, Condor. Since then Thoroughbreds, some Hanoverians, and some East Prussian stallions have been employed in greater numbers. All stallions are sent, in the autumn of their third year, to the Stallion Testing Centre at Westercelle.

In 1819 Oldenburg's first horse-breeding act was passed, to be amended in 1897 and again in 1923, which version is still in force. This act lays down that the entire responsibility for the breed, including the licensing of stallions, is delegated to the Society of Breeders of the Oldenburg Horse in Oldenburg, a fact which possibly explains the high degree of uniformity of breed type.

The Rhenish-German Cold Blood

In the first part of the present century this breed was numerically the biggest in Germany, and the most widely disseminated. The intensification of agriculture and industrialization had resulted in a general demand for a heavy draught breed. In the Rhineland in 1876 a cold-blood horse was declared to be the target of breeders, and at the same time the Belgian Horse was recognized as a breed, after some experimentation with British cart-horses such as Suffolks and Clydesdales. But, in close association with the country of its origin, the Belgian Horse was systematically developed in the Rhineland, and after the First World War was officially deemed to be the Rheinisch-Deutsches Pferd (Rhenish-German Horse).

During the first decades of this century the breed expanded into most areas with intensive arable farming, particularly in Westphalia and the province of Saxony—though here, right up to the First World War, both Shires and Clydesdales were also bred. The Rhenish-German Horse became more popular, however, wherever arable farming was practised, its chief qualities being early maturity, efficient food conversion, and good temper. In almost every area it was the Belgian stallions who were used to maintain the requisite type.

In the Rhineland, in Westphalia, and the Saxe-Anhalt a heavy type was preferred, whereas in the other areas a medium-sized horse found favour. After the Second World War the heavy types ceased to be justifiable economically and the Ardennes type grew in popularity, though with increasing mechanization the demand for them showed a decline. Now breeding has almost ceased in the once-important region of the Rhineland. A few isolated pockets still remain in Westphalia, Lower Saxony, and the Palatinate, where, for a long time, the Ardennes type has been preferred.

The Schleswiger (See Plate 58)

The Schleswiger is bred in the northern-most area of Germany, in Schleswig-Holstein, and it traces back to the Jutland Horse from Denmark which had established itself in the district of Tondern and the neighbouring west coast.

In the beginning British Yorkshire Coach horses, and even Thoroughbred stallions, were used to improve the Schleswig Horse, but methodical selective breeding was commenced in 1860. In the last century this medium-sized horse, very mobile and possessed of an extremely equable temperament, was in great demand for pulling buses and trams. In 1888 the breeding standard was recognized, and three years later came the formation of the Society of Schleswig Horse-breeding Clubs.

Until 1938 the breed was maintained by the regular use of Danish stallions, but from this time onward selection was done within the breed, very largely in an attempt to breed out the somewhat flat ribs, the long barrel, and the flat and soft feet. A medium-sized, active horse was always the target. In common with the Jutland Horse, there was always too much hair on the fetlock, which may well be the fault of the widespread use of the stallion Oppenheim, who is believed to have been a Shire.

In order to accelerate progress after the Second World War, two French cold-blood stallions were imported, one a Boulonnais and the other a Breton. The former undoubtedly had the stronger influence on the the breed.

Chestnut is the predominant colour in the Schleswiger, but bay and grey are by no means unknown. The governing body is the Society of Schleswig Horse-breeding Clubs in Kiel.

The Württemberg Horse

The Royal Studs exercised a very profound influence upon warm-blood breeding in Württemberg, particularly in the main Stud and stallion depot at Marbach, which was founded in 1593 on the chalky soil of the Rauhe Alb mountains, and whose influence prevails to this day.

The smallholdings of Württemberg called for a hardy and unassuming warm-blood horse which was easy to handle. Originally the breeders tried to produce this type of animal by crossing the indigenous horse with Arab stallions. Later more strength was recruited through East Prussian and Norman stallions, and to some extent by the use of Oldenburg, Nonius, and even Suffolk and Clydesdale sires, though the latter were a short-lived experiment.

The prototype was finally attained by the middle-sized, compact Anglo-Norman stallion Faust, who was of Cob type. He produced a lot of very useful horses with depth, hardiness, and a good temperament, which were at the same time good food converters. Later crossing experiments with Thoroughbreds, Holsteins, Oldenburgers, and Anglo-Normans were not successful, although some stallions from Brandenburg and Hanover were used to advantage.

Most recently the breed has been improved by East Prussian stallions, most notably by Julmond, who has proved to be a very reliable transmitter of the desired conformation and characteristics. His progeny can be regarded as good representatives of the present day's multi-purpose performance animal.

Breeding is under the direction of the Society of Horse Breeders of Württemberg in Stuttgart, who also look after the Stud Book registrations.

The Zweibrücker

The Eichelscheid-Zweibrücken Stud in the Palatinate, an area of great historical importance, was started in 1752, although already in the sixteenth century horses with Oriental blood were to be found in the then existing Studs of the princes and bishops.

In Zweibrücken both Arab and Turkish stallions were mated to Thoroughbred mares, and in addition Anglo-Norman stallions were used. The high reputation accruing to the Zweibrücker Horse is indicated by the fact that around 1800 the Studs of Trakehnen in East Prussian, and later Neustadt an der Dosse (Brandenburg) introduced Zweibrücker stallions.

The Stud suffered heavily in the wars of the French revolution and also in the War of Liberation in 1814. One of the stallions rescued from the French by the Austro-Hungarians was Nonius Senior, later famous as the founder of the breed which bears his name in many countries adjacent to the Danube (see p. 57).

Re-establishment of the breed was started in Zweibrücken with Orientals, English Thoroughbreds, and Normans, the last-named being especially successful in the development of a stronger type of horse. The same tendency was followed later by importations of stallions from Hanover and Oldenburg. The use of the Oldenburg did not come up to expectations, and it nearly resulted in the loss of the typical Zweibrücker characteristics.

In additions to Gidrans and Amurath II, other Cob-type Norman stallions provided so beneficial an effect upon the breed that they were resorted to time and again until very recently. Only in the last few years, when the emphasis switched from agricultural to sporting requirements, were East Prussian stallions used, particularly in the vicinity of the East Prussian Stud at Birkhausen, which was formerly part of the Stud of Zweibrücken.

The governing body of breeders and compilers of the Stud Book is the Society of Horse-breeders of the Palatinate in Kaiserslautern.

THE FRENCH REPUBLIC

To achieve long-term success in horse-breeding continuity of effort should be combined with a consistent policy, never at the mercy of passing fancy or the prejudice of individuals, especially as the latter may seek a short-term advantage at the expense of the future of what should be regarded as a national heritage.

Throughout its history the Administration of the French National Studs has shown the necessary perseverance and provided the enduring support without which such long-term projects as the selection of horses for breeding cannot prosper.

In feudal times the great seigneurs bred the war-horses and Palfreys they needed for war or for tournaments. After the break-up of the feudal system, successive governments took care to ensure a supply of horses sufficient for the needs of a centralized state. The wars of the kings of France absorbed a greater and greater number of horses as reign succeeded reign. It even became necessary to import horses from Spain and from the Germanic countries at great cost to the royal treasury.

By a decree of the Council of Louis XIV dated October 17th, 1665, Colbert involved the French Sovereign officially in horse-breeding activities. This decree created the corps of Gardes-étalon, who were made responsible for providing officially approved stallions for the benefit of French horse-breeders. Each of these stallions was marked on the thigh with a crowned 'L'. After being dispersed by the Revolution, the establishment of National Stallions was restored by Napoleon in 1806. The approved stallions were distributed between six Studs and thirty-six stallion depots.

The wars of the Empire and the armies of occupation between them exhausted the resources already strained by the Napoleonic campaigns. But the Imperial organizations survived, and the Vicomte de Castelbajac, Peer of France and Councillor of State, created L'Ecole des Haras in 1822. This guaranteed regular recruitment of Les Officiers des Haras who were responsible for the administration of stallion depots, of which there are now twenty-two.

The Administration of National Studs controlled racing in France until the foundation of the French Jockey Club in 1833 which took over part of the task. However, it still retained control of the breeding of working horses. The military disasters of the Second Empire and the depredations of the occupying forces necessitated the passing of the law of May 24th, 1874—a veritable Charter for National Studs—which defined the future policy of governments of the Republic regarding horse-breeding.

Under this law, often amended but never repealed, the number of National Stallions (today about 2000) and the sum necessary for their upkeep are fixed in the National Budget. New stallions are bought each year from funds raised from a tax of 1 per cent on the turnover of the Pari-Mutuel on all race courses in France, and are distributed between depots. During the breeding season they are scattered about in groups of two or three, or occasionally more, at countless places in France for the use of breeders. At the end of the season, in July, they reassemble in their respective depots.

Apart from this Government activity the Ministry of Agriculture has decreed that before any breeder may put his own stallion to public tud it must undergo an examination, which is repeated annually. Consequently, each stallion is kept under permanent surveillance by the officers of the Studs, who thus safeguard each breed against sires who might produce undesirable characteristics.

Finally, the Administration of Studs periodically organizes a number of competitions for stallions, mares, and fillies at which the best breeders of working horses are awarded prizes, some of which (those *de conservation*) are intended to encourage breeders to keep certain females of real quality rather than to sell them for an immediate profit.

The progress of mechanization has set back, and to some extent has ended, the breeding of work horses formerly indispensable for national defence and for work on the roads and in the fields. Nonetheless, the work of Colbert continues today in the important part which the Administration plays in the raising and use of saddle horses as well as in the surveillance which it exercises over the organization of races and the Pari-Mutuel.

The increasing interest in the saddle horse in France is further stimulated by the riding societies which doubled in number between 1962 and 1968, and now have a membership of nearly 100,000 regular riders. These flourishing organizations are systematically supported by the French Government through the Ministry of Agriculture who, in five years, have increased the yearly subvention from 1,250,000 to over 11,000,000 francs.

The Anglo-Norman Horse (See Plate 73)

The French Trotter and the Anglo-Norman Saddle Horse derive from a common ancestor in the original, fairly common, Norman mare. Stallions brought home from Hanover and Mecklenburg by the victorious armies of the First Empire had already left their mark on this foundation stock, and since then the general standard has been influenced by the evolution of the Trotter brood mares, who constituted the pick of the breed. At the turn of the century Trotters and coach horses were bred from the same stock.

When the growing popularity of the motor-car began to threaten the prosperity of the Norman coach-horse breeders, they turned their attention to the production of saddle horses for remount purposes. They thus created a division, which has now become clearly defined, between the racing-trotter type and the Anglo-Norman riding horse.

The latter, with many infusions of Thoroughbred blood from stallions standing at the National Stud depots, began to excel at cross-country work. The most famous sires were Orange Peel, Lord Frey, and Ivanhoe; more recently Ultimate and in particular Furioso. Bought soon after the Second World War from a training establishment near Reading, in England, Furioso was sold for £800 to a commission of Officiers des Haras. They did not require him for his racing record, which was poor, but for his conformation, his exceptional limbs, and his excellent action and natural balance. He died recently at the age of twenty-five, after a brilliant career at stud with the Haras du Pin (Orne), during which he topped the Thoroughbred sires of horse-show winners for ten years consecutively. Among his progeny were some first-class showjumpers who were exported all over the world.

At the time when the horse seemed to have little future, the Studs encouraged breeders with Thoroughbred and half-bred stallions of riding type—especially those which conformed with the weight-carrying Thoroughbred formula of General Blacque-Belair, who presided over the army remount service from the end of the war of 1870 until the start of the First World War.

Starting from their two Stud depots—the Haras du Pin, and that of St Lô (Manche)—the breeders have spread their influence far beyond their own rich grass country, into Anjou, Vendée, even into the Charollais in the centre of France, by supplying stallions to the depots at Angers, La Roche-sur-Yon, and Cluny. The rich soil and damp climate of the Luçon Marshes and the banks of the Loire have produced the saddle horse of Vendée—an impressive horse, with stronger action and somewhat less quality than the Norman, but with an admirably developed chest and shoulder. But in the centre of France the harder climate, more marked difference between the seasons, and poorer soil have resulted in the Charollais, a real riding animal, lighter-boned but closer-coupled than those already mentioned.

Dams are selected at shows for brood mares and fillies, organized by the National Stud and the Société des Chevaux de Guerre, the latter founded in 1907 by M. Maurice de Gasté, a tireless

[71]

worker for light-horse breeding. Anglo-Norman stallions are bought annually at Caen, having been previously judged not only on conformation but also—since showjumping is now the prime outlet—on their action and performance over fences.

Since the end of the Second World War the Swiss Army has sent a buying commission to Caen each year, which is a useful outlet to replace the now defunct French remount service. Horses are collected from all over the country by M. Alfred Lefevre of Falaise and dispatched to Switzerland at regular intervals, where they are entrusted to farmers who are liable for national service. These men look after them, work on the farm throughout the week, and on Sundays, dressed in their uniforms, ride them on manoeuvres.

Today, thanks to their size and courage, the Anglo-Normans can compete with Irish horses, which are rightly acknowledged to be the finest riding horses in the world.

The Ardennais (See Plate 74)

The Ardennais is a fashionable horse. Its coat, form, character, and make-up in general fit in with today's taste. The most common colours are bay and roan. In addition, being more thick-set than any other cart-horse, short, stocky, close to the ground, with muscles well covered with flesh, and an enormous bone structure, it is built like a heavy tractor, perfectly suited to farm work. Finally, it is endowed with an exemplary gentleness, and its docility makes it an incomparably useful agricultural tool, especially as good carters are becoming rare; a child can lead this horse at will.

Reared in a harsh climate in the French Ardennes in Lorraine, in Champagne, and in the foothills of the Vosges, it is hardy in any circumstances. Winters are severe in these regions, and the animals spend them in stables made warmer by the fact that they are built in the middle of the farm buildings. In fine weather they are put out in meadows, where they have the advantage of natural food, but in the Ardennes they are kept in stables as late as April. They are perfectly adapted to their surroundings and do well there, growing to a size that no other breed could reach in similar conditions.

In former times the Ardennais was smaller and also more lively, and there can still be found in Bassigny, a little area of old France, on both sides of the upper Marne around Chaumont, some of those Ardennais post-horses which, it is said, were the only ones to bring back the wagons of the Emperor from the disastrous Russian campaign.

But it is the heavy Ardennais from Thiérache or Lorraine which is preferred. In this form it is the farm animal of eastern France, and takes the name of the "cart-horse of the north". There it is more important than in the Ardennes, its birthplace.

The popularity the Ardennais enjoys in the farmers' minds is so great that it is nearly as numerous as the Percheron, and this popularity is growing to such an extent that the breed's Stud organization has had to limit its further expansion in order to preserve this admirable breed.

The last War decimated the regions considered to be the birthplace of the breed. Those horses which escaped disaster were mediocre and lacking in consistency, and the animals which came as replacements as soon as hostilities were over were a motley mixture from Denmark, Brabant, the Netherlands, and Hanover. The true French Ardennais, which one would have liked to see back again, had almost disappeared in the turmoil. It was therefore necessary to have recourse to importing great numbers of choice stud animals from Belgium and the Netherlands to fill the gaps. This aim should by now have been fulfilled. The breeders of the Ardennes cannot be encouraged too often to refrain from yielding to the ease of importing animals in this way, and to choose from native stock the most likely to preserve the qualities of the breed so as to make the Ardennais the truly French horse it once used to be.

The Boulonnais (See Plate 76)

Although of different ancestry, the Boulonnais, with as much of the Oriental in its make-up, is so like the Percheron that it is possible to confuse them. The first infusion of Eastern blood is said to come from the Numidian Cavalry which stayed on the coast of Boulogne before setting off with the legions of Caesar for the conquest of Britain. Then the Crusades and the Spanish occupation of Flanders successively brought to the Boulonnais mares renewed doses of this Oriental blood which still runs in their veins.

The mares were sorely tried by the last two Wars; in the First the front was drawn up on the edge of the Boulonnais area, and twenty years later the mares, scarcely built up again, suffered losses from which they have once again miraculously recovered. During the months following the end of hostilities breeders had to scour Belgium to find the scattered remnants of the breed. But these misfortunes could not dry up the sap of the Boulonnais, firmly rooted in its native soil.

Point-to-pointing at Limpsfield   69

Lipizzaners at the Spanish Riding School, Vienna 70

Bulldogging at Calgary   71

72 The courbette, *one of the figures performed by the Cadre Noir de Saumur, France*

In spite of its having become heavier, like its brothers of other breeds, in conformity with the demands of trade, the Boulonnais has retained its elegance and its unique expression. This is even more majestic than the Percheron's and it has handsomely set ears. It has not the 'strong points', the strong frame and build of the Percheron, but the harmony of its unbroken lines, the graceful rounding of its muscular parts, the fineness of its body tissues, with their plentiful distribution of little veins which stand out, make the whole animal look as if it were made of polished marble.

Formerly, light-coloured coats were preferred, but it has become clear to breeders of Boulonnais horses that farmers want horses with some colour, and that they must return to those colours which used to be found in the birthplace of the breeds. Coloured coats are not only tolerated but actually sought after nowadays.

The Breton (See Plate 68)

There is one breed of cart-horse which reflects the special character of the province which gave it birth. There is no horse like the Breton, not only in France but throughout the whole world. This is because it has derived from the sides of the Black Mountains, whence it has spread over all the Breton peninsula, special qualities of endurance, liveliness, and looks.

These little hairy animals, reminiscent of the horse of the Steppes, whose faults are redeemed by a hardiness which has no equal, can still be found in the regions of Carhaix, Gourin, and Rostrenen.

The absorbent quality of the Breton has been in its favour, in that it has profited by numerous additions of foreign blood, but has kept, in spite of all this, the original character of the 'pony' of the time when the National Provincial Stud was at Langonnet, right in the middle of the mountains. After the wars of the Empire period were over, a few Oriental stallions were at this Stud. But the resumption of relations with England also played an important part. Just as Norfolks were being imported into Normandy to develop trotting ability, and to add brightness to the step of their horses, a large dose of the same blood was given to the horse population of Brittany, and this is still to be seen today.

Those in charge of military remounting were, for their part, very active in Brittany, where the horses provided the Horse Artillery with an inexhaustible supply of the 'light cart-horses' which were its pride and joy. The demands of the Army did, fortunately, preserve the Breton Horse in a form still very different from its fellows and much appreciated abroad.

But it too has been subject to the general tendency over the last fifty years for all breeds of cart-horse to move towards the 'heavy weight', like the Belgian Horse. However, in this pursuit of weight the Breton comes in a good last. It has not been able totally to resist the trend, however, and it must be said that infusions of Ardennais and Percheron blood in the Dinan area have marked the start of a progressive increase in the weight of mares on the richest soil like that of Châteaubriant and the north coast of Brittany.

Horse meetings in Brittany are attended with fervour, often even with passion. The competitions and tests to which stallions were, and are, rightly submitted, in former times by the remounting authorities and today by the National Studs, are occasions for Folk Festivals, gay with the head-dresses, costumes, and ribbons of the country where the horse is king, whether wearing a saddle or a collar.

The capital of the Breton Horse is, without doubt, Landivisiau, in the middle of North Finistère. Commercial activity is intense there. It draws horses from all parts, and merchants from the whole of France, North Africa, Spain, Italy, Switzerland, and Japan come there for supplies of horses.

In Italy, Spain, and the Balkans, where all breeds have been tried, they always come back to the Breton, which gives at least equal service, and responds to what these countries have the means to offer. Its adaptability does not extend to work only; in cross-breeding it is ideal for improving primitive breeds, bringing them closer to the cart-horse type.

The Breton has also worked wonders in North Africa, where farmers needed to have a more powerful animal than the local horse. Crossed with the latter, the Breton produces a highly successful half-breed, which fills agricultural requirements, uniting as it does the size of the cart-horse with the resilience of the native animal.

The French Anglo-Arab (See Plate 67)

Anglo-Arabs originated in Britain, where they are controlled by the Arab Horse Society, who keep a special register for them. The breed is based on a mixture of Arab and Thoroughbred blood. Anglo-Arabs are bred in many countries, and the French variety is particularly interesting because it includes crosses between Arabian and Thoroughbred stallions with native mares carrying an ancient strain of Eastern blood.

[73]

We know that the south-west of France was occupied by the Moslems some 1200 years ago, and it is said that after their defeat and subsequent withdrawal across the Pyrenees, they left as a legacy of their occupation a horse population of Eastern descent. This is the stock upon which the French Anglo-Arab is based. It is maintained that the brood mares of the south of France have still retained the imprint of the Eastern stallions ridden by the invaders. These horses, the result of countless years of selective breeding, astonished the people of that time by their high courage, their balanced action, and their endurance, as well as by the nobility of their appearance.

They soon became acclimatized to the French environment, and retained throughout countless generations the close-coupled conformation and other distinctive characteristics, although they lost a little size. Thus for centuries these horses have prospered from the Pyrenees to the Loire, known by the names of the different districts to which they had gravitated—Iberian, Navarrese, Bigourdane, and Tarbaise.

During the Monarchy, the Revolution, and the Napoleonic Wars, the horse population was reduced to such an extent that it was necessary to revitalize it with a fresh injection of Arab blood. This was provided by the Cavalry Units of Soult and Murat, home from the Spanish campaigns.

From the time of his Egyptian Wars, Bonaparte showed a marked preference for Eastern-type horses. The greys which he is seen to ride in the paintings of Meissonier may have been Arabs— or, perhaps even more likely, Barbs, for French Arabs do not so often run to grey, but are more often bays, chestnuts, and sometimes blacks.

About forty years later, under the second Empire, M. Galjot, then Director of the National Stud, had the brilliant idea of crossing the brood mares of the Midi, already strongly impregnated with Eastern blood, with English Thoroughbreds, which were at that time being imported in large numbers from Great Britain, due to the extraordinarily rapid development of racing in France. This policy gave the brood mares of south-west France, in one operation, all the advantages of the two centuries of selective breeding which had been carried out on Eastern horses by British breeders since the days of the Stuarts.

Outside the Basses-Pyrenees and the River Adour basin, which is the true cradle of the breed, Anglo-Arabs are to be found in Medoc, the Causse de Gramat, in the vicinity of Beaumont-de-Lomagne, and in the Limousin. It is in the rich pastures of the Domaine de Pompadour (Corrèze), surrounding the medieval castle given by Louis XV to the famous Marquise, that breeding continues today. Under the control of the National Stud Service, generations of brood mares receive services alternately from Thoroughbred and Arab stallions, in an attempt to breed from the rich soil of the Limousin a more developed type of horse than was possible in the Pyrenees.

The planners have in their minds' eye the evolution of a larger-framed Anglo-Arab, long in the leg, better suited for showjumping from the point of view of size, able to compete successfully in international events with Anglo-Normans and with rivals from all over the world.

Today, the total number of brood mares, only a few hundred, is spread throughout the south-west. They are served by National Stud stallions, some of them pure-bred Arabs, brought from their homes by successive buying commissions—some from Arabia proper and from Egypt, others from Tunisia where the local tribes have jealously preserved the essential characteristics of the race. But the Barb, found in the Maghreb, has always been studiously avoided by breeders interested in the evolution of the Anglo-Arab.

It is indeed a pleasure to see the remarkable gifts of the Thoroughbred and the natural qualities of the Arab so happily associated today in the most delightful of riding horses.

The French Thoroughbred (See Plate 66)

This is not the place to recount the history of the English Thoroughbreds which are found today in the French Studs, for they are all, whatever line one traces through the maze of pedigrees, descended from horses registered in the (British) General Stud Book. When England was at the height of her prosperity she was the cradle for this breed of horse. Later the Thoroughbred followed the migration of wealth across the Channel and came to flourish in France during the Second Empire and the *Belle Epoque*, when the Duc de Morny was launching the Deauville and Longchamps race courses.

The first Thoroughbred stallions to cross the Channel were imported by Queen Marie Antoinette's Master of the Horse, the Prince de Lambesc; but Thoroughbred-breeding has never known a more brilliant period than the middle of the last century. The Stud Farms and training establishments owned by members of the French aristocracy and the world of high finance were filled with them, and among the leading owners were many whose memory is perpetuated today in the names of races run each year at the leading courses near Paris—the Comtes de Berteux, de Lagrange, d'Hédouville, and Messieurs Aumont, Rieussec, Lefebvre, and Pereire.

Like its Arab ancestor, the English Thoroughbred is the improver *par excellence* of the common breeds. Since the Stuart kings initiated selective breeding for racing in the seventeenth century the Thoroughbred has contributed nobility, conformation, and a close-coupled, muscular frame to cross-breeding. Some of these qualities are inherited from its Eastern forbears, while others have been gradually acquired through generations of carrying riders across every type of country. Its limbs have lengthened and improved upon those of the Arab so that, crossed with brood mares deriving from the coach and carriage horses of our ancestors, it has played a part in producing French cavalry remounts up to the start of the Second World War.

The best breeding establishments have developed around Lisieux and Argentan, in the Calvados and Orne departments respectively. More than two-thirds of Thoroughbreds in France are to be found here, partly due to the proximity of the Paris and Deauville race courses, and partly to facilitate transport of the mares to neighbouring stallions. There are, however, a few well-known breeding establishments situated somewhat outside this centre, notably those of Mme. Jean Couturie a little farther south in the Sarthe and Comte Roland de Chambure in the Bessin region near Bayeux.

Others remain in the Paris area, where the first Stud Farms were established a century ago—Jardy, for instance, now owned by M. Marcel Boussac, which lies adjacent to St Cloud race course at the very gates of Paris. The fame of the Jardy Stud dates from the time when Flying Fox arrived there to mark a milestone in the history of French breeding. He was bought at Newmarket in 1900 by M. Edmond Bland, after the Prince of Wales as under-bidder had pushed up his price to the then fabulous sum of 37,500 guineas. But times have changed, and now it is the American breeders who go to France to buy the best performers for staggering sums. The owner of Sea Bird, M. Ternynck, recently leased him for five seasons to the United States for 1,500,000 dollars.

In different countries the method of selection varies. In France, where race programmes have changed little over the years, the Thoroughbred has a reputation as a stayer. Elsewhere, sprints for two-year-olds have become fashionable, enabling a horse to start racing younger and to run more often, so that the American race horse now specializes in a distance of 1400 metres.

Numerically, French Thoroughbreds are only tenth in the register of European breeders. It is thus surprising that they have been successful in international racing over the last twenty years.

The French Trotter (See Plate 65)

The Americans had already been breeding a Trotter on English lines for more than a hundred years when the Norman coach-horse breeders, backed by the Administration of the National Stud, decided to do the same in about 1835. As a basic breeding stock they chose the all-purpose breed found in their own pastures, the horse who carried them out hunting and drew their carts and carriages when they went to market.

This breed had already been refined by infusions of Arab and German blood when Napoleon's armies returned home from their campaigns. Immediately after the raising of the Continental Blockade the French public became intensely aware of everything English. As with fashion in dress, horse-breeding did not escape the general craze. But here, instead of attempting to improve the coach horse by direct cross-breeding with the English Thoroughbreds which were gradually filling the stables of the aristocracy, the planners had recourse to English hunters, then unknown in France. One was Young Rattler, who is to be found in every French Trotter's pedigree.

These half-bred stallions progressively modified the heavy Norman mares and prepared them for the essential improvement brought about later by English Thoroughbred sires, among them The Heir of Linne and Sir Quid Pigtail, who left their mark on the breed. Then with the temper and the blood already improved, and Normandy horses being exported for high prices all over the world, the sole remaining quest was for the style of the English light carriage horse. This was found in Norfolk, and used to such effect that the French Trotters even today retain their Thoroughbred qualities and the general conformation of the Norfolk Trotter.

Since then there have been certain other out-crosses—with American Trotters, or again with the Trotters selected for the court of the Tsar by Count Orlov (see p. 111); these were often greys, a colour extremely rare elsewhere. But the Norman breeders, safeguarding their interests, have always refused to allow these 'intruders' to take part in races on which selection is based, or to be entered in their Stud Book. Up to the Second World War the Stud Book was open to Anglo-Norman Horses able to prove a trotting record of 1 minute 42 seconds to the kilometre in a public race. In 1942 the Stud Book was closed to all animals not born of a previously registered sire and dam, which marks a milestone in the history of the French Trotter. To find a similar one we must go back to the beginnings of the breed in 1733.

Among the very many breeders who have contributed to Trotter-breeding, mention must be made of M. Olry-Roederer for his work at the Haras des Rouges-Terres, which lies at the heart of an astonishing collection of similar establishments in the Merlerault region (Orne). From this fertile valley the breed has fanned out over the whole of France, where it has successfully replaced the coach horse and the remount. Now that both are superseded by the car, Vendée, the Charollais region, and the south-west have all become outposts of Trotter-breeding.

Into this typically military but rural atmosphere were born the mounted trotting races, still kept on the race cards today and at which the French are very proficient. Long ago, when horses had to be kept in readiness for general mobilization, these races had their meaning. Today they are merely a picturesque anachronism.

French Trotters can hold their own in Italy, Germany, the Scandinavian countries, and the U.S.A. Jamin, a worthy representative of Rouges-Terres, entirely French in origin, went to the States some ten years ago and beat the best American horses on the fast heavily-banked tracks of Roosevelt Raceway, to which he was entirely unaccustomed.

In conformation the French Trotter has retained many of the points of its working forebears, being raw-boned and sometimes lacking quality, but it has also inherited their toughness and endurance and a boundlessly willing temperament.

The Percheron (See Plate 75)

When one thinks of the cart-horse one breed which readily comes to mind is the Percheron, the best-known variety and the most widely distributed over the four corners of the earth— *e.g.*, England, Canada, the United States, and Argentina.

Situated on the borders of Normandy, Maine, Touraine, and Beauce, the Percheron area, made up of fifty cantons, encroaches on the Departments of Orne, Sarthe, Loir-et-Cher, and Eure-et-Loir. But, maps apart, it differs from the regions surrounding it both by the richness and freshness of its earth and by the prominence of its hills. The sides of these hills, many of them wooded, shelter grassy valleys which converge at the valley of the Huîsne, whose winding stream forms in the very heart of Perche the principal artery of this pretty part of France.

Over a smaller area, meadows and arable land complement each other on a typical Percheron farm. Its stables house scarcely more than two or three brood mares, which stop work only when foaling. The mares are, therefore, scattered, and it is difficult to discover their quality and importance: very few of them are taken to compete in the contests organized by the Percheron Horse Society. The stallions, on the other hand, are kept in the hands of a few families of breeders who control most of the breeding, and the semen from their best stallions is granted to the farmers of Perche only on condition that they themselves return an option on the animal to be born. Foals with a future are thus skimmed off by the big undertakings which are staggered along the valley of the Huîsne to be sold as stallions, either to the breed's Stud organization or to principal breeders—a perfect cycle from the foal to the old horse, linking together those in charge of the birth.

The Arab ancestry of the Percheron came first from the Oriental stallions which the Lords of Nogent, Bellême, and Mortagne kept in their grasslands; later, the breed's Stud organization was to continue this tradition, and, at the beginning of the last century had assigned Arabs to the Bonrétable stable of stallions.

Then, as stage coaches and, subsequently, the Parisian omnibuses disappeared and the only work left to the Percheron was in the countryside, the region turned to breeding an increasingly heavy horse.

But adding weight by selective breeding often leads to loss of quality; the animal is less tightly knit, less lively in its step. However, the Percheron has been able to take on the imposing size of a modern cart-horse without losing its character.

The beauty of the Percheron lies in its strongly built frame, like a piece of sculpture, with all the quality of the Arab. It has sloping shoulders like a saddle-horse, a pointed chest with a prominent breast-bone, and well-placed hind quarters. Finally, it has a splendidly wide body, which enables it to cover a fair amount of ground without its back appearing disproportionately long, so that such a massive animal is able to move in perfect balance, with supple and flexible steps which amaze any visitor when a Percheron, weighing nearly a ton, is set to perform an extended trot. The Percheron is often accused of having the faults which go with these qualities; it is certainly a blood-horse, generous in the extreme. Whole, it shows its most noble qualities, but it requires a specialist hand, one who is able to appreciate its keenness to work. Carters have been known to leave farms in Beauce where only geldings were required because they so loved to work with the Percheron, eager and incomparable when it extends itself to the full. Once castrated, it loses its 'crest' and much of its muscular power.

NORTHERN EUROPE

BELGIUM has been recognized for centuries as a country well suited for breeding and rearing heavy horses, and from time immemorial Belgian horses have maintained their well-earned reputation for courage combined with tractability and power combined with speed in action. Their substantial forehand and solid bone construction have been reinforced at intervals by the introduction of foreign blood, but Belgian breeders have never crossed their magnificent heavy mares with Arabian, English, or French stallions as has been done in neighbouring countries.

In modern times Belgian governments have promoted the breeding of heavy draught horses, but in spite of this their numbers have shown a steady decrease in recent years, especially since 1951, when only 30,000 foals were born as against 45,000 in earlier years. Since 1951, there has been a marked influx of horses from the Baltic States and from Eastern Europe.

In spite of increasing mechanization in industry and a ten-fold increase in the number of tractors throughout the country, the Belgian Heavy Draught Horse has held its own well as far as agriculture is concerned; there are still about 80,000 horses on Belgian farms, but the use of horses in industry has shown a marked decline.

Besides the traditional heavy horse, about thirty Studs are engaged in breeding Thoroughbreds, while Trotters—mainly half-breeds—are most popular in areas where *Epreuves hippiques* are to be found. A Stud Book is kept. Several varieties of ponies are also bred, by far the most popular being the Shetland, for which a separate Stud Book is kept.

The Ardennes

The Ardennes is the older of the two breeds of heavy draught horse in Belgium. The full name by which it is known to the French-speaking world is *la race de trait Ardennaise*. A number of heavy breeds throughout Europe are descended from this ancient stock, which was mentioned by Caesar in his *De Bello Gallico* as a hard and untiring working horse, owned by a German tribe which lived on the west bank of the Rhine.

Marshal Turenne expressed his admiration for the Ardennais horses. They also won praise from Napoleon, when, during the war of 1812, they proved to be the only horses capable of dragging his artillery across difficult country.

There are very few Ardennais horses of the old type left; the modern breed has been influenced by the Belgian Draught Horse. The present-day Ardennes is a stocky animal standing between 15·1 and 15·3 hands. The usual colours are sorrel, roan, bay, and chestnut. The Ardennes is an especially economical feeder, and is noted for having an extremely kind nature, coupled with a lively disposition. It is particularly suitable for work in hilly districts like the Ardennes country—and Sweden, which breeds its own type of Swedish Ardennes. The Belgian breed is mostly found in Luxembourg, Liège, and Namur.

The Brabant (See Plate 77)

Although Belgium, like most other European countries, was subjected to the dominion of foreign troops who brought with them horses of alien blood—such as Arabian, English, and French (of unspecified breeds), and, of course, Spanish—and was also subjected to pressure in the form of the demands of their own people for lighter cavalry horses, the breeders of the Belgian heavy horse never swerved from their objective.

[77]

They practised severe selection—even inbreeding was favoured where exceptional qualities were present—and in this way definite lines were established. Thus a heavy horse of exceptional utility and great draught-power was developed. This became known first as the Flanders Horse, and more recently as the Brabant or *race de trait Belge*. By about 1870 three native groups were firmly established, and these differed one from the other only by minor points of conformation. The stallion Orange I is regarded as one of the pillars of the Brabant breed; he was the founder of the *Gros de la Dendre* line—massive, heavy, deep bay horses. The second group, the *Gris du Hainaut*, had dun, sorrel, or grey colouring, and the founder of this line was the stallion Bayard. The Hainaut greys were of more elegant conformation.

The bay horse Jean I appears to have laid the foundations for the third group, the *Colosses de la Mehaïque*. These horses stood higher at the wither, were not so well muscled, but were possessed of legs of steel. The Belgian Horse was much in demand, especially after Brillant, a son of Orange I, won the International Championship at Paris in 1878, and in succeeding years at London, Lille, and Hanover. A grandson, Rêve d'Or, became world champion in 1900. The most famous of the modern Brabant breed was Avenir d'Herse, described as a "super-champion".

Distribution of the Brabant Horse covers Flanders, Anvers, Limburg, Brabant, Hainaut, Liège, Namur, and Luxembourg. Brabant blood has 'improved' a number of other breeds on the Continent, while 'Flanders' stallions were imported to Britain several centuries ago, to cross with the three native heavy breeds, particularly the Clydesdale and the Shire.

The *cheval de trait Belge* is a large, massive, and powerful horse. It is thick-set, stocky, and close to the ground, with a double amply muscled croup and broad chest, generally with a proportionately small head. The legs are short and strong, with much feather. The horse has a good striding walk. Stallions average 16·1 to 16·2½ hands and weigh more than 1200 kilogrammes.

DENMARK'S horse population has dropped by about three-quarters in the last ten years, but now seems to have settled down at approximately 35,000.

Besides the breeds described below mention must be made of the famous old Knabstrup breed of spotted horse, long famous in Denmark but now almost extinct, the last of the old pure-bred Knabstrups having been crossed with the Fredericksborg which they greatly resemble except in colour; the Knabstrup colour has persisted, so that Fredericksborgs with Knabstrup coloration are still to be found (see Plate 82).

Horses with Knabstrup coloration have always been in great demand as circus performers, and a large proportion of the spotted horses now to be seen in circuses owe their colour to Knabstrup ancestry.

The most popular breed in Denmark at the present day is the Fjord Pony (shared with Norway—see p. 83) of which there are over 200 stallions and 20,000 mares; next come the Belgian Draught Horses and their crosses, with about 170 stallions and nearly 20,000 mares, and then Oldenburgs (see p. 68) with 160 stallions and about 12,000 mares. The native Danish breeds described below come close behind. There are also about 150 Thoroughbred stallions and about 1000 Thoroughbred mares.

The steady decrease in the numbers of draught horses in Denmark is being partly balanced by a steady, though smaller, increase in the numbers of riding horses.

The Fredericksborg (See Plate 83)

One of the most successful of the many notable Studs founded in the sixteenth century was the Royal Fredericksborg Stud established in 1562 by King Frederick II of Denmark. By this time, the ultra-heavy horses, needed to carry knights in ponderous armour who often rode well over twenty stone, were no longer required, and more active chargers were in demand, both for officers and as troop horses for cavalry regiments. As cavalry tactics gradually changed from medieval conceptions to modern there was an increasing need for chargers which combined courage with obedience, and it was found that horses bred from stock which had been readily trained for Riding School Airs were most likely to prove suitable for military manoeuvres. King Frederick's foundation stock included Andalusian and Neapolitan blood; later, Eastern and British half-bred stallions were introduced, and horses bred at this Stud soon acquired an international reputation as cavalry chargers. The Fredericksborg was considered to be one of the most elegant riding horses in Europe, with a lively but obedient temperament, and with action which was both vigorous and full of scope. It was the forerunner of the 'Pleasure Horse' now so much in demand in the U.S.A.

Unfortunately, the breed's popularity almost proved its undoing. Fredericksborg horses were so greatly sought after for export at high prices that breeding stock was sold freely, and without sufficient regard for the future, until in 1839 the Stud had to be wound up for lack of suitable breeding material.

Fortunately, there were still a considerable number of Fredericksborgs in Denmark and breeding was continued by individual enthusiasts. The breed was found extremely suitable for harness work and for light agricultural tasks. The elegant Fredericksborg carriage horse of a hundred years ago gradually developed into an excellent medium-weight working horse.

A system of registration was started in 1923, since when an average of over 100 stallions and over 1000 mares have been registered every year. The present-day Fredericksborg stands about 15·3 hands and is generally chestnut in colour. The breed is well distributed all over Denmark.

The Jutland Horse

Sturdy, hardy, active horses have been bred in the Peninsula of Jutland from time immemorial. The Jutland breed was mentioned with approval as a war-horse as early as the twelfth century, and throughout the Age of Chivalry these horses were in demand as chargers because they could carry the weight of a knight in full armour and endure the hardships of a campaign.

Many authorities have pointed out the resemblance between the Jutland and the Schleswig Horse (see p. 68) and it is at least possible that some Jutland blood may lie behind the modern Schleswiger, as the province of Schleswig, now German, was once owned by Denmark. In the Middle Ages there were numerous Studs in North Germany, Holland, and South Denmark, all producing weight-carrying chargers, and all no doubt exchanging stallions from time to time.

The best of the present-day Jutland horses are believed to stem from an imported stallion, Oppenheim LXII, said to have been a dark chestnut horse with a white blaze. He came from England and may have been a Shire. The best-known descendant, Oldrup Munkedal, who carried Oppenheim many times in his pedigree, founded the most important bloodline in the modern Jutland breed.

The impact of mechanization has adversely affected the Jutland, like so many other cold-blooded horses, and the breed is now on the decline in spite of its particular suitability for agriculture and for heavy draught work.

FINLAND has nearly 180,000 horses, almost all of them recorded as Agricultural; that is to say, of the draught type, for, as in most Scandinavian countries, many heavy horses are used for forestry.

Only one breed is officially recognized—the Finnish breed described below—and only one Stud Book is kept, but since this was opened in 1907 a small minority of horses have been registered as of the General Utility type, sometimes described as the Finnish Universal. Of some 70,000 stallions and nearly 100,000 mares entered in the Stud Book between 1907 and 1960, just over 7 per cent of the stallions and less than 7 per cent of the mares accepted for entry were of the General Utility type.

Before acceptance in the Stud Book—*i.e.*, at about four years of age—each horse or mare must pass an exacting test and qualify in pulling power, temperament, general soundness of conformation, and in action, both at the walk and at the trot. It must also qualify by covering specified distances in stated times, with loads of different sizes.

The Finnish Horse (See Plate 86)

The present-day Finnish Horse has been bred up from native ponies very similar to those still to be seen in the north of Scandinavia. Over the centuries gradual improvement was achieved by innumerable crosses with both warm-blood and cold-blood stallions from the south.

The objective has always been to develop working ability rather than good looks. Early Finnish breeders would have agreed that no good horse could be a bad colour, and would have added that, if he was sound and willing, there could not be much wrong with his shape either.

The result of selective breeding on these lines is the modern Finnish Horse, very agile and surprisingly powerful for its size (they stand just over 15 hands). They are noted for their staying power and for the excellence of their constitution.

The Universal type which is sometimes used for riding and light transport, as well as for draught, is inclined to be a little more lightly built and cleaner in the leg than the much more common draught type which is noted for its toughness and capacity for endless hard work in very difficult conditions.

THE NETHERLANDS has about 200,000 horses and ponies, of which over 120,000 horses are used by farmers and about 80,000 ponies by market gardeners, the latter figure including many Shetland ponies. Horse-breeding is strictly regulated. Only licensed stallions may be used at stud; no licence is issued without a thorough examination by a qualified practitioner. Originally these examinations were controlled by a Government Department, but an Act of 1939 transferred this duty to the recognized Stud Book societies. They receive an annual grant from the State, to be spent on premiums for suitable animals which are selected in part by their practical achievements in performance tests.

The most popular heavy breed in the Netherlands (no official statistics are available for riding horses) is the Dutch Draught Horse, followed by the Groningen, the Gelderland, the Shetland Pony, and the Friesian Horse. There are also a few Fjord ponies. The Groningen—an off-shoot of the Oldenburg (see p. 68)—is regarded in the Netherlands as a separate breed, and now has a separate Stud Book.

By no means all horses and ponies are used for draught purposes; riding ponies are now extremely fashionable. There are five pony breeding societies and literally hundreds of pony clubs all over the Netherlands. The Dutch Shetland Pony Stud Book Society, established for over thirty years, has more than 5000 members and nearly 40,000 registered ponies.

All breeds mentioned above have recognized Stud Book societies which also operate for Hackneys and Arabians, and there is also the Trotting and Racing Foundation at the Hague.

The Netherlands imports a great number of horses and ponies every year, many of the latter coming from Great Britain. She also exports on a large scale, and buyers come from all over Europe to the Dutch horse sales. All possible steps are taken to promote the export of home-bred horses.

The Dutch Draught Horse (See Plate 78)

The Dutch Draught Horse is a new breed created since the end of the First World War. The objective of the breeders was to produce a heavy horse of quiet temperament, with a good turn of speed. These qualities were particularly needed by small farmers with mixed farms on sandy soil. At the same time it was desired to produce a horse sufficiently powerful to be of use on the arable farms in the sea-clay areas of the Netherlands.

The native breeding stock selected for the purpose consisted of mares of the Zealand type, which carried a distant cross of Eastern blood. They were mated, first to Brabant stallions and then, to a lesser extent, to Belgian Ardennes stallions.

A Stud Book was kept almost from the beginning, and, since 1925, no horses of unknown pedigree have been accepted for entry. Indeed, no horse can be entered until its pedigree has been carefully checked and its identity verified by a sketch of its markings. Each horse, which has been entered in the Stud Book when about two and a half years old, has to undergo a special inspection of conformation before it is accepted for the Preferential Stud Book. Thereafter, it will be graded at inter-provincial inspections at which prizes are offered for the most outstanding specimens. There is also an annual National Show at which conformation, breeding-record, and pedigree are all taken into account.

The present-day Dutch Draught Horse is one of the most massively built and most heavily muscled breeds in Europe. In type it is very similar to its ancestor, the Brabant. It is described as a massive, hard, deep animal, with good feet, well-placed and heavily moulded legs, well-developed forequarters, and an easy active walk and good action in all gaits. It is now by far the most popular draught horse in the Netherlands and is giving great satisfaction to importers.

The Friesian Horse (See Plate 79)

This is one of the oldest breeds in Europe. Its ancestors stemmed from the heavy cold-blooded horses which survived the Ice Ages (see Fig. 4, p. 15). Excavation of the sites of pre-historic villages in Friesland have confirmed that a heavy horse was domesticated there 3000 years ago.

73 *ANGLO-NORMAN*

74 *ARDENNAIS*

75 *PERCHERON*

76 *BOULONNAIS*

77 *BRABANT*

78 *DUTCH DRAUGHT HORSE*

79 *FRIESIAN*

80 *FJORD PONY*

81 *DØLE*

82 *KNABSTRUP*

83 *FREDERICKSBORG*

84 *NORTH SWEDISH HORSE*

85 *SWEDISH WARM BLOOD HORSE*

86 *FINNISH HORSE*

87 *ITALIAN HEAVY DRAUGHT HORSE*

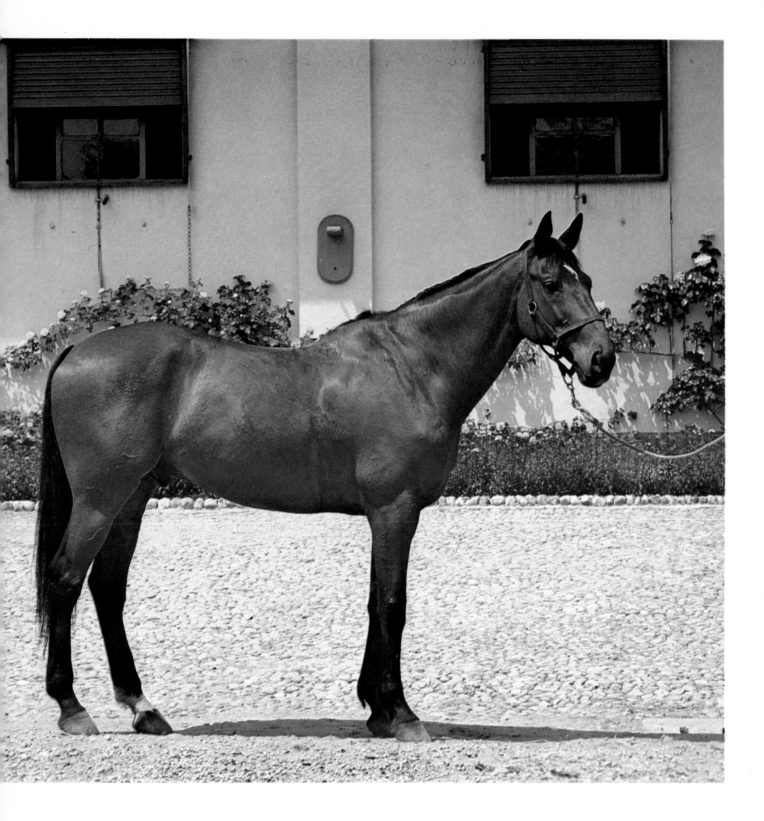

88 *SALERNO*

Early accounts, based on a combination of legend and tradition, suggest that the inhabitants of what is now Friesland herded their horses out of doors all the year round, while the cattle were housed during the winter. The horses appear to have been rather clumsy and heavily built, but capable of the utmost endurance, though they seem not to have been particularly fast.

During the Crusades many German and Friesian knights brought back Eastern stallions which greatly improved the original native breed. A further injection of Eastern blood came during the Eighty Years' War, when part of the Netherlands was occupied by Spanish troops with Andalusian chargers.

The excellence of the Friesian pastures caused horse breeders from neighbouring regions to send young stock to be reared there, and by the seventeenth century Friesian horses had won a wide reputation as weight carriers.

One hundred years later trotting races began to be popular in the Netherlands, and especially in East Friesland. These races were generally sprints over short distances. Friesian horses were found to excel at trotting, and breeders began to concentrate on lighter, faster horses. Possibly as a result of this, the breed became less popular for general use and seemed in danger of dying out.

About a hundred years ago a Stud Book was founded, with one section set aside for the Friesian breed, but, unfortunately, the position continued to deteriorate, and by 1913 the breed was confined to the Province of Friesland, where only three stallions were at stud. A new society was founded to restore the breed, which, from then on, has never looked back, and in 1954 Her Majesty Queen Juliana honoured the society and granted it the title of "Royal".

The present-day Friesian is a sound harness and agricultural horse of about 15 hands, with such a smart and attractive appearance that it is in great demand at horse shows throughout the Netherlands, where matched teams of Friesians, jet black as they now always are, pulling a Friesian gig, with occupants in the national costume, provide a fascinating and popular spectacle.

The Gelderland

The Gelderland is now the most popular harness horse in most provinces in the Netherlands, though Groningen, Friesland, and Drenthe still tend to prefer other varieties. The breed was created in the last century, when stallions from Britain, Egypt, Germany, Hungary, Poland, and Russia were introduced by horse breeders in the Gelder province, to cross with the native mares. Gelder breeders had always been noted for initiative in trying out new breeding systems, and for producing horses which were suitable for their own locality and also attractive to their neighbours.

The best of the descendants of these numerous imported stallions were inter-bred, and gradually a type began to be fixed. In later years Oldenburg and East Friesian stallions were made use of, and in about 1900 Hackney stallions were introduced; since then the only outside blood used has been Anglo-Norman.

The present-day Gelderland is an excellent type of carriage horse, compact, with a good action, and capable of doing light draught work or agricultural tasks in medium heavy land. Some horses are broken for riding, for which they have proved most suitable. The best of these have been found to be above-average showjumpers.

The Gelderland is generally a bright chestnut colour with white markings, but good greys and some skewbalds are to be found. Standing about 15 hands and strongly built, its energetic action and proud carriage stamp the Gelderland as a horse which will always be in demand.

ICELAND is unique in Europe in that it has been occupied by horses, and by human beings, for little more than ten centuries. Scandinavians introduced horses, or more probably ponies, to the island at a time when it had virtually no animal life of any kind. Later, ponies were brought over from Scotland.

In spite of its volcanic nature and the relatively small area available for grazing, Iceland proved a suitable home for the smaller, hardier type of pony. Imports ceased and the existing stock was improved by selective breeding until a distinctive type of pony was created. These became so numerous and were so highly thought of that up to a hundred years ago Icelandic ponies were regularly exported to the British Isles for pack purposes, and, it is said, for work in the coal-mines.

Until this century pack ponies were the principal means of transport in Iceland where no motor roads existed until about sixty years ago, and where minor roads are sometimes impassable to motor traffic in severe weather, especially in the more remote areas. In spite of this the horse population of Iceland has decreased by more than half since 1948, and, unfortunately, is still decreasing.

The Icelandic Pony

Bred from stock introduced by the Norse settlers, with injections of Scottish Pony and perhaps of Irish Pony blood, the Icelandic Pony was considered by disciples of the late Professor J. Cossor Ewart as the prototype of *Equus celticus*—the Celtic Pony—which may have been the common ancestor of all, or nearly all, the pony breeds of Northern Europe.

It has had a stormy history, for the Vikings of Iceland were great exponents of horse fighting, and stallion ancestors of the modern Icelandic Pony were made to fight almost to the death for heavy wagers, guided and sometimes aided by their blood-thirsty owners. A terrible fight between two Icelandic stallions, which started a blood feud, and which ended in a massacre, is described in *The Story of Burnt Njal*.[1]

The present-day Icelandic Pony stands between 12 and 13 hands. Most are broken for riding, and they move with a distinctive action—the amble—now so seldom to be found. They are short and stocky and noted for their good nature and for their extreme hardiness.

Attempts to improve the breed by introducing warm-blooded stallions have hitherto been singularly unsuccessful, and the Icelandic Pony remains today much as it has been throughout the centuries, rough and rugged, but with many virtues and almost no vices at all.

NORWAY has about 50,000 horses, the great majority of which are agricultural or draught horses. It is an interesting fact that in 1967 over one-third of the working horses were seventeen years old or more, which reflects great credit both on the constitution of the Norwegian horses and on the horsemanship of the Norwegian people.

Rather over half of the Norwegian horse population consists of Døle horses, while over one-third are Fjord ponies. Both these breeds are very widely distributed over Scandinavia, and farther afield. Another breed recognized by the Norwegian Ministry of Agriculture is the Lyngen, a stocky pony rather similar to the Fjord, and capable of pulling a surprisingly heavy load.

A famous old Norwegian breed, the Gudbrandsdal, named after the Gudbrandsdal Valley, is believed to have been indigenous to Norway and to have contributed to the ancestry of many Scandinavian breeds. It is now almost entirely merged with the modern Døle described below.

The Døle Horse (See Plate 81)

This horse is very like the British Dales Pony and is probably descended from the same or similar ancestors. The breed is widely spread, but seems to have originated in the north-east part of southern Norway near the Gudbrandsdal Valley, formerly the heartland of the old Gudbrandsdal Horse, now regarded as being embodied in the Døle.

The rich grazing in the mountain valleys provided an excellent environment for developing a very strong and hardy medium-sized horse which could be used for all agricultural purposes. In the eighteenth century the interest in breeding horses failed in a great part of the country, but in Gudbrandsdal the horse held its position fairly well. In the nineteenth century, interest in breeding improved so much that societies to promote breeding were formed and equestrian sports were encouraged.

A number of stallions were imported, and among them was the Thoroughbred Odin, imported in 1834, who had the most lasting influence upon the breed. His blood runs in all Døle pedigrees today. The first exhibition for horses sponsored by the State was held in 1859 in Gudbrandsdal, and here the first stallion of importance to Døle breeding was shown. This stallion was Balder 4 (1849), a great-grandson of Odin. At this time there was a heavy and lighter type of horse.

As horse-drawn implements became heavier, so the Døle horses became more powerful, largely thanks to the influence of a stallion called Brimen 825.

In the 1930s trade for horses continually improved, and during the German Occupation of Norway, when fuel was very scarce, breeding enjoyed an artificial prosperity. At the end of the War both farming and forestry were mechanized, and this caused a serious drop in the value of horses.

Now the demand is again for a lighter Døle Horse, and stallions of Norwegian Trotter stock have been turned out on the mountains with Døle mares. Breeding centres were established by the State in 1962, and it is here that the Døle horses are now being bred.

[1] *The Story of Burnt Njal* (Dent, London, 1911) trans. by Sir George Webbe Dasent; third edition.

The Fjord Pony (See Plate 80)

This pony, also sometimes known as the Westland, has inhabited Norway since time immemorial. The Vikings kept and bred a pony of this type, and there are pre-historic stones on which are engraved horses or ponies fighting in organized combat—a popular sport with the Vikings. These ponies are bred over a wide area in Norway—from Telemark in the south to Finnmark in the north—and are widely distributed throughout Scandinavia.

While the bigger horse breeds have, for the most part, been replaced by tractors, the small Fjord Pony is kept on because it is so well suited for work in terrain where the motor has difficulties in doing a job, or becomes too unwieldy. J. Albrechsten wrote: "A span of well-paired and well turned-out Fjord ponies is one of the things that will beautify daily life for a family living on a farm."

In fact, there appears to be no job which the Fjord Pony is incapable of carrying out—from ploughing to carrying pack up difficult mountain paths and through rivers. In all countries which are subjected to hard snowy winters this horse is invaluable, and can never be replaced by motorized vehicles.

A great number of these ponies have been exported to Denmark and Germany and other central European countries; some have gone even farther afield.

The Northland Horse

Tradition says that the ancestors of the Northland Horse were imported from Russia well over 1000 years ago. There is very little information about them except that they were small and the original colour was probably white with black markings. They may have been similar to the stuffed Wild Horse in the museum at Bergen, which is believed to be identical with the horses described in the poem *Beowulf*. These small horses, sometimes called ponies, have been used for riding and for draught work in Norway for hundreds of years. They were bred mostly by farmers and there is no record of any attempt to standardize the breed until about fifty years ago. In 1916 the veterinary surgeon Olsen organized a show for Northland horses at Tromsø near Hatteng, Lyngen, where typical Northlands were exhibited. In 1923 there were jumping competitions at Mjelde in Tromsøysund. A group of enthusiasts worked to preserve the old breed, and met with a fair degree of success.

A further exhibition was held in 1939, again in Lyngen, for Northland horses, and a plan was made for the improvement of stallions.

In 1944 a stallion, Rimfakse, was nominated as the most typical specimen of the breed for stud purposes, although it was recognized that he was not without faults. He produced several prominent sons who were considered to be of better quality than himself.

After the Second World War breeders were concerned that the old breed might die out. Fortunately, Mr Christen Klafstad bred systematically from the best stock available, and in 1962 he won a major prize with Nordlandssvarten 11, a descendant of Rimfakse. This success gave a great stimulus to other breeders. In spite of these successes, by 1945 registration of Northland horses had fallen to forty-three, of which only six were stallions.

On May 9th, 1967, a meeting of Northland breeders was held at Bodø with a view to stimulating further breeding. As a result of this effort, in the last few years there has been a much greater demand for Northlands and more registrations and there is a good prospect that the number of horses registered will continue to increase.

SWEDEN has seen its horse population halved in the last ten years, but the 80,000 horses now remaining play an important part in the country's economy. Timber represents one-third of Sweden's exports, and half of the timber cut in Sweden is moved by horses, the North Swedish breed being highly regarded for this work.

Working conditions in the forests are so hard that horses tend to deteriorate very fast, and the Swedish Government has instituted an advisory service for horse owners whose animals work in the lumber camps. This is a continuation of the policy stretching back almost a hundred years, during which time the Swedish Government has promoted the breed of suitable horses by means of a direct subsidy. Since 1914 the Swedish Ministry of Agriculture has controlled horse-breeding by a system of stallion licensing.

The majority of pure-bred stallions registered are Swedish Ardennes, followed by North Swedish; half-breds and Trotters are also very numerous. Other breeds registered (in order of popularity) are English Thoroughbreds, Shetland ponies, North Swedish Trotters, Fjord ponies, Welsh ponies, Arabians, and New Forest ponies.

[83]

The North Swedish Horse (See Plate 84)

The North Swedish Horse originates from an ancient breed native to Scandinavia, and is probably closely related to the Norwegian Døle Horse. Since the beginning of this century the breed has been regulated by a systematic breeding programme, and since 1930 no stallion has been accepted for breeding until it has been examined by a specially qualified vet and has also passed two tests, one of pulling logs along a rough track under working conditions, and the other a test of maximum power pulling against an ergometer. Both stallions and mares, when mature, are re-tested for draught capacity with a specially constructed car. The legs and hooves are also checked radiologically.

The Stud at Wangen has been responsible for the development of the breed, and here the importance of good action is much stressed. Breeding stock must combine energy and power with liveliness of gait. Thanks to careful breeding, the present-day horse has an excellent temperament, combined with tremendous courage in pulling heavy loads.

The North Swedish Horse has a sound constitution and is noted for longevity. The stallions average 15·1 to 15·2 hands, the mares being somewhat smaller. Although generally classified as a cold-blooded horse, its action and temperament are more typical of a warm-blooded breed.

The Swedish Ardennes

The first Belgian Ardennes Horse was imported into Sweden almost one hundred years ago, and was crossed with the native Swedish Horse. The results were so successful that the best of the cross-breds were mated together and further Belgian Ardennes were imported. The original Stud was at Blomberg in Vestergötland where breeding was continued on these lines until, within a surprisingly short time, the characteristics of the Swedish Ardennes were fixed so that it bred true.

The climate and conditions in this part of Sweden are similar to those to which the Belgian Ardennes had been accustomed in its native country. This helped the new breed to flourish and eventually to dominate Swedish horse-breeding.

The present-day Swedish Ardennes vary in size according to the part of the country in which they are reared, the larger horses being bred on the plains of Skania, Ostergötland, and Vestergötland, while the small Swedish Ardennes are found in hilly country where the soil is lighter.

There are no large Studs and breeding is done by the farmers themselves, who make the fullest use of this all-round, economical, pocket-sized heavy horse. There has been less demand for these horses in recent years owing to mechanization, but the breed is highly thought of, both in Sweden and in those countries to which it has been exported.

The Swedish Warm Blood Horse (See Plate 85)

The Swedish Warm Blood Horse is descended from Oriental, Spanish, and Friesian stallions which were imported into Sweden roughly 300 years ago. Later on, Trakehner, Hanoverian, and Anglo-Norman stallions were used to improve the breed of those horses which were used for the very high standard of riding which has always been the goal of Swedish horsemen. For the last four Olympic Games the Swedish Team has been mounted on home-bred horses, and has brought home many honours, including a Gold Medal in 1956.

In 1621 a Stud was founded at Strömsholm, which belongs to the King of Sweden. This was probably the first organized Stud in Sweden. Since 1868 Strömsholm has been the home of the well-known Swedish Army Riding School.

The Stud at Flyinge, founded in 1658, which is also a stallion depot, sets a high standard. The mistake has not been made here of using the services of inferior Thoroughbred stallions. Only the best are good enough, as, for example, Darbhanga, a half-brother to Nasrullah, whose offspring have won no less than 960 races in Sweden and 1100 in Scandinavia.

When we look farther into the use of well-known Trakehner stallions it is not surprising to learn that the Swedish Warm Blood Horse generally makes an excellent dressage horse, often of international standard. Sweden exports horses to Denmark, Finland, Germany, Great Britain, Mexico, Norway, and Switzerland. Several Swedish horses have made their names in other countries. Among these was Cetus, a showjumper and dressage horse, who was sold to Canada and became Champion Working Hunter at the Montreal Horse Show in 1965 and 1966.

Perhaps the best-known name associated with this breed is that of Dr Aaby-Ericsson, who tells a charming story against himself, which seems to have originated in West Germany. It is said that "Aaby-Ericsson makes a good bartender; out of his 200-year-old Swedish blood lines he takes the best conformation; to provide bone and joints he uses a little Hanoverian blood; for nobility and temperament he adds Trakehner blood, while the Thoroughbred and the Arab bring elegance and intelligence. In this way he makes an outstanding cocktail."

[84]

SOUTHERN EUROPE

ITALY was one of the earliest European countries to appreciate horses of quality, and the Etruscans were breeding promising specimens nearly 2500 years ago (see Fig. 9, p. 20). Later, the native Italian breeds were coarsened by the stallions ridden in some cases by barbarian invaders and in others by the Roman auxiliary cavalry who were recruited from all over the Empire, including the British Isles. Italian horses were also crossed with the weight-carrying chargers of the Lombards (see p. 19).

Four hundred years ago Neapolitan horses were famous all over Europe. Some were purchased by Britain's King Henry VIII; others went to the Spanish Royal Studs, while others contributed to the foundation stock of the Kladruber and the Lipizzaner (see p. 54).

In recent years the horse population of Italy has been decreasing, the number having dropped by about 10 per cent in as many years. As in most European countries, the greatest reduction has been in the number of draught horses, due to increasing mechanization of transport and agriculture. The reduction has been greater in the plains, for in the mountains the pack-horse still plays an important part.

On the other hand, there is a strong and increasing demand for fast light-draught horses and riding horses. Of about 1500 stallions recorded in use at Government or privately owned Studs, over two-thirds are draught or pack-horses. Of the other 30 per cent, the majority are Trotters, which are extremely popular in Italy. The Italian Trotter is bred mainly from the American Trotter, with some French Trotting blood. Between 1867 and 1881 Italy imported over 300 Hackneys or Norfolk Roadsters from Britain, and one of these imported mares bred the famous Vandallo, who raced 139 times, scoring 101 firsts, and was unplaced only twice. There are now about 3500 Trotting mares in various Studs, and about 150 Trotting stallions, of which the best known is Tornese, who stands only 14·2 hands. In 229 races he is said to have won over 340 million lira (over £225,000). His stud fee is now stated to be £1000.

Trotting races are extremely popular in Italy, where they have been held on the roads from time immemorial. In 1808 a trotting race was held on a track at Prato Del Valle, and since then trotting tracks have sprung up throughout Italy.

Next in popularity after Trotters come English Thoroughbreds, which number about 1000 brood mares and just over 100 stallions. From this comparatively small contingent many very famous horses have been bred, including Nearco and Donatello II. The influence of Italian breeders on the modern Thoroughbred has been out of all proportion to their small numbers and is recognized on both sides of the Atlantic.

There are also a great number of high-class cross-breds, stemming from Thoroughbreds, Arabians, and Anglo-Arabs, all of which are sometimes crossed with the few remaining mares of the two national warm-blood breeds, the Calabrese and the Salerno (see Plate 88). These two breeds are now decreasing in numbers as breeders transfer their attentions to Thoroughbreds and Trotters.

In addition to the three draught breeds described below, there are about 1000 Belgian Heavy Draught horses, mainly used for agriculture. There are also some Haflingers, especially in the mountain districts of the north-east.

The Avelignese Horse

This is a dual-purpose breed used mainly for pack transport in the mountains, but also for light agricultural work. It is bred throughout the mountainous regions of north, central, and southern Italy and also in the province of Bolzano. Breeders work carefully to a standard, and colts likely to make stallions are approved, if suitable, at an annual meeting at Verona.

The Avelignese is a typical mountain horse, standing between 13·3 and 14·3 hands and outstandingly muscular. The horses are generally sorrel or palomino in colour, and are noted for their sureness of foot. They will face mountain trails even in extremely severe weather conditions, and it is claimed that they get to know the tracks so well that in the neighbourhood of their home they can travel by night almost as well as by day. The breeding stock is mostly owned by farmers or carriers, and mares and stallions are invariably worked, the mares being kept on full work until shortly before they are due to foal.

At present, there are over 270 stallions and, it is said, over 2000 brood mares. The breed seems to be more than holding its own and its future seems to be more secure than that of many.

The Italian Heavy Draught Horse (See Plate 87)

By far the most popular heavy horse in Italy is the Heavy Draught Horse, sometimes called the Italian Agricultural Horse. This breed provides nearly 35 per cent of the total number of stallions at Stud in Italy, and is bred for slaughter as well as for work. The breed stems from the French Breton (see p. 73) and is bred chiefly in the region of Venice, and also throughout northern and central Italy. It is noted for its speed in action as well as for its power and docile temperament.

It is an unfortunate fact that increasing competition from mechanization, coupled with increasing demands for animal protein, have led breeders to concentrate more on food conversion, with an eye to slaughter, than on working qualities. A competition for young horses of about $2\frac{1}{2}$ years old is still held annually at Verona, but it seems probable that present-day trends will lead to the eventual disappearance of this useful breed from the agricultural scene, to which in the past it has contributed so much.

The horse stands between 15 and 16 hands high and the usual colours are sorrel or roan.

The Murgese Horse

For many centuries the Murge district near Puglia was noted for its high-quality horses, but some 200 years ago interest in horse-breeding seems to have diminished and almost expired. It did not revive again until the 1920s. The present-day Murgese Horse is a dual-purpose animal showing definite traces of Oriental ancestry from sources which cannot now be identified.

The breed is used mainly for light agricultural work, but is sometimes ridden. Murgese mares are often mated to warm-blooded stallions and sometimes produce outstanding riding horses.

The principal breeding areas are Puglia, Campagna Abruzzi, Basilicata, and Calabria. Breeding is regulated on a voluntary basis, and an annual competition for young stallions between two and three years old is held every December at Martina Franca, near Taranto.

The horses vary between 15 and 16 hands in height and the usual colour is sorrel. There are, at present, over 150 stallions, but no present-day estimate of brood mares is available.

PORTUGAL shares many breeds with her neighbour, Spain. In fact, most breeds in the Iberian Peninsula are common to both countries. The Portuguese horse population has fallen slightly over the years and is now about 75,000, the majority of the horses being 'country-bred', that is to say, of no particular breed. In addition to the breeds described below, Portugal has a number of English Thoroughbreds, mainly imported but some bred in Portugal. There still exist representatives of the old Portuguese breed, the Lusitano (see Plate 93), which used to meet the requirements of the Army Remount Division for supplying cavalry regiments. Lusitanos were also used for light farm work.

This breed is of great antiquity and has a somewhat controversial origin. The horses stand between 15 and 16 hands, the usual colour being grey. Lusitanos are often trained for the Portuguese bullring, for which the highest quality horses are required as the Portuguese system of bullfighting is conducted almost entirely on horseback, but although the Portuguese bullfighter will gallop directly at the charging bull, swerving only at the last possible moment, horses should never be touched, let alone killed, by bulls in Portuguese bullrings.

The Spanish system of bullfighting, so widely publicized by the late Ernest Hemingway and others, and so blatantly developed as an attraction for tourists, is entirely different from the little-known, but much more humane, and incidentally, much more spectacular, system of bullfighting practised in Portugal, described in detail in Appendix III, page 124.

Another Portuguese breed worthy of mention is the Sorraia, found in the plains bordering the river of that name and its tributaries, the Sor and Raia. This horse is noted for its phenomenal hardiness and ability to thrive in areas with poor soil and indifferent herbage. For centuries it was the standard mount of the cowboys in the area. It was also used for light agricultural work. The breed is now greatly reduced in numbers, though the well-known expert Dr Ruy de Andrade, and his son after him, has kept a small pure-bred herd. The horses lack quality and are often palomino or Isabel in colour, but may be grey, and are occasionally striped (*zabrada*), with the dark dorsal stripe of the mule along the spine. Sorraias have luxuriant black manes and tails, and often black tips to their ears. Their height is between 12 and 13 hands.

The Alter-Real (See Plate 94)

In a secluded corner of Portugal's Alentejo Province there still exists a National Stud, the birthplace of a breed renowned for over 200 years. Chestnut, bay, or piebald in colour, standing between 15 and 15·2 hands, the Alter has a small head, a straight profile, tending towards the convex, and a short neck, arched in the Andalusian manner. It is a short, close-coupled horse, with a wide, deep chest, and an ample, well-muscled croup. The forearm is shorter than the cannon, and the upper part of the legs is thick, with big, flat knees and strong hocks. The bone is of fine quality, and the whole effect is that of a well-balanced, strong horse with the legs well placed under the body. Its action is extravagant and showy, with an abundance of knee flexion and, consequently, a somewhat restricted forward movement. Highly strung and full of courage and energy, it tends to be temperamental and even violent.

The Stud was founded by the House of Braganza in 1748 in Vila de Portel, whence it moved to its present site in 1756, coming under the direct administration of the Royal Household shortly after 1770. It was started with some 300 Andalusian mares, almost all of them from the area around Jerez de la Frontera in Spain, where the finest Andalusian horses were to be found.

Horses from the Stud helped to furnish the Royal Manege in Lisbon, and in the reigns of King João V and King José about 150 horses were maintained there. It was very much a centre of interest, and exhibitions were given in the style still used at the Spanish Riding School in Vienna.

The Stud flourished and its fame continued until 1821, when it was sacked by the Napoleonic invaders who stole the finest animals. With the abdication of King Miguel in 1834, a further series of disasters overtook Alter. A great part of the land, formerly given over to pasture, was confiscated, the number of breeding stock was reduced, and the Royal Stables were abolished by order of Prince Pedro de Alcantara and Queen Maria II.

After these misfortunes, the work of reorganization was begun by the introduction of heterogeneous Arab stallions and horses from England, Normandy, and Hanover. These experiments with alien blood caused the breed to begin to deteriorate, but they continued due to the influence of the Italian-born Queen Maria Pia, who was extremely interested in the Arabian Horse.

This decline was accelerated by the efforts of a French veterinary surgeon named Cantaloup, whose attempts to 'Arabize' the breed were eventually defeated by the decisive influences of the land, pasture, and climate. Eventually the disastrous series of experiments was finally abandoned.

A further effort was made to re-establish the breed by the introduction of Andalusian Zapata mares (a particularly pure strain—see p. 89) and a few Spanish stallions. It will be seen that up to this time the Alter owed its best qualities to the foundation stock of Andalusian Thoroughbreds.

The Stud had settled down once again when, with the advent of the Republic in 1910, the Archives were almost entirely destroyed and valuable data lost. In 1932 it was taken over by the Ministry of Economy, who began the work of reconstruction by the reduction in the number of mares from a hundred to forty of the best examples, of which only twelve were used with two of the finest stallions. This did much to improve the situation.

It is a curious fact that, in spite of so much cross-breeding, the Alter retains its original characteristics. It is a splendid riding animal and especially suitable for Haute Ecole, which was indeed its original function. The model for the horse ridden by King José in the famous Black Horse Square in Lisbon was an Alter by the name of Gentil. In 1966, at the Horse of the Year Show at Wembley, London, two pure-bred Alter horses attracted favourable comment.

The Garrano Pony

In the Portuguese provinces of Garrano do Minho and Traz dos Montes the magnificent green pastures of the mountain valleys produce an excellent breed of pony. Though lightly built, Garranos are extremely hardy and are used mainly for agricultural work and for hauling timber.

They vary between 10 and 12 hands and are predominantly dark chestnut in colour, with a luxuriant mane and tail. Their general conformation is excellent, and occasionally one finds a specimen of great beauty. In some cases the ponies have an infusion of Arabian blood, which stems from Arabian stallions sent by the Ministry of Agriculture for mating to approved mares.

The horse fairs at Vila Real and Famalicao have long been famous for the quantity and quality of Garranos to be seen there. In former times, there were traditional trotting races run at a short collected trot, specially taught by the owners of the animals. These races were supported with the greatest enthusiasm and resulted in betting for surprisingly high stakes.

The ponies are in demand for many purposes; the Ministry of War periodically buys Garranos for use as pack ponies for machine-guns and for other military purposes.

SPAIN is one of the areas in which wild horses may possibly have survived the Ice Ages (see p. 15), and rock paintings at Ribadesella in northern Spain,[1] discovered while this book was in the course of preparation, increase the probability that this was so.

We know that the Vandals, with their huge cold-blooded chargers, moved through Spain some 1500 years ago on their way to Africa, and that fifty years later the Visigoths, on their weight-carrying war-horses—possibly improved by Eastern blood (see p. 19)—occupied Spain, where they remained for some 150 years, during which time their stallions must have transformed the original native horses. Then came a series of Moslem invasions, first by the Moors, riding ancestors of the present-day Barb, then Syrians, whose stallions may have been among the forebears of the modern Arabian, and finally another more permanent influx of Moors.

The Andalusian breed and its descendants owe much to the Eastern blood of the stallions brought over by the Moslem invaders.

By 900 years ago, Spanish horses were in great demand as chargers. William of Normandy chose one for his mount when he invaded England, and it carried him to victory at the Battle of Hastings. (See Plate 19.)

At the present time Spain has rather over half a million horses and nearly 35,000 ponies; in each case over half are classified as draught animals, and the large majority are 'country bred'—that is, of no specific breed.

By far the most popular breed of horses in Spain is the Hispano-Breton. Next come two riding breeds, the Andalusian (with its offshoots the Andalusian Carthusian and the Zapateros), and the Hispano Anglo-Arab; there are also about 8000 Percheron horses. Another breed still remaining in Spain, and to a much lesser extent in Portugal, is the Spanish Arab, the best of which are used to breed that outstanding all-round horse, the Hispano Anglo-Arab, described below.

The best-known ponies in Spain are those bred in the mountains of Aragon, from which they take their name. Their origin is quite unknown, but they are extremely tough and hardy and are invaluable for riding or pack purposes on the mountain trails.

For centuries horse-breeding in Spain has been dominated by the requirements of the Spanish Army. Now there are no mounted units except for a few belonging to the National Guard, but the distribution of Government-owned stallions is still controlled by the military. Spain is divided into eight districts, each with a stallion depot, and in some cases a sub-depot also, and these are still administered through the central remount depot in Madrid. The stallions distributed by the depots include Andalusians, Arabs, Anglo-Arabs, and Thoroughbreds, as well as Hispano-Bretons.

[1] *The Sunday Times* (February 2nd, 1969) p. 10.

89   *The Hackney pony stallion, Marden Finality*

90   *Sun and wind in Southern France*

92   *A four-horse team in a typical Oxfordshire village*

The Andalusian Horse (See Plate 95)

In 1476 Don Alvaro Obertus de Valeto left 10,000 acres of land to the Carthusian Monastery in Jerez, where the monks had a number of fine mares. Horse-breeding activities had already started at another Carthusian Monastery in Seville, and in 1490 a third was founded at Cazallo.

These three monasteries were the cradle of the Andalusian breed. It is recognized that this had its origin in stallions introduced during the Moorish Occupation, and it is evident that the foundation stallions must have sprung from a distinguished Oriental breed, though their straight profiles bear no resemblance to the modern Arabian.

On the other hand, the pastures and climate of Andalusia are much like those of parts of Arabia and have had an enormous influence on the maintenance of the breed's qualities.

The Carthusian Studs became famous, supported as they were by enormous wealth, and administered with intelligence and devotion. The monks succeeded in creating and maintaining three superb herds of Oriental origin, with no cross of any foreign blood. In the early days, by Royal Edict, new blood was introduced into the great majority of Spanish Studs, the stallions used being Neapolitans from Central Europe, but the Carthusian monks refused to obey this ruling and continued using stallions of African or Asiatic origin.

These monks were not only guardians of the purity of their breed, they were also strong supporters of the Spanish system of equitation, for, when the French riding style named *Ecole de la Bride* became fashionable in Spain, the monks energetically opposed it and even threatened to excommunicate those who "ride in the style of the bastard school, forgetting that of Jineta who has given so many days of glory to Spain and to Religion".

As a result of the improvements achieved by the monks, their horses became famous, and those bred at the Jerez Stud later became known as Andalusian Carthusians. The ancient Stud Farm still exists in Jerez in front of the old Monastery and bears its original name, "Salto al Cielo" (Leap into Heaven). There, in later days, sick and aged animals were retired to spend their remaining days in rest and quiet. No mare was ever sold.

Andalusian Carthusians are still bred in Spain. A few were successfully hidden from Napoleon's rapacious armies during the Peninsular War, but the majority of the remaining descendants of the Andalusians are Zapateros from the Stud founded by the family of Zapata. This herd was successfully concealed from the invading French, and after 1815 surplus animals were sold to less fortunate Andalusian breeders at high prices.

The original colour of the Zapata breed was chestnut or black, but two grey stallions were introduced about fifty years ago and the breed has since become predominantly grey. The brand of the Zapata family was a bit; this continues to be used to this day. Zapateros have won many awards at leading shows on the Continent and are part of the establishment of the Military Stud at Cordova. They are also bred at private Studs in the areas of Seville, Jerez, and Badajoz.

The Andalusian Thoroughbred is a quality riding horse, its movements low and smooth. The head, straight in profile, shows no Arab influence, though the horse is evidently of Oriental ancestry. The skin is bluish, the usual colour being grey, either flea-bitten or spotty.

The Hispano Anglo-Arab (See Plate 96)

This breed was created by crossing Spanish Arab mares with English Thoroughbred stallions, and sometimes inter-breeding the best of their progeny. It is popular in Portugal where the Thoroughbred stallions used are generally imported direct from England or Ireland. In Spain, on the other hand, large numbers of English Thoroughbred horses are bred, and there are many home-bred, as well as imported, Thoroughbred stallions at stud.

Most Hispano Anglo-Arabs are bred in the provinces of Andalusia and Estremadura. The best specimens are about 16 hands, and the predominant colours are bay, chestnut, and grey.

This is the horse which the Army Remount Commission almost invariably selects for military teams entered for competitions and sporting events, and they are very much in demand throughout the Peninsula for hunting, jumping, dressage, and as Event horses generally. They are also known for testing young fighting bulls (*Derriba de rezes brevas*), a procedure so unusual that it merits a short description. Bulls are bred specifically for fighting from strains renowned for their courage in the bullring. The breeders test young stock to ascertain which have sufficient aggression to enhance their reputation. They know that each young bull has a favourite spot on the ranch to which he will go when free to do so. The young bulls are released one by one from a holding yard, and as each canters away a rider gallops up behind him with a long pole.

The test consists of putting the young bull off his balance so that he falls. Precise timing is the essence of the operation. As the young bull's weight goes forward on to his front legs the rider pushes him off his balance. The bull falls and the rider turns. If the bull is fiery he will immediately rise and charge. The rider avoids the bull who, if spirited, will charge again and again.

NORTH AMERICA

The historical Introduction describes how, about a million years ago, the species *Equus caballus* evolved in North America, and migrated into Asia, Europe, and South America. Centuries after this Indian tribes reached North America, probably over the land bridge which then existed across the Bering Strait, to find wild horses waiting for them. However when the first white man arrived, about 500 years ago, the horse was totally extinct both in North and South America.

We do not know why the horse died out in the New World, but we do know that other species became extinct at about the same time—for example, ground sloths, mastodons, and dire wolves. On the other hand, species like the bison and the pronghorned antelope managed to survive. The most plausible theory is a type of plague or disease which did not spread to the horses in Asia because the Bering bridge had meanwhile been washed away. But this is still conjecture.

Horses were returned to the Western Hemisphere by the Europeans who colonized it. While Christopher Columbus (*c.* 1446–1506) was alive the Spaniards began to utilize the larger islands of the West Indies as horse-breeding centres for Spanish America at large, it being found that horses bred and raised there were much better able to stand the climate. The horses originally shipped across the Atlantic were from Andalusia in southern Spain. These Andalusian horses were of mixed European, North African, and Arabian origin. They showed the sloping rump and low-set tail of the Barb, the broad chest of the native Spanish horse, the endurance and soundness of the Arabian, and, above all, the ability to stay fat on sparse feed in a hot, dry country.

In 1511 Hernan Cortes sailed for Havana, Cuba, for the conquest of Mexico, taking with him sixteen horses, the first to set foot on the American continent since the last aboriginal horses died out some ten thousand years before. There were eleven stallions, including two pintos, and five mares. Although almost constantly at war, the Spaniards and Indians had a common goal—to make as much use as possible of horses and to increase their numbers. In spite of efforts to keep them from acquiring horses, the Mexican Indians were soon mounted.

Horses moved but slowly northward. When Juan de Onate settled in what is now New Mexico in 1598 he explored the territory as far north as Kansas, but found no horses in any part of these regions. Three-quarters of a century later, virtually all the tribes of the Western Plains were well mounted. The Comanches were outstanding as horsemen, as were the Apache tribes in the north. The Indians were, for the most part, indifferent horse breeders, however, doing nothing to improve the quality of their stock. Improvement came only by stealing from the white man. Even the mustangs, domestic horses which had run wild, were superior to the average Indian cayuse, as their horses were called. Nevertheless, the mounted Indian was a formidable opponent.

Horses followed the early European settlers on the Atlantic coast. By 1612 the Spanish were breeding horses in Florida. In 1629 the Reverend Francis Higginson brought horses from England to the Massachusetts Bay Colony, and during the following decades many more followed to the other British colonies, and from Holland to New Amsterdam, now called New York. Whereas in the west horses were used almost exclusively for riding, in the east they were also used for lighter farm tasks (oxen doing the heavy work), for hauling produce, and for road transportation. In 1717 it took two weeks for the Post Rider to make the 250-mile journey from Boston to New York, about 17 miles a day, but a half-century later there was regular and much more rapid service between the principal eastern cities from Montreal, Canada, to St Augustine, Florida. On June 25th, 1777, there was inaugurated the first regular coach service in North America between Boston and New York.

The rocky soil of New England soon forced the settlers of that section to become merchants instead of farmers, so it is not surprising that here was developed the first American breed of horse to become an important article of export. When Charles II established the fashion for racing at Newmarket Heath, and thus laid the foundation for the Thoroughbred breed, England discarded her amblers and pacers (see p. 32). These were preserved in New England, more especially by the planters with large farms on the shores of Narragansett Bay in Rhode Island. Their breed, the Narragansett Pacer, became the rage in the West Indies, the gait being particularly comfortable for those overseeing the sugar-cane fields of these islands. Such was the demand, and so exaggerated the prices paid, that by the end of the eighteenth century the breed was literally sold out, and thereafter ceased to exist. Much of this blood is still found, however, among the ancestors of the Standardbred.

The fashion for horse racing quickly spread to the Colonies. Not long after taking over New York from the Dutch, the British Governor, Nicolls, established a race-ground on Long Island (1666), not far from the present site of Belmont Park.

The Horse in North America Today

Because of a rapid rise in farm wages during and following the Second World War, tractors replaced work horses at a corresponding rate. This brought about a sharp reduction in the total horse population of North America, it being widely prophesied that the horse was on its way out. While the number of horses kept for work was dwindling, that of horses kept for sport was increasing by leaps and bounds. The first major increase was in the number of race horses, for both running and harness racing. During the Second World War, when purchasable goods were strictly rationed and people's pockets were bulging with war wages, the entertainment industries experienced a boom, particularly racing and its attendant Pari-Mutuel betting. In 1940 the total annual revenue derived by the various states from Pari-Mutuel taxes was $16,145,182,[1] while in 1946 it had risen to $94,035,859. This trend has continued, the figure for 1967 being $394,381,913. Similarly, the total amounts distributed in purses for 1940 was $15,911,167 as compared with $139,170,738 for 1967. There has been a corresponding increase in numbers of and attendance at rodeos, which constitute America's second largest group of equestrian spectator sports.

Even more significant for the future has been the increase in the number of riders for pleasure. Among the various explanations for this phenomenon, the most frequently advanced is the reaction against over-mechanization and over-urbanization of our current society, which provides a return to nature, to the wilderness and to animals. Whereas ten years ago an automobile was the ultimate status symbol of the teenage group, today a horse is at the top.

Estimates contained in a special research project conducted by Theracon, Inc., of Topeka, Kansas, indicate that the United States' horse population of 1959, reported by the United States Census of Agriculture as 2,947,900, had risen to 6,380,000 as of January 1st, 1968. Sharp gains in certain states are attributable to the fact that the breeding of race horses is subsidized by a percentage of Pari-Mutuel taxes. California,

[1] $1,000,000 is equal to approximately £418,000.

Massachusetts, Maryland, Delaware, and New Jersey registered gains of from three to five times the 1959 figure, while Florida shows a gain of $8\frac{1}{2}$ times.

The horse population of Canada has been similarly affected by the greatly increased interest in racing of all kinds, which has stimulated the breeding of Thoroughbreds and Standardbreds; the latter received a particular boost by the legalizing of Harness Racing at night on floodlit tracks (see Appendix IV, p. 126). In the State of Ontario the total number of Thoroughbreds and Standardbreds registered annually now exceeds the combined total registrations of all other breeds.

Other horses bred in Canada, in order of the number of registrations, are Arabians, Quarter horses, Belgian Draught horses, Hackneys, Hunters, and Clydesdales. The most popular pony breeds are Shetlands, Welsh, and Icelandic. In former days, a Canadian Hunter was recorded as well as a Canadian Horse, but the Canadian national livestock records for 1966 show the Canadian Horse Breeders' Association as having made only eighteen registrations during the year—all in Quebec Province.

The most prominent Canadian horse today is unquestionable the Cutting Horse (see Plate 108) which has been developed as a Competition Horse, though its sponsors point out that "a calm, cool performance in actual ranch work" is definitely an asset for competition purposes. The competition itself is packed with action:

> During the two and a half minutes . . . a rider demonstrates the ability of his horse to out-think the cow with terrific short bursts of speed, agility of turns in mid-air, fabulous foot work, and co-ordination between horse and rider that is unexcelled in any arena event. . . . Once seen in action, spectators all over North America are amazed. . . . They all agree that to watch a Cutting Horse in action is indeed a spine-tingling experience.[1]

The Albino

The Albino, or true white horse, has been extolled for centuries in song and story, and celebrated in innumerable legends. Throughout folklore the prancing white stallions and snowy mares seem forever destined to hold young horse lovers spellbound. From serious art forms to second-rate motion pictures the dazzling white steed is the symbol of all that is heroic.

However noble the white horse may be to those of creative imagination, the Albino is suspect to practical, experienced horsemen, and, unfortunately, their doubts are not without foundation.

Albino horses, like other albino creatures, are inclined to certain weaknesses inherent in their lack of colour. Unlike the grey, who may become almost white in its old age, the Albino is stark white at birth. Its skin is not dark at all, but rather is pink, and its eyes, instead of being the ordinary deep-brown colour, are a pale, translucent blue. These peculiarities are the result of the Albino's congenital lack of pigmentation, and subject the horse to adverse effects. The complete absence of pigment in the skin causes excessive sensitivity to sunlight, and the eccentric condition of its oddly pale eyes may cause impairments or defects in vision. Thus, even at best, the Albino begins life with two weaknesses which, for most knowledgeable buyers, are sufficient to confirm their innate suspicions.

One still hears arguments as to whether the Albino is a colour or a breed. However dissimilar Albinos may be in points of conformation, their genes are markedly recessive and create a high incidence of colour fidelity. Albino matings so frequently produce offspring of identical coloration that there is no denying their ability to 'breed true'. In this sense, then, they fulfil the most common criterion for qualification as a breed.

The colour-versus-breed dispute is rendered somewhat academic by a scientific alternative—namely that the Albino is a mutation—which is not always synonymous with ugliness or deformity. Some researchers believe that the stallion Justin Morgan, founder of the Morgan breed, was a creature with such prepotency as a sire that he must have been a mutant.

While scientists direct their efforts towards solving the genetic riddle breeders at the White Horse Ranch in Nebraska are directing their energies towards correcting the Albino's weaknesses, and have had some degree of success in producing Albinos with normal dark eyes, unimpaired vision, and increased tolerance for sunlight. So far, however, Albinos have failed to distinguish themselves in any serious competitions, and until their achievements redeem them from the traditional suspicion aroused by their lack of colour, it is likely that most riders will continue to regard the white horse as the black sheep of the equine family.

[1] From information issued by the Canadian Cutting Horse Association and the National Cutting Horse Association of Canada.

The American Quarter Horse (See Plate 102)

The American Quarter Horse has achieved such widespread recognition as the ideal cow-horse for working the beef herds of the western United States that there is an equally widespread temptation to assume that the breed originated among the lawless cowtowns and cattle kingdoms of yesteryear. On the contrary, the Quarter Horse originally was as eastern as Britain's Atlantic Colonies, and the strain was first bred among the Colonial Seaboard Settlements.

The Colonists who sought their fortunes in the New World found a land that was far from being all milk and honey. The newcomers were blessed only in that they inherited from earlier Spanish explorers a residue of horse stock that was exceptional in quality.

These imported Spanish horses were inter-bred because no out-cross was available. *Equus* had disappeared from the Americas approximately ten thousand years prior to the arrival of the Spaniards. Thus for many years the animals brought from Spain constituted the only members of the species on either the northern or southern American continents. This situation was changed by the importation from Britain of stallions 'of the blood'—that is, sires who were not known as Thoroughbreds, since the breed was not officially 'invented', but who were bred according to the Thoroughbred pattern. By crossing good home-bred mares, descended from Spanish imports, to good English stallions, the colonists cultivated a superior brand of offspring with all the versatility required to accommodate the demands of pioneer life. These horses performed manifold farm chores, hauled goods and wares and lumber at the mill, took the church-going folk to the village by carriage on Sundays, carried the master astride at efficient but comfortable gaits, and demanded so little in the way of food that they could forage for themselves when necessary.

Known for their compact, chunky build (they averaged about 15 hands) and massive, muscular quarters, they had tremendous thrust and pull through the shoulder and haunches, and it was this extraordinary power which established the breed as master of the short-distance sprint.

The English love for racing was no less feverish in the New World than back across the ocean, and though the settlers had little time to clear land purely for sporting purposes, they did not hesitate to transform the main street of the village, or a path hacked out of the wilderness, into a convenient quarter-mile racing stretch. The electrifying starts and explosive sprints of the little pioneer horses soon earned the breed its first name, the Famous and Celebrated Colonial Quarter Pather, now familiar to us simply as the Quarter Horse.

The rise of the Thoroughbred and construction of oval tracks so stimulated the popularity of long-distance racing that the original concept of quarter-mile sprints was altogether abandoned in the east. No longer the star of the 'Sport of Kings', the Quarter Horse was banished westwards where Quarter Horse racing remained alive only as a sporadic frontier pastime.

Over the years the Quarter Horse developed a protective instinct toward other animals, a shrewd capacity to anticipate their actions and to react spontaneously with a skittering stop, a dazzling sprint, a mid-air turn, or whatever was appropriate to head off and to 'contain' each vagrant steer, thus keeping it from harm's way. For this reason, wherever there were cattle there were also Quarter horses, which became indispensable partners to the cattlemen.

Today Quarter horses are found in all parts of the world, including Africa and Australia, where beef cattle thrive in abundance. In the United States about half a million members of the breed are registered, which, with an estimated quarter of a million unregistered, makes the Quarter Horse the most popular breed of all. Equally successful as a horse for range work or a pleasure horse for trail riding, it is also the outstanding champion in all forms of rodeo and western show competition.

The ultimate triumph, however, is its dazzling return to the turf in a recent revival of short-distance racing which has been welcomed with overwhelming public enthusiasm. Indeed, the Quarter Horse now boasts the fattest purse in racing with the All American Futurity Stakes worth a total of approximately 600,000 dollars.

The American Saddle Horse (See Plate 106)

In less than a century the territory of the Ohio Valley, lying west of the Appalachians and the strategic Cumberland Gap, was transformed from Daniel Boone's wilderness of forests and Indians into Scarlet O'Hara's world of lush plantations and cultivated gentlefolk. The local Southern aristocracy was far removed from its rugged pioneer forebears; in horse-flesh, at least, it was now possible to perfect their ideal.

To successful planters, the ideal was a horse which would satisfy aesthetic demands as well as practical workaday requirements. The aesthetic side called for an animal of beauty and distinction, with a faint hint of disdain for creatures of lesser stature. The practical needs called for an animal which afforded incomparable comfort in the saddle, for when these wealthy planters settled down to business their riding took them on journeys which lasted from dawn to dusk.

Speed was not required since the planters did not wish to conduct their surveillance at a canter. Yet the length of the working day demanded endurance, lest the horse succumb to fatigue, and gaits of sublime ease, lest the rider be the one to succumb.

After several generations of selective breeding, Kentucky horsemen achieved the perfect blend of qualities in a horse which was at first known as the Kentucky Saddle Horse and is now officially entitled the American Saddle Horse.

Although the foundation sire of the breed was a Thoroughbred named Denmark (foaled in 1839), it is almost impossible to imagine anything less like the great gallopers of the turf than the Saddler. It has a fleshy, rounded, and compact appearance, as if its entire body (and it is a tall horse, averaging a good 16 hands or more) were literally collected in at either end, condensing itself around some invisible source of energy beneath the saddle. The neck is carried high and its natural arch is very acute. The tail, usually aided by artificial means for the show ring, is similarly carried aloft and arched. Its limbs, less fragile and leggy looking, move with extreme vertical action, climbing high and folding tight to achieve slow, rocking gaits.

Saddle horses come in three models, all of which excel in the show ring, rather at the expense of any nation-wide popularity for normal riding. The Harness Horse is not exhibited under saddle but in light show harness and pulling a light-weight four-wheeled vehicle. It performs at the walk and park trot (animated but never excessively fast), and judges usually place special emphasis on manners as well as on brilliance. The Three-gaited Saddler performs at the walk, trot, and canter, and is properly exhibited with a 'roached' mane and tail—*i.e.*, the mane is completely shaved off and the tail is clipped close at the top and pulled rather thin below.

The most outstanding of all is the Five-gaited Saddler which is exhibited with full mane and tail, the latter often supplemented with artificial accoutrements. As performed by these animals, the simple walk, trot, and canter assume the grace of a ballet, and the additional movements, the 'slow-gait' and the 'rack', are most spectacular. The slow-gait is a true prancing motion, a four-beat pattern in which each foot rises, hesitates in mid-air, and falls in a single, separate sequence. The rack is an all-out, full-speed-ahead, all-stops-pulled version of the slow-gait that on a straight-away can cover a mile in 2·19 minutes and in a show ring can invariable be counted on to bring the fans to their feet in a thunderous roar of applause.

The American Shetland Pony (See Plate 97)

By far the most popular pony in the United States is the diminutive Shetland whose pedigree registrations are now over forty thousand. In order to qualify for registration, they may not exceed the height limit of forty-six inches set by the American Shetland Pony Club. They average a height of about forty-two inches, but occasionally they come in truly miniature proportions, being only twenty-eight inches off the ground. They appear in a wide assortment of colours— mouse, grey, brown, bay, black, chestnut, roan, cream, dun, and dappled. Their small size, however, is not reflected in their price. The great popular demand has recently set values sky-rocketing. At a recent auction pure-bred Shetlands fetched an average price of 1700 dollars. Exceptional stock brings equally exceptional sums. The Queen of Diamonds fetched 30,000 dollars and the fabulous stallion Frisco Pete was syndicated for the colossal sum of 90,000 dollars.

Fortunately for buyers who simply require a small amiable backyard pet, satisfactory Shetlands can be bought for more reasonable sums, ranging from 75 dollars to 500 dollars.

Through selective breeding, quality Shetlands in the United States have acquired consider-ably more refinement than the original 'Island type' which tends to be somewhat coarser of feature, broad-beamed, and stubby-legged. The American version has a more Oriental look and a structural delicacy which belies its renowned hardiness. The ears are dainty, the body and legs of proportionate dimensions, the head gracefully articulated, often with a faint inward dish along the nose which suggests the classic Arabian face. Though mane and tail still grow to luxuriant extremes, the coat is less of a woolly thatch, and has a sleeker, trimmer appearance.

The Shetland's adaptability has rendered it useful for all manner of purposes. It is at home in both Western and English tack and goes well in harness. Hunter types are shown under saddle over two-foot pony-course fences. Saddle types are shown with weighted shoes, toes worn long, and artificially set tails, and they prance through their gaits with impressive action and elevation.

In harness rig they can be used for anything—from quietly pulling the baby's go-cart to stepping lively in long, multi-team hitches. In shows they are usually exhibited either in harness-pony classes, where manners, style, and brilliance are emphasized, or in pony-roadster classes, where a somewhat brisker pace is in order.

As it happens, however, the latest fad in Shetlands is not in the show ring, but on the race track, where they trot with lightweight, scaled-down, two-wheeled racing sulkies. Shetlands are the basis of a new sport of pony racing which offers a dazzling world of excitement for children and a taste of racing in make-believe—without the harsh reality of Thoroughbred costs to dampen the fun for parents.

The American Thoroughbred (See Plate 104)

Though the word Thoroughbred had yet to come into use, horsemen of the eighteenth century, particularly in England, were regularly crossing Arabian and other stallions of Eastern blood with indigenous mares—a system which sometimes produced race horses of incredible swiftness. Equine literature of the times was rife with reference to 'bred' horses, indicating those produced by this formula. The first such animal to arrive in North America was Bulle Rocke, a son of the Darley Arabian imported from England in 1730.

The American Revolutionary War, however, interrupted the growth of colonial racing and likewise the development of Thoroughbred stock, but shortly after the cessation of hostilities the first true Thoroughbreds were imported from England to form the bedrock of native American racing blood, and to contribute to the mighty Thoroughbred dynasties which would arise in the New World—all descended in the male line from the English scions Eclipse, Matchem, and Herod.

The first post-war import was a rather small grey stallion named Medley who arrived in 1784. He was followed by Shark, a stallion who had established himself in a brilliant racing career in England. Of far more crucial consequence to the strength of American bloodlines, however, were the two succeeding British imports, Messenger and Diomed.

Messenger's offspring included not only a host of most successful Thoroughbred racers (among the more recent is Kelso who, upon retirement a few years ago, was the leading money-winning horse of all time with earnings just short of two million dollars), but horses whose penchant for specialized gaits constituted a major contribution to the formation of new breeds. To this single stallion may be traced the blood of both Rydsyck's Hambletonian, founder of the Standardbred, and Denmark, founder of the American Saddle Horse.

Diomed arrived at the ripe age of twenty-one, having been bought for only fifty guineas. In his racing days he had won the first Epsom Derby, but in latter years was labelled as such a bad foal getter that the stud fee he commanded was a mere ten dollars. However, Diomed's son Sir Archy outclassed all rivals in his day to become the first truly important native-bred American stallion. His illustrious grandchildren included American Eclipse, supreme in his own generation, and the incredible filly Haynie's Maria.

During this period—between the Revolution and the Civil War—American racing ceased to be a diversion confined to country gentlemen. Its popularity has increased regularly from that time until the present day, when, with attendances totalling about fifty million people annually, Thoroughbred racing is unquestionably the biggest spectator sport in the U.S.A.

The North American Thoroughbred industry is backed by a huge financial investment. Recently, within one year nine stallions were syndicated at sums between 1,000,000 and 2,500,000 dollars. The total value of Stud Farms, race tracks, and Thoroughbred racers in the U.S.A. is now estimated at over 5,000,000,000 dollars.

The American Welsh Pony

Of the several types and breeds of Welsh Pony, the one which has captivated American owners is the Welsh Mountain Pony, so much so that in the United States any reference to a Welsh Pony is taken to mean the Welsh Mountain variety. As with the Shetland, the American type of Welsh Mountain Pony has been developed on lines particularly suitable for the U.S.A., though in this case the difference between the American and the original variety is not so great.

The American demand for the little Welsh import and its home-bred relatives is strong, and since it numbers far fewer than the Shetland, rendering the quality Welsh a semi-exclusive animal, the purchase price is even steeper than that of its Scottish counterpart. The cost of a good pure-bred specimen is rarely lower than $1000 and $2000 is a far more likely quotation. As the supply increases, these extravagant sums will be somewhat reduced.

The standards for registration set by the Welsh Pony Society of America are simple restrictions as to size and colour—the maximum permitted height is 12·2 hands and the coat must be of solid coloration. (As it happens greys, especially pale and white-haired types, and chestnuts are particularly prevalent in the United States.)

It has been the great good fortune of these imported ponies to rouse the interest of breeders who are not ordinary run-of-the-mill dealers, but rather genuine enthusiasts for the breed.

Thanks to such good influences, the attributes of the strain have not been harmfully exploited. For example, the naturally snappy carriage, well-flexed neck, compact, stylish conformation, and bouncy, elevated action make the Welsh Pony a perfect candidate for smart harness show classes in which it might have been exhibited with long hooves, weighted shoes, and artificially enhanced tails. Fearing that these excesses might reduce the pony's usefulness for children's pleasure riding and its extraordinary suitability as a youngster's hunter, the American Breed Society has tactfully discouraged any temptations which would convert an ideal little companion into a hot-house neurotic. Protected by an organization and devoted following of such integrity, it is certain that this widely admired strain will prosper in the New World.

The Appaloosa (See Plate 99)

Of the various colour types for which registries exist and in which serious attempts at selective mating are being undertaken in order to develop patterns which reproduce 'true', the Appaloosa comes closest to what may be considered a fully fledged breed.

Like the Pinto's, the Appaloosa's coat results from hereditary spotting genes which induce distinctive dual coloration wherein white may appear in combination with any other solid body colour, roan being the most common. There, however, any significant similarity between the two ends, for in direct contrast to the broad blotches and utterly random shapes and forms which define the Pinto coat, the Appaloosa pattern usually assumes an organized, measured character with spotting designs that are regular and relatively precise. In quantity the spots may be innumerable, and placed, often with remarkable consistency, in a near perfect circle or elipse. Invariably the pattern is emphasized most acutely over the hips and loins.

In giving its official description of these markings, the Appaloosa Horse Club specifies:

> Most individuals will be white over the loin and hips with dark round or egg-shaped spots. Spots vary in size from specks to three or four inches in diameter. Some Appaloosas carry the spotting all over the body, but it is usually dominant over the hips. Others will show white over the hips without the dark spots in the white. Still others will appear mottled all over the body, or will show white specks or spots with dark background.

Beyond the prominence of its polka-dotted coat, the Appaloosa bears other features which, though admittedly far less dazzling to the eye, are nonetheless perhaps equally significant as these side characteristics transmit with extreme fidelity from one generation to the next—even in instances where the coat design does not fulfil official specifications. Thus, for example, in a case where the spots have a disappointing 'washed out' look and the Appaloosa's coat is virtually indistinguishable from an ordinary roan, the animal may nevertheless be identified as being of the strain by the presence of the following traits.

First, the area surrounding the 'seeing' parts of the eye (*i.e.*, iris, cornea, pupil, etc.) is notably white in colour, just like the human eye, though a completely different shape. Second, regardless of the individual's coat coloration, the skin beneath will always have a mottled, muddy appearance with an overall pink and grey splattering that is usually particularly evident around the nostrils and muzzle. And third, the hooves, similarly, are parti-coloured, invariably marked with vertical black and white striping which is quite visible in the surface growth of horn.

Appaloosas, like the original stock of so many other types, were first brought to America by the Spanish. A good number of these horses drifted northward by one means or another and fell into the hands of the Nez Percé Indians. This tribe of unusually excellent horse breeders lived in north-eastern Oregon near the Palouse river (hence the corruption, Appaloosa) and developed animals of such quality that the merits of their stock were specifically noted in the journal of Meriwether Lewis, in the Lewis and Clarke expedition of 1806.

In October 1877 the Nez Percé were wiped out by the U.S. Army in a battle that lasted a total of six days. From the legacy bequeathed by the vanquished Nez Percé, the Appaloosa has recently grown at such an astonishing rate of popularity as to become one of the Big Five breeds in America, ranking behind only such traditional favourites as the Quarter Horse, the Thoroughbred, the Standardbred, and the Shetland Pony.

The Canadian

From about 1665 draught horses, trotters, and pacers were taken to Canada from Normandy and Brittany, and by a century later a definite type of Canadian Draught Horse had been fixed.

93 *LUSITANO*

94 *ALTER-REAL*

95 *ANDALUSIAN*

96 *HISPANO ANGLO-ARAB*

97 *AMERICAN SHETLAND PONY*

98 *PONY OF THE AMERICAS*

99 *APPALOOSA*

100 *PALOMINO*

101 *PINTO*

102 *AMERICAN QUARTER HORSE*

103 *MORGAN*

104 *AMERICAN THOROUGHBRED*

105 *STANDARDBRED*

106 *AMERICAN SADDLE HORSE*

107 *TENNESSEE WALKING HORSE*

108 *CANADIAN CUTTING HORSE*

A hundred years ago this was described as an excellent, hardy, general-purpose animal resembling a small Percheron. Thus the variety spread gradually throughout Canada and also the U.S.A.

After the British defeated the French in Canada, Canadian horses, and especially riding horses, were crossed with English breeds. For example, the first crosses between Canadian Trotters and English Thoroughbreds were very successful in trotting races and became known as Frenchers.

Both varieties of Canadian horses went out of fashion and became scarce, but in 1885 a Stud Book was opened, and ten years later a Breeders' Association was founded. Since then animals have only been admitted to the Stud Book on inspection.

Both varieties survived but are now found mainly in the province of Quebec. The light draught type is feeling the effects of mechanization, but the hunter type is flourishing. The main breeding centre is the Agricultural Research Station at Deschambauld, Quebec, which now has five Canadian stallions and about thirty Canadian mares, as well as other breeds. This Station is experimenting in crossing Canadians with Thoroughbreds and Standardbreds.

The Morgan Horse (See Plate 103)

The Morgan, like the Quarter Horse, is a breed whose heritage is entrenched in the history of colonial America. Unlike the Quarter Horse, however, the Morgan family owes its being to but a single phenomenal stallion.

It has never been definitely determined when or where this horse was born. The region in which he is supposed to have made his first appearance is West Springfield, Massachusetts. Here, tradition asserts, in the early 1790s the dark bay two-year-old colt was tendered to an impoverished tubercular inn-keeper named Justin Morgan in payment of a debt.

Mr Morgan named the colt Figure and returned home with him to Randolph Centre, Vermont. Not long afterwards Justin Morgan died and his horse passed from one owner to the next, each time confronted with some new task which was lowlier and drearier than the ones before. He changed hands in a dozen or more transactions until finally, under the charge of his last owner, a farmer named Levi Bean, he was assigned the degrading duty of pulling a manure spreader and denied stabling or shelter even in the icy grip of the harsh north-eastern winters.

Meantime, the stallion's original name of Figure was altogether forgotten. Everyone referred to him as Justin Morgan's horse which eventually became just plain Justin Morgan. Also quite forgotten was the breeding of Justin Morgan, as the stallion is hereafter called. One account maintains that he was sired by a horse named True Briton.

It has been established that, at the approximate time of Justin Morgan's birth, a stallion named True Briton did exist—a celebrated racer who defeated Old England in a pre-Revolutionary 'match' race. It is conceivable that this illustrious racer might have sired the anonymous brown colt who later became known as Justin Morgan.

Information about the dam is vaguer still. Some claim she was of the family sired by the imported stallion Wildair (who belonged to the same owner as True Briton) from whom such notable modern sires as Nearbo and Nasrullah are descended on the maternal side. Others believe she was simply an obscure local mare from the Connecticut Valley.

Although so little is known of Justin Morgan's background, it is certain that the horse had a remarkable constitution and possessed extraordinary strength. Measuring only about 14 hands and weighing approximately 800 pounds, he survived, unsung but undaunted, through a lifetime of gruelling labour and miserable treatment, working from dawn to dusk before a plough, hauling loads of goods through mud that was axle deep, tearing roots and stubborn stumps from earth to be cleared for planting. After hours, he was often stood at stud for bargain rates, and was matched against all comers in merciless weight-pulling contests.

He also possessed the gift of speed. On holidays or special occasions he was given time off from work to race both in harness and under saddle—and never once was beaten. Word of his feats, and those of his descendants, soon spread through Vermont, and ultimately all New England. It became increasingly obvious that Justin Morgan was a sire of unprecedented prepotency, so exceptional in transmitting his qualities, even to size and predominantly dark coloration, that he is considered by some to have been a 'genetic sport'—an inexplicable deviation from the norm.

Though today's Morgan horses are doubtless more refined than Justin Morgan might ever have dreamed possible, structurally they are replicas of their diminutive but mighty ancestor. However dandified their airs in the show ring exhibitions—ranging from harness classes to roadster classes, pleasure-horse classes to old-fashioned weight-pulling contests in collar and working harness—Morgans are still rugged individualists with an endurance capacity equal to the Arab's. Their compact size and kind nature belies their extreme physical strength, and it is the happy mixture of all three which has brought the Morgan nation-wide popularity as a safe, economical, handsome all-purpose horse for the entire family's enjoyment.

[97]

The Palomino (See Plate 100)

The Palomino is a 'colour breed' of a sort quite different from either the Pinto or the Appaloosa. In the first place, the properly marked Palomino is never a parti-coloured animal but rather a solid-coated horse which, much like ordinary single-coloured horses such as bays or chestnuts, should not have any areas of white at all on the body. Beneath the hair, the skin overall should also be of uniform colour—the same greyish-black that likewise underlies the coat of ordinary solid-colour horses, and the mane and tail must be the familiar flaxen or cold silvery white. Limited white markings—the traditional blaze and socks and conservative variations thereof—may decorate the lower legs and face.

In order to qualify for admission to the Palomino Horse Breeders of America registry, an animal must meet exacting specifications, not only for markings but for the precise shade of coat hue as well. White markings on the legs may not advance beyond the knee or hock, and white hairs on the face may not be so abundant as to cause a 'watch' or 'clock' eye as often occurs when the ornamental splash is excessively lavish. To be officially acceptable, both eyes must be the customary dark-brown colour. Furthermore, in the flaxen mane and tail no more than 15 per cent of the hairs may be of darker tone. The *pièce de résistance* is, of course, the body hue itself which should be of exactly the same glint as newly minted gold and may permissibly be no more than three shades darker or lighter.

There are no guidelines to conformation beyond the fact that applicants to the Palomino Horse Association registry should, at maturity, weigh between 900 and 1300 pounds and be between 14 and 16 hands high. For stallions or mares to qualify for the breeding registry, it is required that one parent be recorded among the P.H.B.A. listings. The other must be of either Arabian, Quarter Horse, or Thoroughbred blood lines.

There is a second unique feature which distinguishes the Palomino from its eye-catching kin —namely, the genetic factors which govern its coloration. Unlike the spotted varieties, this coat colour does not result from the presence of a special 'Palomino gene', nor a combination of genes, nor other such easily traceable hereditary factors. The Palomino coat, in fact, may occur in any traditional pure-bred strain (admittedly these cases are infrequent) where spotting of any sort has been virtually 'bred out'. Thus it is theoretically possible for a Palomino Thoroughbred to exist, while conversely it is inconceivable for a Pinto Thoroughbred to exist.

Producing Palomino coloration is not in itself difficult. The interaction which occurs at random among non-colour breeds and results in the 'surprise' Palomino can be deliberately brought about through at least four known crosses with essentially satisfying effects. The primary crosses are as follows: first, Palomino to Palomino, which produces an average ratio of two Palomino offspring to one chestnut and one Albino offspring; second, Palomino to chestnut, which produces an average ratio of one chestnut to one Palomino foal; third, Palomino to Albino, which produces an average ratio of one Palomino to one Albino offspring; and fourth, chestnut to Albino which produces only Palomino foals.

Of the four methods, the last is obviously most consistent, but also results in a colour that is often flat, dull, and washed out. For this reason the second crossing—namely, Palomino to chestnut—is often preferred for this produces the richest and most dazzling golden glint.

The Pinto (See Plate 101)

The Pinto Horse, equally familiar as the Paint or Calico, is a colour breed whose members by definition are not determined through standards of conformation or structure, or by family lineage, but by their coat coloration which manifests the presence of hereditary spotting genes.

The typical Pinto coat is characterized by its large, random-shaped patches of white set against any other solid colour, and splattered over the entire body, not just the usual marking points of the legs and face. In cases where the contrasting colour is black, the Pinto may also be known as Piebald. Where splashes of white are combined with any colour other than black, the horse may be classified as Skewbald.

Spotting patterns are further defined according to which of the two colours dominates the coat. The 'Ovaro' type is a Pinto coat in which the horse's solid colour dominates the pattern and forms an overall base for the irregular splashes of white. The 'Tobiano', on the other hand, is a Pinto whose dominant, basic coat is white, and whose patchwork of solid coloration are decorative markings secondary to the white.

These distinctive markings are not achieved merely by mating a white horse with another of solid, darker coat. Two mono-coloured horses will not produce duo-coloured offspring unless one or both of the parents has specific spotting genes inherited from a Pinto ancestor.

The American Indians were not oblivious of the fact that a spotted pattern was a natural camouflage. Whether or not this accounted for their special affection for the Pinto, the extent of their preference for spotting was such that they did not hesitate to apply the paint brush on horses too sparsely endowed with colour by Mother Nature.

Cow-hands, too, held the Paint in great favour, frequently paying a much higher price for the privilege of getting a spotted animal. Apparently their owners were fully pleased with the choice, for nowhere is the Paint extolled with more sentiment and longing than in the traditional songs and the rambling tales of the American West.

A recurring point in the testimony of wranglers and cattle-men who swore by the supremacy of Pintos was their characteristic ruggedness, their extraordinary capacity to survive the rigours of the country. In modern times Pintos have proved their excellence over fences and established themselves as fully the equal of other breeds in the hunting field. When their background contains a supply of Thoroughbred blood, the result can be a model of conformation.

Since spotting has been bred out of most of the pure-bred strains—the Arab, the Thoroughbred, the Standardbred, etc.—the horse whose coat has Pinto markings automatically reveals itself to be of impure pedigree and may suffer the prejudices of those whose only interest in colour is whether the blood is blue. As Pinto breeders achieve more faithful transmission of colour patterns and arrive at more uniform standards of conformation, this attitude will be overcome and Pintos will be welcomed without hesitation by the entire horse community.

The Pony of the Americas (See Plate 98)

Horsemen in the United States seem to suffer from a national inferiority complex about native ponies much as American drivers do about native motor-cars. For the miniature equine equal to the Rolls the conscientious American pony buyer almost invariably turns to some importation from the British Isles. The resulting lack of dedication towards wild indigenous types casts an unfortunate shadow on America's pony record, for though there is indeed an abundance of handsome native strains, particularly among the coastal islands and shoreline marshes of the Atlantic seaboard, there is but one officially recognized, legitimate home-grown type which is a defined breed, and has been accorded enough interest to effect organization of a Stud Book and registry. Even so, this is in no sense a wild pony (nor for that matter, notably independent of direct British influence) but rather the deliberate creation of a single person— Mr Leslie Boomhower of Mason City, Iowa, who founded the 'Pony of the Americas'.

In 1956 Mr Boomhower, an experienced horse-breeder, conducted an experiment in which a Shetland Pony stallion was crossed with an Appaloosa mare. The outcome was altogether pleasing—a miniature edition of a full-sized Appaloosa, complete with coat design of small spots consistently shaped in the form of a circle or ellipse, of the customary coin-size dimensions, and with greatest emphasis over the hips and loins. The full assortment of other characteristics peculiar to the 'App' also marked the new type of pony: eyes always encircled by white, vertical striping on the hooves, and mud-coloured skin spattered with light and dark mottling, always most obvious around the muzzle. Frequently referred to as 'varnish' marks, the muddy mottling around the mouth and nostrils may also be found about the jowls, eyes, tail, and sheath or udders.

The show-ring success of Mr Boomhower's first colt, Black Hand, soon led to the formation of a Stud Book with the experimental champion pioneering as Number One.

To qualify for registry, mature ponies must fulfill Pony of the Americas Club specifications and display the characteristic markings which distinguish the strain. Foals are granted tentative registration upon application and at the age of three are examined by a veterinarian or Club inspector to verify these qualifications and measure the animal's height, which must be no shorter than 11·2 nor taller than 13 hands to meet official standards.

The Standardbred (See Plate 105)

The earliest American horses to race between the traces were roadster strains known as Canadian and Narragansett Pacers—native stock but doubtless related to contemporary British counterparts called Norfolk and Lincoln Trotters. From these colonial types emerged sires who founded significant families, such as the Copperbottoms and the Hyatogas, but their swiftness was soon exceeded by star performers of the Morgan breed.

These families and historic champions figure importantly in the development of the Standardbred—but the most important is a horse named Hambletonian 10, who appeared in 1849 and is better known as Rydsyck's Hambletonian. On both sides of his lineage, Hambletonian 10 traces to Messenger, the imported Thoroughbred acknowledged as being among the most prominent sires. Not always, however, were the mares bred to Messenger of similarly elegant blood lines and when mated to ladies of colder background the great Thoroughbred stallion produced horses with a special flair for trotting. One of these descendants was Rydsyck's Hambletonian whose own stature at stud was such that some 90 per cent of all Standardbreds stem from this single ancestor.

The Standardbred swiftly developed into a formal recognized breed, its name derived from the old custom of testing untried harness racers to determine if they could go the mile within a specified 'standard' or time allotment before official permission was granted for them to compete. Today the standard is 2 minutes 20 seconds for the mile—a heady speed at anything less than the gallop it would seem, but generous enough when one considers that half a century ago, without benefit of the improved tracks and highly perfected sulkies of modern times, the immortal Dan Patch completed the mile in less than two minutes flat some thirty times.

Non-Standardbred horses may compete in Standardbred events, as opposed to the Thoroughbred racing restrictions which limits entries to registered Thoroughbreds, provided the fact that they are non-Standardbred is noted in the racing programme. Nowadays, however, such an entry is rare, for the Standardbred has developed the traditional roadster's gaits to a peak far beyond the capacity of other horses, and the breed has assumed its rightful, honoured place as companion to the American Thoroughbred.

The Tennessee Walking Horse (See Plate 107)

The attractions of the Tennessee Walking Horse are such that the breed has given rise to the saying: "Ride one today and you'll own one tomorrow." The soft, fluid, gliding gait—half walk, half run, and altogether gentle and relaxing—for which the strain is famed may not be quite the cup of tea of members of the riding community made of sterner stuff and seeking more ambitious activities like hunting, showjumping, or polo. Yet it would be hard indeed to find a breed that has given greater public relations service to the horseman's community at large; nothing has ever more swiftly disarmed the reluctant rider or introduced larger numbers of dedicated converts into the equine owning fold than the Tennessee Walker. Intimidated novices, whether haunted by an unfortunate past experience or just congenitally shy of horses, and even riders of higher skill, perhaps unhappily grounded due to injuries or the infirmities of advancing age, on the first hand gain a wondrous sense of reassurance and, on the second, can recapture the pleasure of a sport they despaired of having to forego—all because of the liquid motion and guaranteed bounce-proof ride offered by the Walker.

Less frequently touted, but certainly no less important to the breed's appeal, is the splendid disposition also peculiar to this fine Tennessee riding horse which is considered to be among the most naturally amiable and even-tempered of all horses.

Historically, the development of the Tennessee Walker closely parallels that of his cousin, the Kentucky Saddle Horse. Both arose through a lengthy process of selective breeding which began when the first hardy pioneer settlers forged westward across the Appalachian Mountains to establish scattered primitive outposts in Kentucky, Tennessee, and Missouri.

The initial populace of gnarled mountaineers eventually became a group of landed gentry who wished to be mounted on animals no less stylish than themselves. Yet their horses had also to be endowed with extreme endurance, for when the menfolk were not engaged in sipping mint juleps, they spent long hours in the saddle surveying the far extents of their land, supervising the cultivation of crops, and administering general plantation business. Speed was of no consequence since careful, leisurely inspection was the purpose of such tours. Of much greater importance were gaits that would offer maximum comfort and not leave the rider exhausted.

The foundation stock with which breeders began was a veritable colonial potpourri—the blood of Canadian and Narragansett Pacers, laced with some Arab, Thoroughbred, Morgan, and Standardbred blood. (When the Tennessee strain was officially organized into a breed, as recently as 1935, the stallion designated as the foundation sire was a Standardbred named Black Allan who was an utter failure on the harness track owing to his predilection for attempting to race at the walking gait.)

Tennessee Walking horses (or Turn-Row horses as they were once called owing to their customary job of inspecting the crops by 'rows') have become highly popular for riding; their registrations now total over 30,000, and so enthusiastic are their owners that at the Annual Walking Horse Show at Shelbyville in Tennessee, the classes attract more entries than at any other horse show in the country.

SOUTH AMERICA

THE ARGENTINE'S horse population is about 3,700,000 according to the latest United Nations statistics,[1] the great majority being Criollo or Criollo crosses. Horses still play a major part in the Argentine economy, partly because they are essential for transport in the wilder mountain regions, and partly because a large proportion of the petroleum used has to be imported, as local production cannot keep pace with the ever increasing demand of the cities. This has restricted mechanization in rural areas.

In addition to the breeds described below, the Argentine has many Thoroughbreds imported from Britain and the Continent, some excellent Arabians, and various heavy draught horses, especially Percherons, which are used for crossing with Criollos for agriculture and transport purposes. Many of these are bought by the Army.

Some outstanding cross-bred horses are imported from Brazil, especially from the region of São Paulo, where experimental breeding has been carried on for many years.

The Criollo (See Plate 113)

The chief source of information on the Criollo or Criole is the book *El Caballo Criollo* by Dr Emilio Solanet of the Agricultural and Veterinary Faculty of Buenos Aires, a prominent breeder of Criollos and one of the greatest authorities on the breed. Unfortunately, this book is hard to obtain in Europe.

The first horses to reach South America were brought over by Columbus on his second voyage in 1493, and were disembarked at San Domingo, whence they spread to South and Central America and to Mexico. The first importation which had real significance for the Argentine was in 1535. This consisted of a hundred Andalusian stallions and mares, together with light draught and other transport horses, which were landed by Don Pedro Mendoza, the founder of Buenos Aires. Later, when the city had been sacked by the Indians, many of these horses escaped, and bred so freely that fifty years later thousands were running wild. Some herds were reported to exceed 20,000 in numbers.

The Andalusian stock from which these sprang is fully described on page 89. Dr Solanet traces the North African (Barb) blood, which, in his opinion, predominated in the best Andalusians originally imported, and which explained their stamina and ability to survive rigorous conditions.

The horses which ran wild in the Pampas were subject to severe privations; rough winters and summer droughts automatically culled those which lacked the utmost physical resilience. They were also hunted by the Indians. The survivors became accustomed to a shortage of water and inadequate nutrition, and the best of these, caught and used by later settlers, were given the name "Criollos". They carried their owners and heavy packs across the endless plains and climbed the severe passes which crossed the Andes, and became extraordinarily hardy and capable of the utmost endurance.

About one hundred years ago the Criollos were nearly ruined by injudicious crossing with stallions imported from Europe and the United States. These produced a faster, more elegant horse, but one which lacked the necessary resistance to hunger and disease.

About sixty years ago, Argentine breeders combined to re-create the Criollo as it originally had been. By severe selective breeding from the best remaining specimens, the breed was gradually re-established, and in 1918 a Society was formed to promote the breed which now features in the Argentine Government Stud Book.

The modern Criollo has many of the virtues of its ancestors, and is particularly famed for its endurance. For example, the Swiss Professor Aimé Tschiffely decided to prove their stamina by

[1] *Animal Production* (published by the Food and Agriculture Organization of the United Nations), vol. xxi, "Summary of Livestock Numbers", Table 100, p. 288.

travelling from Buenos Aires to New York, a distance of 13,350 miles. The journey involved crossing the Condor Pass at a height of over 18,000 feet at a temperature well below freezing, and crossing a desert in Equador at a temperature of 120 degrees Fahrenheit, where the horses had to travel over ninety miles without water.

Tschiffely was given two Criollos by Dr Solanet, mentioned above, which had recently been obtained from a Patagonian chief. One, Mancha, was a dun gelding aged fifteen, the other, Gato Cardell, was a piebald, a year older. Riding them alternately, the other carrying his pack, and impeded by every imaginable obstacle including saddle sores due to bites from vampire bats,[1] Tschiffely averaged over twenty-six miles every day during this amazing journey. Gato Cardell lived to be thirty-four and Mancha to be thirty-seven. It is claimed that neither had a day's illness in his life.

The Criollo stands about 14 hands and is generally dun, often with white markings, but skewbalds and piebalds are also found. The Criollos are regularly exported from the Argentine to Brazil, Paraguay, Uruguay, and Venezuela.

The Polo Pony

Polo came to England a hundred years ago, introduced from India by British officers who had discovered this ancient game while serving on the North-west Frontier.

The game soon spread to America and to other parts of the world. At first the native ponies of each country were employed, making the game level as far as the pony power was concerned and putting a premium upon the players' individual skill. Chinese ponies were played in Hong Kong and Shanghai, Arabs in Egypt and the Sudan, and both Arabs and countrybreds in India.

But it was not long before the superiority of the better-bred Australian ponies asserted themselves, and by 1914 they dominated the high-goal games in India which was then the recognized polo country of the world.

In Britain Sir Tresham Gilbey and others had begun to breed a special type of miniature blood hunter standing about 14·2 hands. The Polo Pony Stud Book was founded upon native pony mares crossed with dwarf Thoroughbred stallions. The original height limit of 13·2 hands was steadily raised to 14·2 hands, and then, after the 1914 War, abandoned altogether.

Competitive international polo between the U.S.A. and England had been going strong— in fact England won the Meadowbrook Cup in 1914 for the last time. Both the American and British teams were mounted on little dwarf Thoroughbred or nearly Thoroughbred ponies.

At first, after the lifting of the height limit, players tended to put size and pace before any other consideration, but gradually the consensus of opinion decided that the best height for a pony was about 15·1 hands, give or take an inch. Players agreed that a short-striding pony was easier to hit the ball off and quicker to turn than a long-striding race-horse type. The standard requisites of the Polo Pony have always been the same—*i.e.*, speed, stamina, courage, balance, and a temperament neither sluggish nor madly excitable.

In the Argentine and on the cattle ranches of Western America the cow-pony proved adaptable to polo but was common in appearance and lacking in speed. They were useful as beginner's ponies and being inexpensive to buy and ship were much in demand for second-class polo.

The ideal type of international pony was still the American or English Thoroughbred; the Argentine breeders, with their enormous resources of cheap production, had, from 1900 onwards, realized the value of Thoroughbred blood and kept upgrading their stock by continual import of the best stallions, until by 1930 the Argentine Pony was indistinguishable from an English Thoroughbred in looks, but was tougher and with better bone.

After 1930, high-goal American polo saw more Argentine ponies playing than any other type, and then came the 1939 War with a cessation of polo for six years, except in the Argentine. During that time numerous Argentine ponies were bred on the best lines.

In the post-War years fewer players capable enough or with time to spare for training ponies existed in Britain, and by 1947 when polo started again in England and America the Argentine players dominated the scene; their ponies were the main source of supply for first-class polo.

There are now many Argentine Polo Studs which produce annually an enormous output of ponies surplus to their owners' requirements.

Since the average height of the Argentine is somewhere around 15·2 hands, and since nowadays only mares that have proved themselves in the game are bred from, it is fair to assume that the Argentine Polo Pony can now be considered as a separate breed.

BRAZIL has a huge and increasing horse population which, according to the latest United Nations statistics, is now over 9,000,000. Apart from Thoroughbreds, Arabians, and a few European draught horses, horse-breeding is dominated by the requirements

[1] A. F. Tschiffely: *Tschiffely's Ride* (William Heinemann Ltd, London, 1947; eleventh reprint), p. 94.

of the Army, which cannot be fully mechanized because of the terrain and the inaccessibility of the mountainous regions.

The army will provide stallions to approved breeders who have forty or more registered mares, aged between four and fourteen years, provided that these are of satisfactory conformation and meet the requirements of a vet.

Smaller breeders can send any registered mare to the nearest Army Remount Centre for service. The Army usually supplies Arabian or Thoroughbred stallions for cavalry purposes, and lightly built, fast-moving Bretons of the old 'post-horse' type for draught. The cross-breds are quite satisfactory provided they are supplied with forage and cover in severe weather, and are not turned out to fend for themselves.

São Paulo City, the largest in Brazil, has for years been famed for its magnificent race course and its horse-breeding expertise. It is also the headquarters of the Brazilian Jockey Club. The State University at São Paulo has an important Department of Animal Industry which includes a long established Research Foundation investigating horse-breeding and related problems.

The Crioulo

In 1541 Alvar Nuñez landed on the Brazilian coast near Santa Catarina with a fleet carrying a number of horses—Alters from Portugal. These spread and bred like the descendants of the Spanish horses landed in and near the Argentine. Their modern descendants are mostly rather smaller than the Criollo, and different types appear in different parts of Brazil. In addition to the Mangalarga and the Campolino described below, the Crioulo in north-east Brazil is known as the Nordestino, while in the State of Goiás it is called the Courraleiro. These areas have poor soil and worse grass, and these two varieties are particularly well able to survive on the very minimum of sustenance. A better variety of Crioulo is bred in the Rio Grande do Sul, from which it takes its name. During the last forty years, many stallions have gone from this area to improve the native horses in other parts of Brazil.

The Mangalarga

During the last century Brazil imported fresh draughts of selected stallions from Spain and Portugal, which were used to improve the native horses. One of the best of these stallions, named Sublime, was sent to stud in Minas Gerais, where he founded the Mangalarga breed, sometimes known locally as the Junqueira.

The Mangalarga is larger than the Crioulo, going to about 15·4 hands. It sometimes has a peculiar gait called "marcha", which is described as being between a canter and a trot. Attempts have been made to improve Mangalargas with warm-blood stallions. The most successful cross-breeds for riding purposes come from Arabian, Anglo-Arab, Thoroughbred, or Trakehner stallions.

In 1840 Cassiano Campolino set out to improve the Mangalarga, as it was in those days, by selective breeding. He succeeded so well that a separate variety known as the Campolino now flourishes in the State of Rio de Janeiro and the neighbouring regions. These Campolinos are good saddle horses and excel in hardiness. Some thirty years ago, the Military Institute of South Brazil organized an endurance test lasting many days, in which all horses had to exist on what they grazed during the ride. Over the long distances involved the Campolinos did extremely well and all native varieties far excelled imported horses.

PERU used to receive more Andalusian and other Spanish breeds than any other country in South America because Lima was for centuries the headquarters of the Spanish occupation forces. The first horses were brought by Pizarro and Almagro in 1531 and 1532, and regular supplies of remounts enabled Andalusian horses to be bred pure in and near Lima for hundreds of years.

Inevitably some horses escaped and 'went wild'; their descendants, the Peruvian type of Criollo, are sometimes called Saltenos. They stand lower than the Argentine Criollo and are noted for their soundness and lively action. Besides the variety described below there is a larger type standing over 14 hands and occasionally reaching 15, known as the Costeño, which shows very evident traces of its Spanish ancestry. The best of them make excellent saddle horses. There is also the Serrano, a heavily built mountain pony distinctly lower than the Costeño, which is most useful for light draught work on the highland plateaux or as a pack-horse.

In the cold and inhospitable Cordillera Mountains, at heights well over 10,000 ft, the Morochuquo branch of the Criollo family is invaluable for pack transport and as saddle ponies. More heavily built than most Criollos they seldom exceed 13·2 hands and regularly carry astonishingly heavy loads over the steepest mountain passes. Like most mountain ponies they are remarkably sure-footed and have no fear of heights at all.

The Peruvian Stepping Horse

Descended from imported Spanish horses which had run wild, improved by later importations and by selective breeding, the Peruvian Stepping Horse has been developed into a national breed, distinguished by its action, which is believed to be unique in South America. For centuries Peruvians have concentrated on finding horses to travel over vast plains and mountain passes, with the least possible fatigue to their riders.

The gait which has been associated with this type of riding horse for generations is considered to be so special as to constitute a racial characteristic, and thus to distinguish the Peruvian Stepping Horse from other Criollos. This action appears to be extremely similar to that ancient gait, the amble, formerly in general use throughout Europe, but now forgotten except by enthusiasts for 'pacing'.

There can be no dispute that the Peruvian Stepping Horse will cover great distances at a remarkable speed. Like all the Criollo family, it has enormous endurance and is at its best in difficult conditions.

Soon after the last war, the National Association of Breeders and Owners of Peruvian Stepping Horses was formed by a group of enthusiasts who were authorized by the Peruvian Government to stimulate the breeding of the best type of Stepping Horse, both for riding and for light draught and agricultural purposes.

A modern Stepping Horse is a good-looking animal, standing between 14 and 15·2 hands. They can be all colours, but are most often bay or chestnut, sometimes with a white blaze.

VENEZUELA'S horse population has increased remarkably in recent years; in 1965 it was over 40,000, more than double the pre-war figure. Many Criollos in Venezuela have been ruined by unsuitable crossing, as formerly happened in the Argentine.

Venezuela experiences long droughts and very hard winters. The pastures are poor and working conditions are not always good. Numerous attempts to increase the height of the Llaneros, described below, to make them come up to the size desired for Army remounts, have not been very successful, as what the taller animals gain in speed they lose in stamina.

Some years ago a trial was made of 140 half-bred horses specially imported from the Argentine. These were issued to a cavalry unit before the annual manoeuvres. At first they seemed excellent but after a short time they began to weaken, and before the manoeuvres were completed they had to be withdrawn. The native Llaneros went through the whole series of exercises without turning a hair.

The Llanero

The best of this breed have the graceful formation and the lively gait of their Andalusian ancestors and for this reason are sometimes called Andadores. All Llaneros tend to be smaller, finer, and lighter than other Criollos because of the very hard conditions in Venezuela.

The best Llaneros make excellent cow-ponies. They generally stand 13·2 to 14 hands; when over 14·2 an outside cross is suspected and the animal is generally found to lack stamina when compared to the smaller pure-bred rival.

Although the Army objects to their small size it has yet to find a larger animal which can compete with the Llanero in stamina and endurance or which can stand up to the trying conditions in Venezuela. In spite of their small size, it is said that Llaneros can carry a load of 2 cwt or more at a good pace throughout daylight hours every working day for months on end.

[104]

109   *Polo at Windsor with the Prince of Wales*

111   *Richard Meade riding The Poacher, winner of the Three-day Event at Badminton, 1970*

112   *The American-owned Nijinsky winning the 1970 Epsom Derby. He was bred in Canada and trained in Ireland.*

THE U.S.S.R.

Asiatic Russia may well have been the area in which horses were first domesticated, and that relic of the Ice Age, Prjevalski's Horse, still exists in a wild state on the eastern frontier (see p. 14). Horses have been bred systematically in what is now the U.S.S.R. for as long as in any other country, if not for longer.

Because the territory of the Soviet Union consists of so many geographical regions, each with different terrain and economic conditions, it is the Soviet Government's policy that each zone should strive to produce two or three breeds of horses, either improved local breeds or breeds from other areas, particularly suited to the biological and commercial characteristics of that particular locality.

A total of forty breeds and breed groups are now recognized, of which twenty-five were in existence before the Revolution, ten have been developed since, and five have been imported and are now regularly bred in different regions of the U.S.S.R. The imported horses consist of English Thoroughbreds, Arabians (which are kept pure-bred), East Prussian horses of Trakehner type, Furiosos, and French Percherons.

Some other local breeds are not yet officially recognized. The final responsibility for improving the standard of pedigree horses throughout the U.S.S.R. lies with specialists in the Ministry of Agriculture and the All Union Research Institute of Horse-breeding. Experienced specialists also advise Studs and the horse-breeding centres of collective farms. The Ministry of Agriculture publishes official Stud Books in addition to those produced for every individual breed. The best Russian horses are exhibited every year at the U.S.S.R. Exhibition of Economic Achievements as well as at exhibitions in towns and cities throughout the U.S.S.R. Commissions of experts judge these horses and nominate champions in every breed.

State Pedigree Studs are responsible for improving many breeds of horses, their main task being to develop high-quality horses of different types for agriculture, as well as for riding, sport, and racing. The main method of improvement is by selective breeding within each variety, but riding horses which have already had a warm-blood cross are often improved by further crossing with Thoroughbreds or Arabians. It is strictly forbidden to inter-breed Thoroughbreds, Arabians, and Akhal-Tekés.

Except for draught horses and native steppe and forest types, horses of all breeds are tested between the ages of two and four years, to evaluate their potential for riding purposes or for trotting. The horses are classified into groups, each of which must conform to a specified standard for the breed concerned. The best horses are classified as élite, the next as first-class, while horses which are no better than satisfactory are graded second-class. Horse breeders select breeding stock, especially stallions, for pedigree use from those whose measurements and working propensities conform to the standard required for the élite group of the breed concerned.

Improvement of agricultural horses is achieved at State breeding farms which maintain stallions of the most popular breeds. These are provided by contract with the State authorities, and help the collective and state farms to play a crucial rôle in the improvement of Russian agricultural horses.

The Central Government gives general encouragement to the horse-breeding operations of each State and actively promotes the export of horses. It also sponsors commissions for selecting and importing outstanding animals for breeding purposes.

In addition to the eighteen breeds described in detail below, mention must be made of breeds such as the Anglo-Kabardin, created by crossing Kabardin mares with imported Thoroughbred stallions, a process started about one hundred years ago. The cross-breds were bigger and faster than the original Kabardins (see p. 109) but retained the breed's desirable qualities. The resultant cross-breds have been inter-bred for so long that a definite type has now been fixed and the Kabardin Stud Book has a special section devoted to Anglo-Kabardins.

Another interesting breed is the Bashkir, a local breed from Bashkiria on the southern foothills of the Urals. The special qualities of this breed were recognized 130 years ago, and breeding centres for them were first set up in 1845.

In Bashkiria mares have been milked since the earliest times. A modern Bashkir mare of good quality is said to yield an average of 2000 litres (approximately 440 gallons) of milk during a lactation period of seven to eight months. This milk is much used for the production of *kumiss*, a drink which is considered to have dietetic and medicinal as well as alcoholic qualities. Stallions and geldings are used as dual-purpose horses—either under the saddle or harnessed to sleighs. Bashkir troikas are said to cover seventy-five miles a day over the snow.

An interesting breed not widely known is the Jomud Horse which shares with the Akhal-Teké (see p. 107) the distinction of being descended from the ancient Turkmene Horse. The Jomud has great powers of endurance, and took part in the now famous ride from Ashkhabad to Moscow, nearly 2700 miles, including 225 miles of desert which were covered in three days with a minimum of water. Jomud horses are smaller than Akhal-Tekés and are considered to be nearer the Arabian in conformation.

About seventy years ago the managers of the Kustanair Stud began crossing Kazakh mares (see p. 110) with Don and Strelets stallions. Later the stallions of other riding breeds were introduced. By 1950 a definite type had been fixed, now known as the Kustanair breed. These horses are well made, of medium height, and with all the characteristics of a riding breed. They are sometimes raced on the Alma-Ata, Rostov, and Lvov tracks. In colour they are usually chestnut or bay. In spite of being primarily riding horses, they are also used in harness on collective stud farms in Kazakhstan.

Latvia has always produced a good stamp of heavy horse, originally created by crossing local mares with Oldenburg stallions (see p. 68). The modern Latvian Harness Horse is a heavy animal with a well-developed body; it moves well at the trot. It is bred, for the most part, at collective and state farms in the Latvian S.S.R., and has taken prizes in competitions for heavy horses open to the entire Soviet Union.

In the far northern part of European Russia, in the valley of the river Pechora near the Arctic Circle, there exists a local breed—the Pechora—regarded by Russian experts as the descendant of a typical aboriginal Forest Horse. In the summer these horses are herded in the moors and meadows of the river valley, but the winter is so severe that stabling is provided and some hay is made available. Small, but with comparatively long bodies, they are used to draw sleighs or as pack-horses, although they are not capable of carrying heavy burdens.

Another interesting local breed is the Viatka Horse—or Pony, as it is sometimes called—which is found in the basins of the Viatka and Obva rivers. It has been noted for over a century as being particularly suitable for use in Troika sledges. This breed has a peculiar trotting gait which is well suited to snowbound roads and tracks. Viatka Troikas are said to have covered 160 kilometres (about one hundred miles) in twenty-four hours. The horses are generally grey in colour, with an aboriginal dark dorsal stripe.

Another very ancient breed is the Zhmud from Lithuania, which Russian experts believe has been bred in the Baltic area since the Bronze Age. These horses are small, but well built and compact, with good action both walking and trotting. They are said to trot twelve miles within an hour on country roads. Some have been broken for riding and even for competition work. One Zhmud stallion won a restricted class in a jumping competition open to the whole Soviet Union.

Russian horses of less importance, but well thought of in the regions where they are bred, include such saddle breeds as the Kushum and the Ukrainian, both of which are half-bred, showing some Thoroughbred influence, a heavy draught breed in Byelorussia, and Steppe breeds such as the Adaev, the Buriat, and the Transbaikal. There are also breeds in upland districts, with the particular qualities necessary for traversing mountainous trails and passes: the best known of these not fully described below are the Azerbaijanian, and the Tushin.

The forest areas of Russia have some well-established local breeds and types, including the Estonian Klepper, the Mezien, the Minusin, the Obvin, and the Tawda.

The Russian Ministry of Agriculture has kindly provided measurements of the eighteen breeds described below, and details of the speeds attained by the racing breeds; since most of these are little known outside the Soviet Union it is thought that the figures will be of interest. Measurements are given in centimetres. For readers not accustomed to metric measurement, it may be helpful to know that 100 centimetres is almost exactly 10 hands, so 150 centimetres is almost exactly 15 hands, and so on; also that 1 kilometre is approximately three-fifths of a mile.

The Akhal-Teké (See Plate 121)

The Akhal-Teké is a very ancient breed. Study of horse skeletons found during archaeological excavations at Anau near Ashkhabad has shown that horses of fine bone and elegant conformation were bred in the territory of Turkmenia as far back as 2500 years ago.

Over the centuries the history of the Akhal-Teké has been so closely associated with the history of the Turkmenian people that it is sometimes confused with the original Turkmene Horse. In the Middle Ages Turkmene horses, and later Akhal-Tekés, were exported in large numbers to Russia and European countries where they were extensively used at stud. The modern Akhal-Teké is marked by a particularly majestic appearance, unusual conformation, and light but strong bone. The measurements of an average stallion are:

Height, 157·2 cm; length of barrel, 158·1 cm; chest, 174 cm.

A characteristic feature is the short silky tail, and many Akhal-Tekés have very small manes and forelocks. Various colours are found—bay and light bay, black, chestnut, grey, and sometimes cream. There is very often a pronounced metallic bloom, either golden or silvery, to their coats, which looks amazingly beautiful in the sunlight.

This breed is unique, not only because of its antiquity, but because the methods of horse-breeding traditionally used in the oases of Central-Asian deserts are so very unusual. Throughout the year the Turkmens kept their horses tethered and under blankets. They fed them with light but highly nutritious food such as pellets containing mutton fat, barley, and alfalfa. Akhal-Teké horses are well adapted to a hot climate and are capable of covering great distances through desert conditions. In 1935 a group of Turkmens riding Akhal-Teké and Jomud horses travelled 4300 kilometres from Ashkhabad to Moscow. This journey became famous, partly because it included 225 miles of arid Kara-Kum desert which were covered in three days, virtually without water.

Akhal-Tekés have earned a high reputation throughout the Soviet Union by their successes in all forms of competition. They have won races on innumerable occasions and also excel in dressage. For example, the stallion Absent won a gold medal for dressage in the 1960 Olympic Games in Rome, and four years later he won a bronze at Tokyo. His sire had excelled in the high jump, and many other Akhal-Tekés have achieved fame in other forms of competitive horse-sport.

The best Akhal-Tekés are bred in Turkmenistan, particularly at the Ashkhabad Stud; they are also bred at the horse-breeding departments of Turkmen collective farms, and in a branch of the Tersk Stud in northern Caucasia. Originally, the Turkmens kept no Stud Books, though they could remember with accuracy the pedigrees of their horses for many generations. Now Stud Books are prepared systematically and issued periodically. Only pure-bred Akhal-Tekés are allowed to be bred from or to be entered in the Stud Book.

The Budenny (See Plate 122)

This breed was evolved in the Rostov region between 1920 and 1950 by crossing Don mares with Thoroughbred stallions. These produced what were known as Anglo-Dons. The best of these were inter-bred, and after a very strict selection the best of their progeny were used at stud. The foundation stock consisted of only 10 per cent of the mares and 5 per cent of the stallions from the original total of Anglo-Don cross-breds that were available. The selected cross-breds were kept on the best possible pastures and in the winter were stabled and given the highest possible level of feeding; they were then further tested on race courses and in riding clubs. Only the best were used eventually for the production of the Budenny breed.

The present-day Budenny Horse is good tempered and well made, with a massive body and strong legs. The average measurements of a stallion would be as follows:

Height, 163·4 cm; length of barrel, 164·8 cm; chest, 188·8 cm.

Budenny horses were originally intended mainly for military purposes and a great number of them were used in the Russian cavalry divisions now no longer in service. Today horses are widely used in various equestrian sports and take part in races throughout the Soviet Union. The record time for a two-year-old Budenny over the distance of 1200 metres is 1 minute 16 seconds, while three-year-olds have covered 2·4 kilometres in 2 minutes 38 seconds, and adult Budennys have covered 7 kilometres in 8 minutes 25·5 seconds.

Budenny horses have won many steeplechases, including that at Pardubice (see p. 53), and other competitive events, both in the U.S.S.R. and in international competitions. The horses are noted for their endurance which has been established in tests over long distances. The stallion Zanos covered 309 kilometres under the saddle in twenty-four consecutive hours (twenty hours in action with four hours of rest), while he and another stallion together travelled 1800 kilometres in fifteen days.

Budenny horses are still bred mainly in the Rostov region and chiefly at the Budenny and First Cavalry Army Studs. A Stud Book is regularly published.

The Don Horse (See Plate 123)

The Don breed was widely known as the horse used by the Don cossacks as far back as the eighteenth century. In earlier days Don cossacks had ridden a rather small horse of the Nogai (Tartar) type, which from time immemorial had been distributed over the Steppes in the area of the Black Sea and the Don.

Don cossacks kept their horses in herds on the vast Steppe pastures. Captured stallions of southern breeds, such as the Karabakh, Turkmene, and various Persian breeds, were set free to breed with the herds, and from them the Don Horse has inherited some characteristic features, including its original colour—chestnut with a golden sheen. In the nineteenth century there was a certain amount of crossing with English Thoroughbreds, Strelets, and other breeds, but from the beginning of this century the breed has been kept pure and no outside blood has been introduced.

Throughout the year the horses are still kept in herds on the Steppe pastures. In winter the Don horses must forage for themselves and scrape away the snow to get at the food lying underneath it; only when conditions are particularly unfavourable are they also given a little hay and occasionally grain. The Don is one of the few breeds adapted to the hardships of life when herded on the Steppes.

The present-day Don Horse is relatively tall with a massive frame. The measurements of an average stallion are:

Height, 162·6 cm; length of barrel, 163·6 cm; chest, 190·8 cm.

Typical Dons are well made with a long deep body and a sound constitution. They are renowned for their endurance in all forms of work, for this is an all-purpose working horse successful both in harness and under the saddle. It is particularly used by shepherds in the live-stock-producing regions of the Steppe and in semi-desert zones in the south-east European part of the U.S.S.R., Kazakhstan, and Kirghizia.

Don horses regularly compete in races throughout the Soviet Union, though they are successful mainly in the long-distance events. In 1951 the stallion Zenith established a record by covering 311·6 kilometres in twenty-four hours (twenty hours in action with four hours rest).

The best Dons are bred in the Budenny Stud and the Zimovnikov Stud in the Rostov region, and also in Kirghizia and Kazakhstan. They are also bred in collective and state farms throughout these regions. A Stud Book of pure-bred Don horses is published from time to time.

The Kabardin (See Plate 117)

This breed has been known since the sixteenth century but became famous late in the seventeenth. Kabardins are derived from aboriginal mountain horses improved by crossing with southern breeds (Karabakh, Turkmene, or Arab). Some influence was also exerted by the horses of nomad Nogais who used to roam the Steppes of Northern Caucasia.

The Kabardin is the best mountain breed in the Soviet Union. It has a remarkable ability to climb steep slopes and will carry its rider safely over very narrow cliff trails and across fast running streams. These qualities are due to its calm temperament, well-built frame, and stout but relatively short legs. The average measurements of a stallion are as follows:

Height, 152·7 cm; length of barrel, 153·0 cm; chest, 175·6 cm.

The normal colours are bay and black. The breed is popular far outside the country of its origin and is distributed in many regions of the Caucasus, where it is valued not only as a reliable means of transport but for local competitive purposes. Races are run in the area, and, although less fast than specialized riding horses, Kabardins are well suited for local equestrian sports, and particularly for riding in the mountains and long-distance journeys; for example, in the winter of 1935–36 they were used for a trial round the Caucasian ridge when they covered a distance of 3000 kilometres, under extremely adverse conditions, in thirty-seven days, and showed themselves to have greater endurance than any other breed tested.

The best Kabardin horses are bred at the Malokarachayev Stud and also at some of the collective farms in the Kabardin-Balkar Autonomous Republic.

The Karabair (See Plate 120)

This breed comes from Uzbekistan and is regarded as one of the most useful of Central Asia. It is particularly used in areas where irrigation farming is practised. The origin of the breed is lost in antiquity, but excellent horses bred in the territory which is now Uzbekistan are mentioned in descriptions of military campaigns some 2400 years ago. Since then, for many centuries Karabairs have been used as dual-purpose harness and riding horses.

Their size and conformation have much in common with Arabian horses, though Karabairs are not so elegant or so graceful in action. At the same time they have sound constitutions, exceptionally powerful legs, and an amazing endurance in work. The measurements of an average stallion are as follows:

Height, 154·0 cm; length of barrel, 154·0 cm; chest, 176·8 cm.

The principal colours in the breed are bay, chestnut, and grey. They are raced over the Tashkent courses and have done well in races confined to local horses. They are also employed in equestrian games which are very popular in Central Asia and especially in the little known game of 'Kok-par' which has been described as "A mixture of polo, pig-sticking, mounted Rugby, all-in-wrestling from the saddle, and superb horsemanship."[1] The game is played by teams which can be of any size. Officially, the object is to secure the carcass of a stuffed goat and carry this through the opponent's goal. Unofficially, it is often played with no goals, very few rules, and numerous casualties. The game requires great strength, endurance, speed, and flexibility, and the horses that have been successful in this game are considered to be particularly valuable.

Karabairs are bred at the Dzhizak Stud near Samarkand and also at some collective farms in Uzbekistan. A Stud Book is kept for the breed.

The Karabakh (See Plate 118)

This breed originated in the Karabakh uplands between the rivers of Araks and Kura in Trans-Caucasia, that is, in Azerbaijan.

The Karabakh has been influenced by a number of famous Oriental horses, such as the Arabian and the Akhal-Teké, and by Persian breeds. It became widely known in the eighteenth century when Karabakhs were exported in large numbers to many areas, including the Don Steppes, where they played a prominent part in the formation of the Don breed.

The Karabakh is a typical mountain riding horse, rather small, good tempered, energetic, and with a good action in the walk and the gallop. The average measurements of a pure-bred stallion are:

Height, 146·5 cm; length of barrel, 146·5 cm; chest, 163·0 cm.

A feature of the Karabakhs is their colour; this may be chestnut, bay, or dun, but like several Russian breeds it has a well-defined metallic sheen, generally of gold.

[1] Mandrake in *The Sunday Telegraph* (November 3rd, 1968), describing the Afghan version of the game.

Karabakhs are used for riding purposes, for long journeys in the mountains, and also in the Caucasian equestrian games including Chavgan, a variety of polo, and Surpanakh, which could be described as mounted basket-ball. Karabakh horses have been frequent winners in equestrian competitions open to the entire Soviet Union. They are sometimes raced on the Baku course. A record time for two-year-olds over 1·2 kilometres is 1 minute 30·4 seconds, while adult horses have covered 2·4 kilometres in 3 minutes 2 seconds.

Karabakh horses are bred at the Akdam Stud in the Azerbaijan S.S.R. In order to improve their conformation and their working qualities pure-bred Arab stallions are sometimes used.

The Kazakh

Excavations of burial mounds dating back some 1300 years revealed the skeletons of nomads buried together with their horses. Study of the equine bones found have shown that by that date horses were already being bred in the region of Kazakhstan, and that they resembled modern horses very closely, both in size and in conformation. Kazakhs are typical Steppe horses, well accustomed to pastures which are semi-desert and where frequent droughts and temperatures of up to forty degrees centigrade in summer and down to minus thirty degrees centigrade in winter are not unknown. Sometimes the snow is fifteen inches deep, but even under these adverse conditions Kazakh horses are expected to find their own food on the pastures.

Reared in these conditions, the horses are rather small and have relatively long and deep bodies. The measurements of a typical stallion are:

Height, 143·0 cm; length of barrel, 151·0 cm; chest, 176·0 cm.

The colours vary from bay to chestnut and from grey to black. Greyish, piebald, dun, and dappled colours are found occasionally. The breed is used under the saddle, for herding cattle, for journeys across country, and also compete in some of the national equestrian sports, especially in the long-distance events, the so-called 'baiga'. The stallion Tshan covered 100 kilometres in 4 hours 6 minutes, while many of the better Kazakh horses can cover 300 kilometres in twenty-four hours (twenty hours in action with four hours at rest). Some horses amble as opposed to trotting and these are especially valuable for riding purposes because the gait is so comfortable. It is still a common practice to milk mares and the milk is often made into *kumiss*. The daily yield of mares is approximately ten litres of milk. Kazakh horses are also widely used as meat-producing animals and are grown up to a weight of approximately 450 kilograms (9 cwt).

Kazakh mares are particularly fertile when crossed with stallions of better quality breeds— *i.e.*, with Thoroughbreds, Don horses, or Heavy Draught horses. They are bred at many collective state farms in Kazakhstan while the Mugodzhar Stud is concentrating on selective breeding with a view to improving the standard of the breed as a whole.

The Lithuanian Heavy Draught Horse (See Plate 115)

The origin of this breed dates back to 1879 when a Zhmud horse-breeding society was formed in Lithuania. Zhmud horses were crossed with various breeds with the intention of obtaining bigger horses. Crossing with the Swedish Ardennes proved to be especially effective.

Five hundred and sixty Swedish Ardennes were imported into Lithuania, including 175 stallions. Only the best cross-breds that corresponded in type and conformation to the strong, good-tempered agricultural horse that it was desired to produce were used by the breeders of what became the Lithuanian Heavy Horse.

As the result of prolonged selected breeding with Zhmud-Ardennes crosses the Lithuanian Heavy Draught Horse was evolved and became officially registered in 1963.

The measurements of an average sized stallion are:

Height, 157·2 cm; length of barrel, 164·2 cm; chest, 199·2 cm.

These horses are well made with a long broad body and powerful, relatively short legs. They have a fine head with a broad forehead inherited from the Zhmud. They are mostly chestnut in colour, but some of the horses are bay and red.

Lithuanian Heavy horses are good natured and have good free action, both in the trot and in the walk. Working qualities are of a high standard; they will cover 2 kilometres in 7 to 8 minutes in an ordinary harness, the best result so far obtained being 2 kilometres in 5 minutes 24 seconds. They have great pulling power and are invariably prize winners in pulling competitions and in contests between heavy horses open to all the Soviet Union.

Lithuanian Heavy Draught horses are bred at the Neman, Sudav, and Zhagar Studs as well as at horse-breeding branches of collective and state farms. A Stud Book is kept.

The Lokai (See Plate 119)

Lokais are bred in Tadjikistan in the valleys and mountainous regions formed by the western ridges of the Pamirs. The breed originated in the seventeenth century. The constitution and conformation of Lokais have been influenced by the Arabian and Karabair breeds. The measurements of a typical stallion are:

Height, 151·0 cm; length of barrel, 151·5 cm; chest, 172·0 cm.

The colours are grey, bay, and chestnut; as with many Russian breeds they often have a characteristic golden tint. Not infrequently horses are found with curly hair; sometimes the curls are so thick as to remind one of astrakhan fur.

Lokais are indispensable for work in the highlands and are often employed at an altitude of 3000 metres above sea-level. They have very hard hooves and regularly work unshod on rocky trails. They are used as saddle and pack horses and are often entered for local equestrian sports; they are also raced on the Dushanbe course. The record time for two-year-olds over 1·2 kilometres is 1 minute 22·9 seconds, while adults have covered 7 kilometres in 9 minutes 12·2 seconds. They are bred at the horse-breeding departments of collective and state farms.

The Novokirghiz

Novokirghiz horses are bred in the Kirghiz S.S.R., especially in the mountain regions of Tien Shan, at altitudes between 2000 and 3000 metres above sea-level. The breed was evolved by crossing the under-sized aboriginal Kirghiz Horse with pure-bred riding breeds and with the Don Horse. This crossing was begun about a hundred years ago. When random crossing had achieved some improvement in the original breed, other methods of breeding were introduced and selective work with the best of the cross-breds was carried out. After a number of generations of selective breeding the new variety was officially recognized and was registered in 1954. The measurements of an average stallion are:

Height, 153·2 cm; length of barrel, 157·1 cm; chest, 180·8 cm.

Novokirghiz horses are well made with long broad bodies, relatively short legs, and very hard hooves. The large volume of their chests is due to their extremely well-developed lungs which makes it possible for them to live and work in the mountainous areas.

Novokirghizs are mainly used under the saddle for journeys on mountain trails and also to control herds of cattle when these are driven from one seasonal pasture to another, from the valleys in winter to high-level meadows in the summer.

They are sometimes raced on the Frunze course. The record time for two-year-olds over 1·2 kilometres is 1 minute 20·8 seconds, while adults have covered 7 kilometres in 8 minutes 42·6 seconds. Carrying a rider and a pack load of 150 kilograms (nearly 3 cwt) Novokirghiz horses have covered 110 kilometres of mountain trails, crossing high passes, in 11 hours 10 minutes.

These horses are bred in herds on mountain pastures. The best stock is to be found at the Naryn and Kirghiz Studs, as well as at horse-breeding departments of collective farms.

The Orlov Trotter (See Plate 124)

This breed dates back to 1778 when Count Alexei Orlov commenced breeding at the Khrenov Stud. He mated a stallion called Polkan (descended from the famous white Arabian Smetanka) to a dun Dutch mare and produced the celebrated grey stallion Bars 1 who was born in 1784. This stallion had valuable qualities, later developed by inbreeding and inherited by the modern Orlov Trotters. He was described by contemporaries as a tall horse of elegant conformation, with outstanding action, especially in the trot. He was mated to selected mares of similar origin—i.e., cross-bred Arabian-Dutch.

Orlov Trotters were already widely known by the beginning of the nineteenth century and had become one of the most famous breeds in Russia. An important part in the improvement of this breed has been played by systematic tests of Trotters on race courses. In Moscow trotting races were first held in 1799 and took place generally in winter with the horses racing with light sleighs. In 1834 the Moscow Trotting Society came into being.

The improvement of Orlov Trotters in terms of speed can be seen from the following figures. In 1836 the champion was the stallion Bychok who covered 3·2 kilometres in 5 minutes 45 seconds.

Thirty years later the stallion Poteshny covered the same distance in 5 minutes 8 seconds. By 1894 the record was reduced to 4 minutes 46 seconds. At the present time the record for this distance is 4 minutes 20·3 seconds.

It is important to note that although always used on race courses Orlov Trotters have never been purely race horses. They have also been employed in drawing coaches, phaetons, and Russian troikas. Also, they have long been used to improve agricultural horses.

For that reason horses for breeding have always been chosen not only on the grounds of speed but for other qualities as well. The breeders have always preferred horses of a good height with a substantial frame and attractive conformation. Other valuable qualities of Orlov Trotters include a sound constitution, high fertility, longevity, and the ability to become acclimatized in the different conditions from northern regions of European Russia to Central-Asian areas.

The measurements of an average Orlov stallion are:

Height, 162·6 cm; length of barrel, 164·5 cm; chest, 184·6 cm.

The usual colours are grey, bay, black, and chestnut. They are bred at a great number of Studs, the best known of which include Khrenov, Moscow, Tula, and Perm.

The Russian Heavy Draught Horse

This breed was founded about one hundred years ago at a number of Stud Farms, mostly in the Ukraine, which crossed local cart-horse mares with Ardennes and Percheron stallions and also with selected Orlov Trotters. Resulting cross-breds were selected for inter-breeding with a view to producing a powerful horse for agricultural work, which would be hardy and not unduly massive, as it was required to work fast. Success was achieved within a few generations and Russian Heavy Draught horses won a number of awards at the Paris Exhibition of 1900.

The present-day horse has a long powerful body on relatively short legs, which permits the horse to develop great traction power. The horses are energetic and active and are known for their good nature. Their normal colouring is chestnut or dark chestnut and the measurements of an average stallion are:

Height, 148·5 cm; length of barrel, 158·4 cm; chest, 184·5 cm.

Russian Heavy Draught horses have done well in competitions open to the whole Soviet Union. One stallion trotted 2 kilometres in 5 minutes 36·4 seconds with a load of 600 kilograms (nearly 12 cwt) and it is claimed that a team of three Russian Draught horses once drew a vehicle containing no less than seventy persons.

The breed is distributed throughout collective and state farms in the Ukraine, the Urals, and in other localities. The best horses are bred in the Novo-Alexander and the Kuedin Studs.

The Russian Trotter

This breed was evolved by a long-term programme of selection between crosses of Orlov and American Trotters. As early as the nineteenth century the American Trotter began to surpass the Orlov Trotter on the race course, and as a result the best Orlov mares were crossed with outstanding American stallions, including the world-record holder of its time, Cresceus. Altogether 156 American stallions were used, of which, however, only half a dozen produced offspring which have played a prominent rôle in the formation of the Russian Trotter.

Although faster than Orlov Trotters, Orlov-American cross-breds were smaller and less handsome and were poorly suited for effecting improvements in agricultural horses. Therefore, a subsequent selection was concentrated both on increasing their speed and also on improving their size and conformation. This phase of the breeding had practically been finished by 1940.

The Russian Trotter of today has almost exactly the same measurements as the Orlov Trotter. The measurements of an average Russian Trotter stallion are:

Height, 162·0 cm; length of barrel, 162·6 cm; chest, 183·0 cm.

In some respects the conformation of Russian Trotters is reminiscent of their Orlov and American ancestors—i.e., a well-proportioned, slightly convex head, a long and elegantly arched neck, powerful shoulders, a deep broad chest, and stout legs. The colours are usually black, bay, or chestnut.

Races take place on most of the race courses in the Soviet Union, the fastest time being recorded on the Moscow, Odessa, Kharkov, Kuibyshev, Perm, and Alma-Ata courses. Adult Russian Trotters are recorded as having covered 1600 metres in 1 minute 59·6 seconds, 3·2 kilometres in 4 minutes 10·4 seconds, and 6·4 kilometres in 8 minutes 55 seconds.

113 *CRIOLLO*

114 *VLADIMIR HEAVY DRAUGHT HORSE*

115 *LITHUANIAN HEAVY DRAUGHT HORSE*

116 *SOVIET HEAVY DRAUGHT HORSE*

117 *KABARDIN*

118 *KARABAKH*

119 *LOKAI*

120 *KARABAIR*

121 *AKHAL-TEKÉ*

122 *BUDENNY*

123 *DON*

124 *ORLOV TROTTER*

125 *TERSK*

126 *WALER*

127 *BARB*

128 *PERSIAN ARAB*

A number of Russian Trotter stallions have successfully competed in international events in different European countries.

Russian Trotters are bred in Studs and horse-breeding departments at collective and state farms. The fastest horses are bred at the Lavrov, Elan, Dubrov, Zlyn, and Smolensk Studs. A State Stud Book of Russian Trotters is kept.

The Soviet Heavy Draught Horse (See Plate 116)

This breed was formed by improving local horses with crosses of Belgian Brabants, Ardennes, and Percherons. This crossing was carried out on a wide scale in a number of regions in European Russia in the latter half of the nineteenth and the early twentieth centuries. The best specimens among the cross-breeds were chosen and were then used for selective breeding. The formation of the breed was completed by 1940. Soviet Heavy Draught horses are less massive, more mobile, and better adapted to the Russian climate than their counterparts in Western Europe. The measurements of a typical stallion are:

Height, 160·0 cm; length of barrel, 167·2 cm; chest, 203·1 cm.

These horses have the conformation typical of harness horses. They possess a long body, stout legs, and an excellently developed muscular system. They are good tempered but energetic in work. They will trot a kilometre in 3 to 3½ minutes harnessed to a cart carrying 1300 to 1500 kilograms (over 15 cwt). A stallion has pulled a load of 21,750 kilograms (over 21 tons).

In competitions for heavy horses open to the whole Soviet Union, Soviet Heavy Draught mares have become national champions in drawing weights against the clock.

Soviet Heavy Draught horses are the most popular agricultural horses in the U.S.S.R. being both the most widely distributed and the most numerous heavy horses in the country.

They are bred mainly at the Pochinkov and Mordovian Studs, and also at numerous horse-breeding departments of collective and state Studs in the Gorky, Ivanovo, and Vladimir regions as well as in other places. A National Stud Book is kept.

The Tersk Horse (See Plate 125)

This breed was evolved between 1921 and 1950 at the Tersk and Stavropol Studs in the Northern Caucasus. The breed was formed with the deliberate intention of preserving the type of the old Strelets Horse which was famous in the latter half of the nineteenth and the early twentieth centuries, but which unfortunately practically died out during the First World War, at the end of which only two stallions, Cylinder and Tsenitel, were surviving.

The Strelets breed had been produced from pure-bred Arabians mated to Anglo-Arab mares from the famous Studs of Orlov and Rastopchin. They were considered to incorporate the best characteristics of the Arabian breed and were repeatedly awarded major prizes at international shows; for example, they received gold medals at the World Exhibition in Paris in 1900.

At the end of the First World War the two surviving stallions possessed well-defined features of the Arabian breed. They were of light-grey colour and had a characteristic silvery sheen. There were obviously too few Strelets to attempt pure breeding, so crossing with pure-bred Arabs and with cross-bred Arabs was begun. The resulting cross-breds were chosen very carefully for conformation, the strictest selection being made and the Strelets type being taken as a model.

After thirty years of selective work the type was sufficiently fixed for the new breed to be recognized and it was called the Tersk. Tersk horses are very like pure-bred Arabs in appearance, but they are larger. The measurements of an average stallion are:

Height, 154·0 cm; length of barrel, 154·5 cm; chest, 179·0 cm.

Most Tersk horses are of light grey or even white colour, often with a silvery sheen. Some have a flesh-coloured skin which shows through a white coat, creating a pinkish appearance.

Their gentle disposition, good ability for dressage, and striking looks have made the Tersk Horse very popular for circus work, and famous circus riders give brilliant performances on Tersk horses, not only in the Soviet Union but in many other countries.

From May to October races are held every Sunday at Pyatigorsk race course in which pure-bred Arabians compete against Tersk horses. The best time of a two-year-old Tersk up to the present moment over 1·2 kilometres is 1 minute 21·2 seconds, while three-year-olds have covered 2·4 kilometres in 2 minutes 40·2 seconds.

Tersk horses are very well suited for cross-country riding. They are bred at the Stavropol Stud situated sixty kilometres from the original Tersk Stud, which now has only pure-bred Arab horses.

The Toric Horse

This breed was produced at the Toric Stud in the Estonian S.S.R. Breeding began in 1894 when the Norfolk Roadster Hatman was introduced into the Stud. Hatman is recognized as one of the more important foundation sires of the breed. He was mated with mares of the local Estonian breed often called Kleppers; the offspring consisted of horses of uniform type with massive frames suitable for agricultural work. These qualities were consolidated by inbreeding to the foundation sire on a substantial scale. Other Norfolk Roadsters and some Orlov Trotters were introduced, great attention being devoted to the selection of horses whose conformation was free from defects and who possessed good working qualities.

The average measurements of a modern Toric stallion are:

Height, 157·0 cm; length of barrel, 162·0 cm; chest, 193·0 cm.

Toric horses are exceptionally well made with a long muscular body, short powerful legs, and a good free action both in the walk and the trot. They are noted for their good temper and are distinguished by their great working capacity and endurance. In weight-pulling trials a burden of 10,640 kilograms (nearly 10½ tons) has been moved by a single horse, while a distance of 10 kilometres has been covered in 25 minutes 10 seconds with a substantial load. Every year Toric horses show remarkably good results in competitions for heavy horses open to the whole Soviet Union. They have won championships both for drawing a heavy burden against the clock and in weight-pulling competitions. This breed is to be found in nearly all collective and state farms in Estonia. The best horses are bred at the original Toric Stud. A Stud Book is kept.

The Vladimir Heavy Draught Horse (See Plate 114)

This breed was evolved in the Ivanovo and Vladimir regions by crossing the local horse with Clydesdales and Shires. Breeding was started in 1886 at the Gavrilovo-Posadsk State Stables.

By 1920–25, a large number of cross-bred horses had been obtained. Subsequently, inter-breed crossing was discontinued, and the best cross-breds were mated with each other so as to consolidate their best qualities. This phase was finished by 1950.

Vladimir Heavy Draughts are massive, but very mobile and energetic, horses. The average measurements of a stallion are:

Height, 160·6 cm; length of barrel, 164·7 cm; chest, 196·4 cm.

The usual colour is bay. They are well made, having a body of moderate width, though long, and have stout legs and a sound constitution. Their special attribute is the combination of great pulling power with adequate speed in action.

In competitions for heavy horses open to the whole Soviet Union, the Vladimir stallion Grozny trotted 2 kilometres in 4 minutes 54 seconds with a load of 600 kilograms (over 11 cwt). The mare Kartinka walked this distance in 14 minutes 38 seconds with a load of 2500 kilograms (nearly 2½ tons). Vladimir Heavy Draughts are bred at collective and state farms of the Ivanovo and Vladimir regions. The best horses are found at the Yuryev-Pol'sk and Gavrilovo-Posadsk Studs.

The Yakut Horse

This is one of the most remarkable breeds in the world. The Yakuts' territory, which extends far beyond the polar circle, includes some of the coldest areas of the Northern Hemisphere, the average winter temperature being minus 40–50° C. Yakut horses graze on grasslands in the valleys of the Lena, Yana, and Kal'ma rivers and also on taiga glades, and dig out their food from under deep snow. No less stamina is required of Yakuts during the brief summer, when the animals are attacked by myriads of blood-sucking insects.

The Yakut Horse is used under the saddle, for pack transport, and in harness. It gives good meat and milk. On festive occasions, Yakuts are raced and compete in equestrian games.

Typical Yakuts stand up to 135 centimetres at the withers, and are distinguished by a massive long body and a deep chest. The best specimens stand up to 145 centimetres or even more. Their chest measures up to 200 centimetres and they weigh 500 to 550 kilograms (about 10 cwt).

Their skin is covered with luxuriant hair which is directly associated with the cold climate in which they live. On the body the hairs may be 8 to 10 centimetres long.

There are two well-defined types of Yakut Horse—the southern type, which is close to the Mongolian Horse from which type the Yakut is derived, and the northern type, which is larger. The origin of the latter has yet to be confirmed. It may have come from the white Tundra Horse whose remnants have been found in the valley of the river Yana (see p. 15).

The usual colours are light grey, greyish, or mouse-coloured. Many have a dark latticed pattern on their shoulders. In order to improve this very useful horse, the best specimens have been selected for inbreeding, and horse-breeding farms have been organized for this purpose.

OTHER NATIONS WITH BREEDS OF IMPORTANCE

AUSTRALIA was entirely without horses until they were imported by Europeans about two hundred years ago. The first arrivals came from South Africa and also, possibly, from South America, but European stock was soon being imported, and good English Thoroughbreds and pure-bred Arab stallions were in demand. The country is eminently suitable for horse-breeding and the Australians were successful in producing admirable saddle horses. It has been claimed that between Waterloo and the Crimean War "Australia possessed probably the best saddle horse in the world."[1] At the time of the First World War the Australian Waler was still recognized as one of the finest cavalry mounts in the world.

Inevitably, Australia became the principal source for the supply of chargers to the mounted units in the Indian Army.

At present Australia has about half a million horses of all ages. The official statistics are somewhat misleading in that they are often restricted to adults. For example, the actual total before 1965 was 520,000 of which 37,000 were under twelve months old—a thousand more than in 1964, which suggests that numbers are not likely to decrease. Of the remainder, about 23,000 were classified as adult draught horses—appreciably less than in 1964—while the balance, made up of riding and dual-purpose horses, showed a marked increase. Breeding of racing Thoroughbreds in Australia is increasing, more than 11,000 pure-bred mares being registered each year.

The Waler (See Plate 126)

About 160 years ago the light horses bred in New South Wales had won an enviable reputation and came to be known as Walers, from their place of origin. In the beginning all the settled districts of Australia were known as New South Wales; consequently all saddle horses shipped from these settled parts of Australia became known as Walers. After Australia was later subdivided into separate States this general term for the Australian-bred saddle horse still persisted.

Originally Walers were sired by Arabians, Thoroughbreds, or Anglo-Arabs out of the best available local mares, but as time went on these mares became increasingly clean-bred, and by the beginning of this century the Waler was close to being a pure-bred Anglo-Arab, in many cases with a preponderance of Thoroughbred blood.

In the First World War Walers were in demand as chargers for the Indian Army, while Australia herself provided a cavalry division mounted almost entirely on Walers, which played a leading part in defeating the Turks. Throughout the campaign Waler remounts were supplied in large numbers from Australia, the horses selected being mostly between 15 and 16 hands and of every colour except greys, which were not preferred for war in the desert.

At the end of the War Australian quarantine laws made it impossible for any of these Walers to return to Australia, so they were mainly destroyed in the desert by orders of the Australian Government. A bronze memorial in Sydney honours the memory of the horses which "fought" to free Palestine and to break the Turkish yoke. The inscription states that it was erected

By Members of the Desert Mounted Corps and friends, to the gallant horses who carried them over the Sinai desert into Palestine, 1915–19. They suffered wounds, thirst, hunger, and weariness almost beyond endurance, but never failed. They did not come home. We will never forget them.

[1] R. S. Summerhayes: *The Observer's Book of Horses and Ponies* (Frederick Warne and Co. Ltd, 1968; revised edition), p. 44.

This memorial virtually marked the gravestone of the Waler. But it is true that Australia continued a flourishing export trade of Waler-type horses until 1932. After this year the demand declined, not only for export but for home use, with the advent of the motor-vehicle, although many sheep and cattle stations in Australia still breed a superior type of stock horse. The same principle is followed of using a Thoroughbred sire over station mares for this purpose. Australian horsemen have always favoured the Thoroughbred cross in their stock horses.

Australian saddle horses of indeterminate breeding are sometimes still called Walers even today, but experts agree that, at the present time it would be difficult to find sufficient Walers of the standard of 1914 which could be used for cavalry purposes.

JORDAN includes a great part of what was originally known as Palestine—the "Promised Land" of the Old Testament. Horses were bred there from very early times and the largest contingent of chariots in the alliance which fought against Assyria 2500 years ago came from King Ahab of Israel (see p. 22). As he could contribute no cavalry, his horses were probably not up to the weight of an armed horseman.

About 1200 years ago, the Arabs of Palestine, known as "Tributary Arabs" to the Romans of Constantinople, formed a substantial part of the latter's cavalry in the war against Islam, and by then there can be no doubt that excellent chargers were being bred in what is now Jordan.

United Nations statistics show that the total number of horses in Jordan has fluctuated since the War, but seems to have settled down at about 10,000, of which the best are unquestionably at the Royal Stud described below.

The Jordanian Arab

For centuries the Jordanian Arab, sometimes known as the Desert-bred Arab, had been completely neglected as a breed. The best stallions were regularly exported, and for years grinding poverty forced Bedouins to accept even a few pounds for any foal, except only the very best bred of the females—*i.e.*, those coming from the strains which had been kept *asil* (pure-bred) for countless generations.

Continual breeding to a few bloodlines in a relatively small area may probably have led to some degree of inbreeding; it is certain that only a few bloodlines were preserved and that only the most promising young stock of these bloodlines were kept—in other words, there was most severe culling for generation after generation.

About ten years ago the Royal Jordanian Stud set about collecting and preserving the few remaining ancient bloodlines in the country. A thorough search was made and mares of purest lineage were discovered, in some cases drawing ploughs, in others carrying mounted policemen. Stallions of the rarest blood languished near the goat-hair tents of minor sheikhs far out in the desert. Good luck and much hard work served to trace the pedigrees of high-quality animals from over the border in Iraq or from the Beirut Race Course.

A nucleus was gradually built up of beautiful horses with tapered muzzles and high-held plumed tails. Every one was authentically *asil*. They show the *mitbah*, the characteristic arch at the top of the crest, and the concave profile, the *jiblah*, which is more pronounced in mares.

MOROCCO contains part of the fertile strip near the Mediterranean coast of North-west Africa, formerly known as Mauretania. It is possible that a wild horse may have survived the Ice Ages in this part of Africa (see p. 15). If this was not the case, as the region was totally surrounded by deserts and the sea, horses could only have reached it through the agency of man.

The earliest horse breeders known in Mauretania were the Phoenicians, who developed colonies there, including Carthage whose armies were noted for their cavalry 2200 years ago. By this time the Numidians and other African nations were well mounted and renowned as cavalry.

About 1600 years ago the Vandals rode their weight-carrying chargers into Spain, crossed the Strait of Gibraltar, and established an Empire in Mauretania. During their century of occupation, their heavy cold-blooded horses left a permanent mark on the horse population.

Next came a series of Islamic invasions which converted the inhabitants to Mohammedanism and impregnated their horses with Eastern blood. Tradition suggests that the first Islamic cavaliers came largely from Syria and Egypt, and later the Moslems enlisted great numbers of North African cavalry, to help them to conquer Spain.

Throughout the centuries of Turkish rule, Eastern remounts were regularly brought into Mauretania so that the principal native breed, the Barb, is often regarded as being of Eastern blood, though, geographically speaking, it comes from the western end of the Mediterranean.

The Barb (See Plate 127)

The Barb, formerly known as the Barbary Horse, is historically one of the most important, as well as one of the most controversial, breeds of horses. Barbs originated in the north-west corner of Africa—*i.e.*, in what is now Morocco, Algeria, and Tunis, a fertile haven surrounded by deserts and the sea. This area was sometimes known as Barbary, and old writers referred to its inhabitants as the "Moors". It was always known for its horses and, nearly two thousand years ago, the "dappled Moorish" breed was praised by Oppian as the best stayers known to him. In later centuries the Barb has been praised for its speed rather than for its staying power, which shows the effect of the great injection of Eastern blood described below.

Some thirteen hundred years ago, the Moslems conquered Barbary, thus introducing Eastern blood. The horses they introduced would have included desert-bred Arabians. The Arabian and the Barb have several things in common. Both are desert-dwelling descendants of horses which had originated in good grass country, but had been moved into areas where the quality of the grazing had deteriorated, and where even drinking water sometimes became scarce. Generations of privation have caused modification of conformation from which, in the case of the Arabian, "a terrible beauty is born", but when we consider the Barb, the wonder is not that the original Barbary Horse, with its large proportion of heavy diluvial Forest blood, has shrunk in stature and in substance, but that it should have survived at all.

Barbary horses, with all their virtues and faults, were well known in England by the time of Queen Elizabeth I, and Thomas Blundevill places them second in his list of horses, "beginning first with the Turke because he cometh farthest".[1]

The main asset which the Barb breed had (and has) is a remarkable turn of speed over short distances, coupled with endurance at a slower rate. Other assets, at the time when horse racing was first being taken seriously in Europe, were its availability and relatively low price. While the Turks occupied the eastern half of the Mediterranean from Albania to Egypt, the Barbary Coast was for years open to traders. Then, in 1662, the Barbary port of Tangier became the property of King Charles II of Britain as part of his wife's dowry; in the twenty-one years he occupied it, numerous Barbs were exported to Britain and throughout the Continent. After he handed it over to the Moors trading rights were extended to European nations, and the export of Barbs continued, so much so that by two hundred years ago inferior Barbs could be bought anywhere in North-west Europe at a low price. "They could be met with very common in the hands of our nobility and gentry, or, if you send to Languedoc or Provence in France, they could be bought there for forty or fifty Pistoles a horse."[2]

Many writers in the next few centuries recommended the Barb, both for racing and as a sire of race horses or hunters. For example, in 1686, Richard Blome, writing of "the several sorts of horses most in use", copies Blundevill in mentioning first the Turkish Horse "being extraordinarily swift . . . but the Turks are so unwilling to part with their breeds that of those that come to England, there are very few (if any) good in their kind." Like Blundevill, he next mentions the Barb, of which he states:

> When he is awakened and rode upon his mettle, no horse is more nimble, vigorous and adroit, and better for an Action [battle] of one or two hours. He makes a good stallion to breed Running Horses, [*i.e.*, race horses]—the colts that he gets being generally well winded, fleet and good at bottom [*i.e.*, at staying].[3]

The Barb has frequently been crossed with Arabian and also with other Eastern breeds; so much so that pure-bred Barbs are no longer often seen. Originally, they stood about 15 hands, with flat shoulders and a tail lower than the Arab, from which they also differ in having a "ram-

[1] Blundevill: *The Fower Chiefyst Offices belongyng to Horsmanshippe.*

[2] *The Sportsman's Dictionary or the Gentleman's Companion* (Fielding and Walker, London, 1778), "collected from the best authors, with very considerable additions and improvement by experienced gentlemen".

[3] Blome: *The Gentleman's Recreation.*

[117]

shaped head". Most of all, they differ from the Arabian in their nature; due, perhaps, to centuries of ill-usage, Barbs have acquired a reputation of being bad tempered and inveterate kickers.

In Africa most Barbs were prematurely weaned, insufficiently fed, and worked too young. Nevertheless, when the French occupied most of Barbary from 1830 until recent times, all mounted units of the French African Army rode Barb stallions. They praised the breed for its endurance, its modest demands in the way of feeding, and its weight-carrying capacity, but these qualities are most apparent in Barbs which have been well treated and adequately fed; unfortunately, such Barbs have now become few and far between, except at the Royal Stud of His Majesty King Hassan II of Morocco, where magnificent pure-bred animals are still to be seen.

The constant confusion between Arabians and Barbs in the minds of old-time writers (and a few modern ones also) stems from that fact that in many nations (including France, for example) Arabians are defined as "horses bred in the desert by Arabs". But there are deserts in many countries, and the inhabitants of North-west Africa are often described as 'Arabs' by French writers. For this reason, breeders of French Anglo-Arabs are most careful to make the distinction between Barb and Arabian, which some other continental nations seem to ignore.

IRAN is the modern name for Persia, which has been famed for its horses since the beginning of history. The new name was chosen to emphasize the debt the Persians owed to their Aryan ancestors who occupied the country some four thousand years ago. These Aryans were among the very earliest horse breeders (see p. 18), a fact which is stressed in present-day Iranian literature. For example, that well-known authority Brigadier-General Dr Jahangir Ashidari in his pamphlet *Horses in Ancient Iran*[1] relates how the "Indo-Aryan people . . . ventured to tamé wild horses and trained them so that they became one of the most valuable assets of Aryan culture. . . . With assistance from this nation, horses reached non-Aryan countries." He quotes from traditional Persian sources accounts of how domesticated horses were exported from Persia in very early times to Mesopotamia, Egypt, Greece, and even India, and quotes authority for his contention that the first horses taken into Arabia, about 400 B.C., were brought from Persia through the agency of Phoenician and Mesopotamian merchants and that the modern Arabian is descended, at least in part, from Persian ancestors. He also points out that some of the earliest representations of horses hitherto found in Egypt are attended by grooms dressed, not in Egyptian, but in Persian costumes.[2]

Whether or not we accept that Persia was the main country from which horses were distributed throughout the Middle East there can be no doubt that Persian horses were famous and that the Persian cavalry was for many years almost invincible. For example, King Shaipur I of Persia repeatedly defeated the Roman armies sent against him, and eventually captured the Roman Emperor Valerian. He is said to have used his imperial captive as a mounting stool. These and other Persian victories are commemorated by enormous rock carvings still to be seen in Iran (see Fig. 12, p. 23).

When the Mesopotamians first heard of horses they called them "the ass from the East" as well as "the ass from the mountains" (see p. 16). East of Mesopotamia Iran fills the gap between the Persian Gulf and the Caspian Sea so horses entering Mesopotamia from the East must have come through Persia.

Today Iran has nearly half a million horses—the fifth largest horse population in Asia. Although the country has been modernized to a remarkable degree in a relatively short space of time, horses must remain an essential part of its economy.

The majority of present-day Iranian horses are cross-bred and some 80 per cent are employed in agriculture. Besides the two principal native breeds described below, there are some English Thoroughbreds and some pure-bred Arabians. These are mainly at the Royal Stud or distributed between the Army and private breeding establishments.

In the desert horses are still sometimes ridden bit-less and bareback, but in the towns a high standard of conventional riding is practised. Horse-racing is extremely

---

[1] Part of an official report to the Veterinary Department of the Imperial Iranian Army and issued by the Imperial Iranian Government; p. 7.
[2] *Ibid.*, pp. 54–56.

popular, both on modern lines at race courses such as that at Teheran, or, in the ancient style, over six to eight miles of desert.

The Persian Arab (See Plate 128)

The Persians were racing horses 2700 years ago, and Persian authorities claim that the present-day Persian Arab is a direct descendant of these early race horses. Some Persians assert that these Persian Arabs were the ancestors of the better-known Arabian Horse, and therefore of the modern Thoroughbred. Obviously this is an extremely controversial matter. Mr Summerhayes put it: "There is a theory . . . that Persian horses were the ancestors of the Arabs, which finds a great justification in the looks and characteristics common to both breeds."[1]

The Persian Arabs of today stand rather higher than most Middle-east Arabs—at least 15 hands. They are elegant, noble looking horses, with much fire and speed. They show most of the Arabian characteristics including the large eyes, delicate prick ears, and high tail carriage, but have straight profiles, lacking the typical *jibbah* of the Arabian which we know so well. They are an elegant breed, very fast and with great stamina, and their good legs and feet, combined with innate sure-footedness, make them excellent mountain horses.

The Royal Stud at Farahabad outside Teheran has a number of Persian Arabs, some of which have been bred in the Stud. Experiments have been made in crossing Persian Arabs with Turkomans, with considerable success. They have also had success with Anglo-Persians bred from Persian mares by English Thoroughbreds. One of these, Tahmian, is a favourite pleasure horse of the Shah, while another, Azar, is used for ceremonial purposes.

The Turkoman

The Turkoman, the Jomud, and the Akhal-Teké are closely related descendants of the ancient Turkmene Horse of which Professor W. O. Witt (who occupied the Chair of Hippology in the Academy of Scientists of the Soviet Union) wrote: "The Turkmene Horse possesses the last drop of that valuable blood from which all the breeds of well-bred horses throughout the world have been developed."

Turkmene horses, known in the seventh century as "Turkoman Atti", were noted for their exceptional speed and endurance, and later were prized above all other horses known to the Muslims; for example, they were used exclusively by the personal bodyguards of the one-time rulers of the Mohammedan Empire, the Caliphs of Baghdad.

Turkoman horses owned by the Turkmen (or Tekkes) were recognized as a significant factor in war less than one hundred years ago; Lord Curzon quoted the Russian General Grodekoff: "We ought to take from the Tekkes all their best stallions and mares. They would then at once cease to be formidable."[2]

About the same time, an expert on horses, travelling in Iran, gave his opinion that Turkoman horses were "far and away the best Oriental horses after Arabs that I have seen. In some respects they are superior to Arabs."[3]

Other observers of this period noted with astonishment the Turkmen custom of keeping their horses rugged up throughout the year in all weathers. A report of the Royal Geographical Society in 1885 stated that the horses were covered up winter and summer "with great quantities of felt clothing, which has a tendency to make them delicate and invariably rubs off the mane". The same report mentions that the Turkmen water their horses "as often as they will drink, but at all times after drinking, put them into a gallop until a perspiration breaks out".

These ancient customs are, in the main, observed today. Breeding stallions are kept swathed up from ears to mid-tail in no less than seven rugs, each of which has a traditional name. These rugs are kept on even when the horse is being ridden, and removed only for racing and for stud purposes, and for a few minutes nightly, before sunset, to 'air' the horse before it is rubbed down.

Turkmen delight in racing, and every farmer or man of substance has one or more race horses in which he takes the greatest interest. Turkoman horses and their near cousins, the Akhal-Tekés, normally share the first places in Russian long-distance races and endurance tests.

Modern Turkoman horses continue growing until they are seven years old, at which age they average about 15·2 hands. They are noted for their skins and narrow chests and for their unique action which is described as "floating".

[1] Summerhayes, *op. cit.*, p. 183.
[2] Lord Curzon: *Russia in Central Asia* (Longmans, 1889), p. 129.
[3] *Life and Opinions of Sir Charles MacGregor* (Blackwoods, 1888; 2nd edition) ed. Lady MacGregor, vol. ii, p. 11.

TURKEY was for centuries the source of some of the best breeding stock available to European Studs. For example, the famous Byerley Turk, who features in the extended pedigree of virtually every Thoroughbred, was traditionally regarded as a Turkish Horse. Today, unfortunately, almost all the breeds of horses in Turkey are founded on imported stallions, particularly the Nonius from Hungary.

In addition to the Karaçabey described below, Government-owned Studs cater for Arabians, English Thoroughbreds, Anglo-Arabs, and ponies described as "indigenous", the latter being mainly native ponies which have been improved to a greater or lesser degree by an infusion of Arabian blood. In Kurdistan, a good-looking ornamental-type saddle horse called the Jaf is bred. It is generally rather over 15 hands high, and bay, brown, chestnut, or grey in colour.

The Karaçabey

The long-established Stud at Karaçabey, now run under the auspices of the Turkish Government and supervised by the Director-General of Veterinary Services, lent its name to a breed based on native horses improved by imported Nonius stallions (see p. oo). The result is a good-quality dual-purpose animal of about 16 hands; the best of them make good class saddle horses showing clear signs of their Nonius ancestry. They are popular with the Turkish Army who regularly purchase them as remounts.

The Karaçabeys are also used for light draught work and for agricultural tasks, and sometimes serve as pack-horses in the mountain areas. The breed at present is struggling to hold its own against competition, on the one side from Arabians, Thoroughbreds, and Anglo-Arabs, and on the other side from mechanization, which is becoming increasingly common, both for transport and for agricultural purposes.

A Turkish motto runs: "Sell the Black, never use the Bay, keep the White, but ride the Brown." In spite of this, Karaçabeys are regularly found of every solid colour and a white blaze is not unusual.

APPENDIX I

The Arabian and the Arabian Peninsula

Such is the excellence of the Arabian Horse, and so clearly, for several centuries, has the Arabian peninsula been the chief stronghold of the Arabian breed, that many have come to believe that the Arabian Horse must have originated in the Arabian peninsula itself.

For example, the late W. S. Blunt, father of that well-known expert, Lady Wentworth, supposed that there must have been "a primitive wild horse, indigenous to the Arabian peninsula". Many other writers have supported this belief. Other experts, basing their opinions on archaeological and historical evidence, take a contrary view, for reasons which are summed up below.

Professor Zeuner's map (see Fig. 3) makes it clear that prehistoric horses were, for the most part, far to the north of the Arabian peninsula, and separated from it by the area occupied by the onagers, which, Zeuner states, occupied parts of Arabia.[1] The old horse-like bones so far discovered in the Arabian peninsula have, in every case, turned out to be remains of onagers, not of horses.

The Old Testament, writing of the region north of the Arabian peninsula, refers often to asses and sometimes to camels, but until the time of Moses it never refers to horses. Abraham's possessions are listed in full—his flocks of sheep, his goats, and his asses, but never a horse.

Arabs, sometimes called "Aribi" or "Urbi", feature in many Egyptian and Assyrian records. Tribute extracted from Arab tribes was paid in camels, never in horses. One of the earliest references to Arabian warriors appears in the list of confederate rulers who opposed the Assyrian army some 2850 years ago (see p. 22)—"Ginzibu the Arab" is believed to have been an Arab Chieftain. On this list the Arabs are shown as being mounted on camels.

The Assyrians, who at that time occupied what is now Western Persia and Eastern Iraq, could mobilize some 2000 mounted soldiers. The cavalry of their enemies came from Syria, while the majority of their enemies' chariots came from what is now Jordan. In those days the occupants of these regions were not described as Arabs, though today the inhabitants of Syria, Iraq, and Jordan are generally recognized to be Arabs, and their horses are considered to be Arabians. The inhabitants of these countries have been noted horse breeders for over 3000 years, and many outstanding Arabian horses have come from these regions. For example, the Darley Arabian, which features in the extended pedigree of almost every Thoroughbred (see p. 50), was bought in Aleppo in Syria, while some of the best foundation stock of the Polish Arabians was bought in Iraq, or again in Syria at Aleppo or Damascus.

But the tribes of the Arabian peninsula itself were without horses until comparatively recently. The historical evidence has been summed up by Professor P. K. Hitti, Professor Emeritus of Semitic Literature at Princeton University: "Renowned as it has become in Moslem literature, the horse was, nevertheless, a late importation into Ancient Arabia. This animal, for which the Najd was famous, was not known to the early Semites."[2]

The Professor stresses that "in the early Persian records, the Arabian featured as a cameleer, not as a cavalier". He recalls that the historian Strabo, presumably on the authority of his friend Aelius Gallus, a Roman general who invaded Arabia as late as 24 B.C., denied the existence of the horse in the Peninsula".

From this evidence, it seems clear that the horse was introduced into the Arabian peninsula by the agency of man. South-western Arabia—now the Yemen—was formerly a fertile agricultural area. Some 300 years before Mohammed it was occupied by the Persians whose army consisted largely of cavalry, and who certainly would have introduced horses, which would have flourished south of the great central deserts.

When Mohammed began his ministry in 610, horses were scarce in north and central Arabia, and therefore expensive; they were one of the prerogatives of the wealthier warriors. Horses were quite out of the reach of the ordinary tribesmen and of all but the richest merchants, even in important towns. For example, some eighteen months after he fled from Mecca in A.D. 622, Mohammed led out his followers to attack and plunder a particularly rich caravan, consisting of over 1000 camels, returning to Mecca with priceless merchandise from Gaza. Mohammed's little army comprised 314 men with a total of seventy camels and just two horses. The wealthy merchants of Mecca learned of Mohammed's plan and despatched their strongest force to rescue the caravan. The Meccan army consisted of "seven hundred and fifty camel riders and a hundred horsemen".[3] These figures illustrate the shortage of horses, even in Mecca, the wealthiest city in Arabia at that period.

[1] Zeuner: *A History of Domesticated Animals*, p. 300.
[2] Professor Philip K. Hitti: *History of the Arabs* (Macmillan and Co., London, 1960), pp. 20 *et seq.*
[3] Glubb: *The War in the Desert*, pp. 62 *et seq.*

The earliest mention of horsemen serving with the Moslem armies appears twelve years later, when a Moslem general, Khalid, led a small mixed force of cavalry and camel men from Iraq to Damascus. It may be significant that Khalid, for about a year before this march, had been occupying an outlying province of Persia inhabited by tribes who had a long tradition of horsemanship. Khalid's force "rode camels. The few horses to be used at the time of the encounter were led alongside."[1]

Two years later, when the Byzantine Emperor assembled an army to drive the Moslems out of Damascus, he relied on "auxiliary cavalry recruited from the Tributary Arabs".[2] The "Tributary Arabs" in this case were from south Syria and Jordan.[3] So here again we find a force of Arab cavalry coming from areas outside the Arabian peninsula.

The first reference to a cavalry force raised from inside the Arabian peninsula is in A.D. 639, when a Moslem general invaded Egypt "with a force of 3000 Yemenite cavalry".[4] These were almost certainly mounted on horses descended from those introduced by the Persians into southern Arabia some 300 years before.

Not until the capital of the Moslem world was moved to Damascus in Syria, where horse-breeding had been practised for centuries, do we read of cavalry forming a substantial proportion of the Moslem armies, and, apart from the Yemenese, the earliest Arab cavalry came from tribes whose headquarters were outside the peninsula. By about A.D. 700, Moslem cavaliers had conquered and occupied all modern Turkey, Persia, Palestine, Syria, Northern Egypt, and coastal Cyrenaica, and Islam claimed sovereignty over Tripoli, Libya, and Morocco, whence they soon overran Spain. Apart from southern Russia, all the best known horse-breeding areas in the ancient world were in their power, and undoubtedly the best stallions and mares found their way back to Damascus, whence the most suitable animals, those from other desert areas, would have gone to the Moslem heart-land in central Arabia, where they were moulded by selective breeding into the present-day Arabian.

The evidence suggests that the ancestors of the modern Arabian have been bred by Arabs in the Arabian deserts for something over 1200 years, but not much longer. The probability is that their ancestors had been bred by other Arabs in other deserts for some 2000 years before that.

APPENDIX II

The Ancestors of the Thoroughbred

It has been pointed out elsewhere[5] that the world's present-day stock of Thoroughbred horses all stem from a few dozen particularly prepotent animals, every one of which was being bred from in Britain in the seventeenth or early eighteenth centuries. The most important of them had Eastern or African blood, and it is a historical curiosity that the Thoroughbred was produced at such a great distance from the sources of these stallions, which had to be conveyed round or across Europe to reach the islands where they achieved such remarkable results. All this gives particular interest to the British 'running horses' with which this imported blood was mingled.

Since Britain became separated from the Continent, when the sea-level rose nearly ten thousand years ago, no horses have crossed into Britain except by the agency of man. The first significant imports were the chargers ridden by Roman auxiliaries. They remained in Britain for over four centuries and their stallions must have affected those of the native ponies which had been domesticated. We know from archaeological evidence that these ponies stood only about 12 hands high. Julius Caesar praised them for their speed and stamina.

After the Romans, the Normans introduced new blood. For example, Duke Robert of Bellesme, created Earl of Shrewsbury, imported Spanish stallions to his Welsh estates. Later, the unpopular King John imported a hundred heavy Flemish stallions in an attempt to produce the weight-carrying chargers then required. Edward III imported fifty Spanish stallions for the same purpose, but nevertheless was forced to purchase foreign remounts, mainly from Hainault.

There can be little doubt that returning Crusaders brought Eastern stallions with them. For example, Richard I was presented with some noted stallions by his chivalrous opponent, Saladin, and would almost certainly have sent these horses home to Britain.

Nevertheless, by about 1550, roughly a century before the Thoroughbred began to come out of the melting pot, British horses were still little over 13 hands in height, and King Henry VIII

---

[1] Hitti, op. cit., p. 149.

[2] Bernard Lewis: The Arabs in History (Hutchinson University Library, London, 1958; Arrow edition), p. 53.　　　　　　　　　　[3] Glubb, op. cit., p. 173.　　　　　　　　　　[4] Lewis, op. cit., p. 54.

[5] See the article on "The Thoroughbred Horse", p. 50.

—who, in full armour, rode almost thirty stone—expressed the fear that "the breed of good strong horses might die out". Accordingly, he decreed that land owners must keep herds of breeding mares over 13 "handfuls" in height. He also prohibited the general use of stallions of less than 15 "handfuls", while every Archbishop and Duke had to keep "seven trotting stone horses for the saddle" each of which had to measure 14 hands at the age of three years.[1]

By this time racing had become extremely popular in Britain. The horses raised were variously described as "Galloways", "Running Horses", and "Hobbies". Since Galloways hailed from Scotland and Hobbies from Ireland, it is tempting to presume that Running Horses were the English equivalent of the other two, but this supposes a more precise classification than contemporary evidence will support.

Eastern blood had been introduced by about 1550. Blundevill's book, "The Arte of Riding",[2] lists the breeds of horses then known in Britain. He starts his list with "The Turke because he cometh farthest". Blundevill describes them as "very swift in their running and of great courage". He goes on to state that "All the horses which come from any of the Turkes' domains or the frontiers of his nearest neighbours be called Turkey Horses." This statement may be of importance because, as several writers have pointed out, Blundevill in his list of horses does not mention the Arabian Horse. Much of Arabia (and Syria) was then included in the Turkish Empire; moreover, Turkey cut off these areas from contact with the West because she controlled the coast of the Mediterranean from modern Greece, through Turkey itself, Syria, the Lebanon, Israel, and Egypt to Libya, so any Arabian imported into Britain at that time would have been called a "Turkey Horse".

But it is unlikely that many Arabian horses could have reached Britain before, at the earliest, 1580, when the Turks, for centuries opposed to peaceful contact with Christians, decided to permit trade with certain European countries, including Britain, and received an ambassador from Queen Elizabeth I, who wrote to the Sultan Murad III, pointing out their common interest in the fight against "idolators"—i.e., against Roman Catholics, who comprised a substantial proportion of her own subjects.[3]

After this diplomatic coup, "Turkey Horses"—possibly including Arabians—could have entered Britain more freely in spite of the difficulties involved in the journey. Second on Blundevill's list is "The Horse of Barbary", the modern Barb, which he describes as "little horses, but very swift and able to make a very long cariere [i.e., gallop] which is why we esteem them so much". It seems that Oppian's "dappled Moorish" had acquired speed.

Blundevill's list goes on to mention horses from Sardinia, Corsica, Naples, "The Jenett of Spain", the Hungarian, the "Highe Alamagne", and several other European breeds, ending with "the Iryshe Hobbye". Most writers in the next 100 years or so copy Blundevill's list almost exactly, starting with the Turk, followed by the Barb, and omitting the Arabian.

King Henry VIII acquired "Coursers" from Spain and Italy from 1520 onwards, and established a Royal Stud at Hampton Court, and others at Malmesbury and Tutbury, while James I imported several Oriental stallions, including the Markham Arabian (bought in Constantinople) which is said to have been last in every race it entered.

This horse appears in the list of "Arabians, Barbs, and Turks" which forms the Fourth Part of the fifth edition of the Stud Book.[4] The Introduction to this Fourth Part states:

> The date of the importation of the horses named below is in many cases unknown and can only be guessed at by the date of their produces (sic) besides which they may not have been imported at all but bred in this country [See Dodsworth below]. . . . It is evident from old records that there was a class of horses kept apart as 'running horses' and described as Barbary horses, Spanish Barbs, etc. . . . The horses called Arabian were probably from Persia and Syria.

The introduction goes on to state that the horses shown in the list "are arranged in about the order of date." At the top of the list comes the Markham Arabian, "said (but with little probability) to have been the first of that breed ever seen in England". He is followed by two Barbs and then by Place's White Turk (once the property of King Charles I, though this is not stated). Then comes "Dodsworth, though foaled in England, was a natural Barb, his dam, a Barb mare, was imported in the time of Charles II"; in other words, before "the time of Charles II"—i.e., before 1660—only four Eastern or African horses are named in this section of the Stud Book, where they are described as being one Arabian, two Barbs, and a Turk.

After 1660, King Charles II contracted with several breeders and dealers to supply him with an agreed number of horses and mares every year, many of which he presented to his favourites.

[1] Berenger: *The History and Act of Horsemanship*, vol. i, p. 176.
[2] Blundevill, *op. cit.*, Folio 6 *et seq.*
[3] *Encyclopaedia Britannica*, 1968 edition, vol. xxvii, p. 450.
[4] Published by Messrs Weatherby of London, 1891; p. 388.

On his death, numerous stallions, but only one brood mare, remained in the Royal Stable. This was the period of the famous 'tap-root' mares (see p. 32) from thirty of which every living Thoroughbred is descended. Formerly, it was supposed that most of these mares were of Oriental breeding, but modern research suggests otherwise.

> Only a few of them were imported, the remainder being native [English] bred and of mixed native and Oriental blood. The majority of the foundation sires were Oriental or quasi Oriental. . . . Few were ever certified as to blood or place or origin. . . . One thing emerges with certainty: the percentage of authentic Arabians was meagre, while that of Barbs was proportionately large. . . . This arises from the much greater facility with which both stallions and mares of that strain could be imported.[1]

Many readers will be astonished by the assertion that the Barb played a greater part than the Arabian at this stage of the Thoroughbred's development, because the modern Arabian so completely eclipses the modern Barb, but things were different 300 years ago, and it must not be forgotten that the Barb had been raced (and presumably bred from) in Britain since Blundevill's day, or that Charles II acquired Tangier on the Barbary Coast as part of his wife's dowry. He retained the port for some twenty years, after which it remained open to European merchants who exported many Barbs to Britain and the Continent.

Horses from the East, as opposed to those from North Africa, were seldom seen in Britain in those days. For example, the *Diary of John Evelyn* for December 17th, 1684, includes the following: "Early in the morning, I went to St James's Park to see three Turkish or Asian horses, newly brought over and now first shown to His Majesty." He related that there had been four, but one had died at sea during a nine weeks' voyage. They had been captured from "a Bashaw at the Siege of Vienna". He praised the horses lavishly and stated that the best was offered for 500 guineas, an enormous sum in those days, and that the spectators included His Majesty The King, the Prince of Denmark, the Duke of York, and "several of the Court Noble Persons skilled in horses". Ridden by a German, in full Turkish dress, they attracted huge crowds and were evidently a great novelty.[2]

The three stallions, from one or more of which every modern Thoroughbred is descended, were as follows. Firstly, the Byerley Turk, captured, like the horse described by Evelyn, at the Siege of Vienna, and subsequently used as a charger in 1690 by a Captain Byerley, who later placed him at stud in Yorkshire, the headquarters of the majority of the thirty tap-root mares.[3] The breeding of this stallion is uncertain, but Mr Rathbone points out that he may possibly have carried Turkmene blood. Next comes the Darley Arabian, bought in Aleppo (Syria) in 1704, and certified to be a pure-bred (Maneghi) Arabian. The third, the Godolphin Barb (or Arabian), was bought in Paris about 1730. His ancestory is uncertain and is strongly disputed. (See Plates 23, 24, and 25.)

After 1666, the expression "Running Horse" began to die out and we read of "Breed Horses" and "Bred Horses" which later came to be described as "Thro'bred", and by 1700 the term "Thoroughbred" began to be used.[4] About this time British Thoroughbred horses began to be exported. For example, in 1730 Bulle Rocke, a son of the Darley Arabian out of a mare of less distinguished pedigree, was exported to America (see p. 95).

APPENDIX III
Portuguese Bullfighting

Bullfighting on horseback, with all its traditions and techniques, is essentially a Portuguese art which dates back to the days when wild bulls were hunted with due ceremony on such special occasions as a royal marriage or religious festival. This highly dangerous sport became extremely popular, and eventually the Marquês da Marialva, himself a brilliant horseman, introduced new methods of attack and defence, and laid down principles which hold good to this day.

The Portuguese bullfighter rides an unpadded horse of the highest quality, which must not be touched by the bull, and this in spite of the fact that he will gallop head on towards the charging bull and avoid the horns only by a swerve at the last possible moment.

The horses selected for training for the bullring are mainly country-bred and are often the pick of the horses ridden by the "Campinos" who herd the bulls on the ranches where they are

[1] *Encyclopaedia Britannica*, 1968 edition, vol. xiii, p. 715.
[2] E. S. de Beer (ed.): *The Diary of John Evelyn* (Oxford University Press, London, 1959), p. 783.
[3] Mr G. Rathbone: "The Native British Foundation of the Thoroughbred Horse" in *The British Race Horse* (October, 1966), p. 449.   [4] *Ibid.*, p. 452.

bred. These horses stand about 15·2 hands and move with a high action. They come from generations of ancestors selected for the same purpose, and thus are ideal for working with bulls, having enough courage to face the horn and being sufficiently quick, tough, and powerful to keep out of trouble. They have quiet temperaments and quick reactions, and are thus easy to train. Arabs and English Thoroughbreds have the advantage of being faster, but are usually less suitable in temperament.

The horses selected for training are generally stallions and are not broken to the saddle until they are four or five years old. When perfectly broken and trained in the basic movements they begin training for the bullring. This takes many years, and only a few of the horses which begin training are eventually allowed to appear in the arena.

At an early stage they are tried with a *touro manso* or tame bull—*i.e.*, a bull which is so lazy or unaggressive that he does not launch himself in a full-blooded charge, but will only make half-hearted attacks on the horse and its rider.

This gives the horse more confidence and teaches it to circle a bull and to anticipate its movements. A good bullfighting horse will always watch the bull and not shy away from him. Horses which pass this test satisfactorily may go on to the next stage of training.

Before their education is complete, the horses are schooled in the classical manner to carry out the Piaffe, Passage, Pirouette, and other dressage movements. After this, each horse is trained with the *tourinha*, a wheel with bulls' horns on the front and a piece of cork on the top into which the Cavaleiro will stick his dart or *bandarilha*. A boy runs at the horse with a *tourinha* and the horseman practises different sortés—the name given to the different methods of engaging the bull.

Fighting bulls are bred by ranchers from specially selected cows mated to bulls which have excelled in the arena and which are reserved for breeding. Each spring it is customary to test the cows to see which have inherited the desired courage and ferocity to be used for breeding. Each rancher tests these cows in a small private bullring, and here partly-trained horses can get experience and increase their confidence: the cows are aggressive and fast on their feet, but they are much smaller than the fighting bulls and cannot do the horses any serious harm. Not until a horse is perfectly trained in every aspect of bullfighting, which takes many years, should he enter the arena with a fighting bull.

At the beginning of a Portuguese bullfight the horsemen enter the bullring and compliment the authorities and the public. They display their horses' artistry in the Piaffe, Passage, the Pass Espanhol, and other dressage movements. This interlude is known as the *Cortasias*.

The bull then charges out of the corral into the arena. By now, there will be only one, or, at most, two horsemen remaining to face him. Each Cavaleiro must have a thorough knowledge of the psychology of bulls and must be able to judge the bull's method of attack, his speed, his impetus, and the degree of his aggression. Bulls differ very much in their reactions; every bull has a remarkable instinct for defence and a prodigious memory. He learns to recognize and to anticipate the actions of the horseman, who in turn must anticipate the bull's reactions.

The Cavaleiro decides from which places in the ring he will carry out his sortés, each of which is a manoeuvre with a definite beginning and which proceeds to a definite finality. The bull must be in the appropriate part of the arena before each sorté is begun and must be dominated throughout by the skill of the horse and by the art of its rider.

In the classic *Sorté de Caras*, the bullfighter challenges the bull from in front so that he charges with all his force and weight. At this moment the horse gallops at full speed straight towards him. A few paces before the impending collision—which to the novice spectator seems to have become inevitable—the Cavaleiro turns his horse slightly to the left, away from the bull, who turns his neck to the right in an unsuccessful attempt to gore the horse. At the exact moment when the bull's head is directly under the horseman's arm, with the horns by his stirrup, the horse swings his hindquarters out, away from the bull, and the rider plants a dart at the base of the bull's neck, in the exact position and at the precise angle laid down originally by the Marquês da Marialva, so that had a sword been driven in to its full length the bull would have been killed instantly.

In some sortés, the Cavaleiro guides his horse only with his legs and by movements of his body so as to plant darts simultaneously with both hands. There is a great variety of sortés, each requiring a different technique, but all requiring knowledge, skill, and courage, and supreme horsemanship. The best Cavaleiros are artists in the true sense of the word.

When the Cavaleiro has dominated the bull, young men called *farcados* enter the ring on foot and subdue the bull with their bare hands. Eventually the bull is taken from the arena, dominated but virtually unhurt, and is reserved for breeding if his performance has warranted this, failing which he returns to the country or goes to the slaughterhouse. No bull is ever killed in a Portuguese bullring.

[125]

APPENDIX IV

Harness Racing in the U.S.A.

There was time when lovers of harness racing,[1] considered country bumpkins by snootier members of the Thoroughbred ranks, would often suffer some pointed reminder that Thoroughbred racing was "the sport of kings". The Trotting folk would acknowledge the fact and counter that the harness game owned the rarer distinction of being the pastime of a democracy.

Today the sport needs no defence at all. Ambitious breeding programmes, a high quality of competition, and increasing public interest in such diverse nations as Australia, France, Germany, Italy, Holland, Japan, New Zealand, Russia, and Scandinavia have confirmed this native American game as one of the U.S.A.'s most highly appreciated exports, and an overwhelmingly popular pastime of every conceivable form of society. Surprisingly enough, England, traditionally regarded as the Mecca of the horse-racing world, is one of the few countries in Western Europe in which harness racing has failed to stimulate any noticeable public interest.

In urban areas of the States, Standardbreds frequently make their appearance long after the sun has fallen behind the yardarm so as not to compete with day-time Thoroughbred racing. At these huge metropolitan racing plants, equipped with all the most modern facilities, including the automated mounted starting gate which solved the problem of false starts, frosty beams of light dance down on a sporting pleasure dome, complete with dining rooms and cocktail lounges and an atmosphere throbbing with the breathless excitement of a special brand of crowd which feels compelled to go wherever real action is taking place.

Seated in such a modern stadium, it is hard to believe that harness racing originated two centuries before electric lights existed, and, indeed, before the Republic itself was formed. The genesis of the sport lies in Colonial times when the jarring, rutted excuses for roads traversable by wheeled vehicles began to form a network of communication between the settlements. Since, in the human condition, the desire to race is as inherent as original sin, it was not long before erstwhile innocent carriage folk began to relish a lusty test of their roadster's speed. Preserving their safety and their respectability, the contestants restrained their horses to the more conservative gaits of the trot and pace customarily used by the roadster—the trot being a vastly extended, high-speed version of the natural two-beat trot in which the diagonal legs move in unison, and the pace being a two-beat gait also characterized by speed and extension, but distinct from the trot in that the *lateral* legs function in unison. Though an inclination to perform at the lateral gait is a congenital and usually hereditary tendency, the perfection of the pace is an accomplishment of man's, so that, technically, the gait is considered an artificial movement.

The aura of lace-curtain respectability which attached itself to harness competitions during the nineteenth century had an effect on the popularity of harness racing. Though no formula has yet been volunteered to suggest in what ratio the speed of a Thoroughbred affects the wickedness of man, it is nevertheless true that any smirch upon the gallopers' sport, inopportunely revealed during one of those national spasms of righteousness which occurred towards the end of the last century, would incite the temperance zealots, reformers, and guardians of public morality into a tirade against the entire Thoroughbred community. This, "the sport of kings," was occasionally also regarded as an invention of the devil, and in some states Thoroughbred racing was suspended until the coming of more lenient times.

While harness-racing history had no complete immunity from similar internal scandal, its disorders escaped excessive public indignation because, after all, the horse and carriage was an institution necessary and useful as a means of transportation for all social classes. In principle, the harness horse was a labourer in the vineyard, not a contrivance for man's gaming instincts, and since the animal had an intrinsically respectable function, a turn on the track at race meetings and holidays was too slight a taint to cause a fall from grace.

Then, too, trotting and pacing have traditionally been a sport of the people, of ordinary hard-working folk whose roots lie in the rural towns and villages of the country. Even today, far from the urgency and razzle-dazzle that surrounds metropolitan contests, harness racing prospers as a favourite diversion in agricultural regions, amid a particularly relaxed climate of friendly informality. The feeling was that the activities of honest, salt-of-the-earth people could by no means be as sinful as the murkier sports of aristocrats, known for their vice and degeneracy.

Thus, harness racing thrived without setback until the arrival of the motor-car nearly eradicated the Standardbred Horse and the sport together, except among the most loyal outposts in remote regions. This dismal period of decline prevailed until the 1940's when, at the end of the Second World War, a sudden turn-about occurred. The introduction of the automated starting-gate, the concept of night-time action at the track, and the vast supply of post-War betting money prompted a meteoric rise in harness racing which has continued unabated until the present day.

---

[1] The race horses are driven from a special light vehicle.

Horses and Ponies Illustrated and their Owners

	Breed	Name of Horse	Owner when Photographed	Where Photographed
1	Arabian	Blue Halo	Mrs A. J. Sellar	England
2	Thoroughbred	Crepello	A Syndicate	England
3	Hack	Moonstrike	Miss V. de Quincey	England
4	Cob	Sport	Mrs Z. S. Clark	England
5	Hunter	Monbra	Mrs R. Cooke	England
6	Hackney	Outwood Florescent	Mr M. C. Hughes	England
7	Welsh Pony of Cob Type	Turkdean Cerdin	Mrs J. Crotty	England
8	Cleveland Bay	Mulgrave Rose	Mr T. W. and Mrs D. M. Welford	England
9	Irish Draught Horse	Merrion	Mr Timothy Carey	Eire
10	Children's Riding Pony	Lemington Happy Ending	Mrs Nigel Pease	England
11	Welsh Mountain Pony	Twyford Mazurka	Mrs G. J. Mountain	England
12	Dales Pony	Horsley Miranda	Messrs W. J. and J. W. Dalton	England
13	Fell Pony	Dene Fire Flare	Mrs G. F. S. Newall	England
14	New Forest Pony	Oakley Jonathan	Mr C. Purse	England
15	Connemara Pony	Clonkeehan Tiger Lily and Clonkeehan Water Lily (foal)	Miss F. Lee-Norman	Eire
16	Highland Pony	Glenmuik	Department of Agriculture and Fisheries for Scotland	Scotland
33	Shetland Pony	Glitter of Marshwood	Mrs Maurice Cox	Scotland
34	Dartmoor Pony	Hisley Woodcock	Mrs S. E. Jones and Miss P. M. Roberts	England
35	Exmoor Pony	Bracken Sunrise	Miss L. Lumb	England
36	Clydesdale	Johnston Realisation	Mr James Chapman	Scotland
37	Suffolk Punch	Beccles Dennise	Mr G. E. Colson	England
38	Shire	Grangewood William	Mr E. J. Richardson	England
39	Kladruber	Generalissimus XXVII	Kladruby nad Labem Stud Farm	Czechoslovakia
40	Lipizzaner	Pluto XXVI	Szilvásvárad State Stud	Hungary
41	Murakosi	5734 Szentegát-7	Szentlőrinc Stud	Hungary
42	Furioso	Furioso II	Apaj Stud, Kiskunság	Hungary
43	Nonius	Nonius A XXXIX	Mezőhegyes State Stud	Hungary
44	Shagya Arab	5854 Shagya XXXVI	Budapest Tattersall	Hungary
45	Polish Arab	El Azrak	Janów Podlaski State Stud	Poland
46	Hucul	Wazka	Siary State Stud	Poland
47	Konik	Lis	Polish Academy of Science	Poland
48	Polish Anglo-Arab	Czatownik	Janów Podlaski State Stud	Poland
53	Wielkopolski	Hannibal	Posadowo State Stud	Poland
54	Noric	Frohn-Vulcan XII/1445	Bundesministerium für Land- und Forstwirtschaft	Austria
55	Haflinger Pony	Bärbl	Haflinger Im- und Export K.G.	Austria
56	Einsiedler	Myrta	Kloster Einsiedeln	Switzerland
57	Franches-Montagnes	Udine	Domaine de Bellelay	Switzerland
58	Schleswiger	Friesin 45908	Herr Jürgen Isenberg	West Germany
59	East Friesian	Hestra	Herr Theodor Boekhoff	West Germany
60	Oldenburg	Ulan	Herr Ludwig Kathmann	West Germany
61	East Prussian of Trakehner Origin	Tornado	Frau Rosemarie Springer	West Germany
62	Holstein	Fabulus	Verband der Züchter des Holsteiner Pferdes mit Reit- und Fahrschule Elmshorn e.V.	West Germany
63	Hanoverian	Duft II	Niedersächsisches Landgestüt	West Germany
64	German Trotter	Lord Pit	Gestüt Lasbek	West Germany
65	French Trotter	Patara	Haras du Pin	France
66	French Thoroughbred	Tryptic	Haras du Pin	France
67	French Anglo-Arab	Thalian	Haras de Pompadour	France
68	Breton	Victorin	Haras de Lamballe	France
73	Anglo-Norman	Ultra Son	Haras du Pin	France
74	Ardennais	Coquin d'Acremont and Ruby du Monty	M. Jules Lemaire	Belgium
75	Percheron	Titanic	Haras du Pin	France
76	Boulonnais	Aramis	M. Gérard Calais	France
77	Brabant	Duc van de Viiegweg	M. Albert de Baene	Belgium
78	Dutch Draught Horse	Herman van Halfweg	Me'neer C. J. Erkelens	Holland
79	Friesian	Everlien 4924 Model	Me'neer J. Watzema	Holland
80	Fjord Pony	Maihelten 1692	Indre Sunnmøre hestealslag	Norway

	Breed	Name of Horse	Owner when Photographed	Where Photographed
81	Døle	Vinvara T 1680	Herr Lars Flatla	Norway
82	Knabstrup	Kronplet	Herre Alex Rasmussen	Denmark
83	Fredericksborg	Dercha	Herre Emilius Jensen	Denmark
84	North Swedish Horse	Uno-Malva 18918	Herre E. Swärd	Sweden
85	Swedish Warm Blood Horse	Lansiar	Flyinge Stud	Sweden
86	Finnish Horse	Kajova 6993	Herra Veikko Kinnunen	Finland
87	Italian Heavy Draught Horse	Garmor	Istituto Incremento Ippico, Crema	Italy
88	Salerno	Bargello	Istituto Incremento Ippico di S. Maria Capua Vetere	Italy
93	Lusitano	Domino	Eng. Francisco Lobo de Vasconcelos	Portugal
94	Alter-Real	Guapo	Coudelaria de Alter	Portugal
95	Andalusian	Descarado II	Señor Fernando de Terry	Spain
96	Hispano Anglo-Arab	Nervioso II	Soto Domecq Hermanos	Spain
97	American Shetland Pony	Gambling Sam	Mr Louis B. Gutman	U.S.A.
98	Pony of the Americas	Little Bird	W. F. Artrip, Jr	U.S.A.
99	Appaloosa	Dominion Witch Doctor	Mrs Louise W. Ewing	U.S.A.
100	Palomino	Goldie	Mr Arthur Godfrey	U.S.A.
101	Pinto	Teeter Totter	Mrs A. MacKay Smith	U.S.A.
102	American Quarter Horse	Steel Creek	Mr Arthur Godfrey	U.S.A.
103	Morgan	Blarney Stone	Miss Carol E. Hackney	U.S.A.
104	American Thoroughbred	Nearctic	A Syndicate	U.S.A.
105	Standardbred	Bullet Hanover	Hanover Shoe Farms Inc.	U.S.A.
106	American Saddle Horse	Starheart Sue	Dr and Mrs Donald B. Lurie	U.S.A.
107	Tennessee Walking Horse	Pals Midnite Mitch	Mr S. J. Bell	U.S.A.
108	Canadian Cutting Horse	Blue Hornet	Mr and Mrs Roy A. Ionson	Canada
113	Criollo	Tigra	Col Sir Ian Walker Okeover, Bart, D.S.O.	England
114	Vladimir Heavy Draught Horse	Granit	Urjev Polskii Stud	U.S.S.R.
115	Lithuanian Heavy Draught Horse	Hintaras	Niamunskii Stud	U.S.S.R.
116	Soviet Heavy Draught Horse	Rustem	Soviet Exhibition of Economic Achievement	U.S.S.R.
117	Kabardin	Arbich	Malokarachaev Stud	U.S.S.R.
118	Karabakh	Zaman	H.M. The Queen	England
119	Lokai	Sumbul	Kalinin Collective Farm, Dushanbe	U.S.S.R.
120	Karabair	Final	Dzhizak Stud	U.S.S.R.
121	Akhal-Teké	Polotii	Ashkhabad Stud	U.S.S.R.
122	Budenny	Chimkent	Pervii Konnoi Armee Stud	U.S.S.R.
123	Don	Srachok	Budenny Stud	U.S.S.R.
124	Orlov Trotter	Granit	Moscovskii Stud	U.S.S.R.
125	Tersk	Simvol	Stavropol Stud	U.S.S.R.
126	Waler	Darrouble	The New South Wales Mounted Police Force	Australia
127	Barb	Meftah	Jumenterie de Meknès	Morocco
128	Persian Arab	Jadran	H.I.M. The Shahanshah of Iran	Iran

Thanks are due to Mr Godfrey Argent, for permission to publish his unique picture of a Persian Arab (Plate 128), and to Miss Judith Campbell for arranging the photography; to Mrs Zofia Raczkowska for permission to publish her photograph of the Wielkopolski (Plate 53); and to Mr C. L. Apted for permission to publish his photograph of the Waler (Plate 126)

Acknowledgments for Monochrome Plates

Plate 17	The National Gallery
18	The British Museum
19	above: The Mansell Collection
	below: The Courtauld Institute of Art
20	The British Museum
21	The British Museum
22	The Rijksmuseum, Amsterdam
23	Fores Ltd
24	Fores Ltd
25	Fores Ltd
26	The Mansell Collection
27	Fores Ltd
28	Tryon Gallery Ltd
29	Arthur Ackermann and Son Ltd
30	The British Museum
31	Rothampstead Experimental Station (Harpenden)
32	above: Radio Times Hulton Picture Library
	below: Novosti Press Agency

Plate 49	Paul Popper Ltd
50	P.A.-Reuter Photos Ltd
51	Sally Anne Thompson
52	The Press Association Ltd
69	Fiona Forbes
70	Lichtbildstelle BMfLuf Wien
71	Calgary Stampede
72	Rapho Agence Photographique
89	Monty
90	H. W. Silvester and Bruce Coleman Ltd
91	Novosti Press Agency
92	Frank H. Meads
109	Sally Anne Thompson
110	Sally Anne Thompson
111	Sally Anne Thompson
112	*The Times*

The photograph reproduced on the front of the jacket is of the Arabian Stallion Blue Halo, owned by Mrs A. J. Sellar.

So/9/71